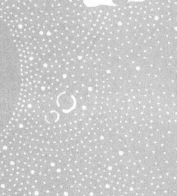

# SEEKING THE SACRED

## ALSO BY STEPHANIE DOWRICK

# SEEKING
## *the* SACRED

### Transforming Our View of
### Ourselves and One Another

# STEPHANIE
# DOWRICK

JEREMY P. TARCHER/PENGUIN
*a member of Penguin Group (USA) Inc.*
New York

JEREMY P. TARCHER/PENGUIN
Published by the Penguin Group
Penguin Group (USA) Inc., 375 Hudson Street, New York, New York 10014, USA • Penguin Group
(Canada), 90 Eglinton Avenue East, Suite 700, Toronto, Ontario M4P 2Y3, Canada (a division of Pearson
Penguin Canada Inc.) • Penguin Books Ltd, 80 Strand, London WC2R 0RL, England • Penguin
Ireland, 25 St Stephen's Green, Dublin 2, Ireland (a division of Penguin Books Ltd) • Penguin Group
(Australia), 250 Camberwell Road, Camberwell, Victoria 3124, Australia (a division of Pearson
Australia Group Pty Ltd) • Penguin Books India Pvt Ltd, 11 Community Centre, Panchsheel Park,
New Delhi–110 017, India • Penguin Group (NZ), 67 Apollo Drive, Rosedale, North Shore 0632,
New Zealand (a division of Pearson New Zealand Ltd) • Penguin Books (South Africa) (Pty)
Ltd, 24 Sturdee Avenue, Rosebank, Johannesburg 2196, South Africa

Penguin Books Ltd, Registered Offices: 80 Strand, London WC2R 0RL, England

ISBN 978-1-58542-866-3

Printed in the United States of America

*Book design by Lisa White*

While the author has made every effort to provide accurate telephone numbers and Internet addresses at the time
of publication, neither the publisher nor the author assumes any responsibility for errors, or for changes that occur
after publication. Further, the publisher does not have any control over and does not assume any responsibility for
author or third-party websites or their content.

*The modern world is desacralized, that is why it is in crisis.*
*The modern person must rediscover a deeper source of his*
*[or her] own spiritual life.*

C. G. Jung

# CONTENTS

# SEEKING THE SACRED

# INTRODUCTION

*Who can tell what miracles*
*Love has in store for us*
*if only we can find the courage*
*to become one with it?*

*Everything we now know*
*is only a beginning*
*of another knowing*
*that has no end.*

Iqbal (1877–1938)

OUR SEARCH FOR THE SACRED MAY be as individual as our fingerprints. Yet it connects us effortlessly to all living beings. It lets us discover what is most treasured and transformative in human existence. It lets us see existence itself as entirely precious. What we regard as precious, we will naturally protect.

From the sacred we may learn enough to keep one another safe.

Seeking the sacred does not distance us from the real; it defines the real. Touching the sacred through and within our everyday experiences, we come to a new sense of who and what we are. *I see the value of your existence. I see myself with new gratitude and respect.* We become freer to live from the inside out.

The sacred is source as well as inspiration for profound inner transformation—for "waking up." It is an opening of the heart and a training of the mind. It identifies holiness and brings it. The sacred is the source of being for many and the meaning of life for many more. It may also be "God," but not inevitably.

The sacred is both simpler and more profound than dogma or "belief" can ever be. Dogma and belief can be instruments of the sacred. Sometimes they are. They may also defile the sacred. Sometimes they do. The sacred may be "That which extends through the universe," as eleventh-century philosopher Chang-Tsai exquisitely expresses it.

*That which extends through the universe*
*I regard as my body*
*and that which directs the universe,*
*I regard as my nature.*
*All people are my brothers and sisters*
*and all things are my companions.*

In the presence of the untried and the infinite, in the presence of the sacred, our seeking may often feel tentative and unskilled. We ourselves may feel directionless sometimes, overloaded at other times. We may wonder if we are taking this search or quest too seriously or not seriously enough. We may prefer finding to seeking. We may understand finding and seeking as one. None of those states of mind is intrinsically more important than the other. Seeking is an unfolding. It is a treasure hunt where everyone wins.

꿈

It enchants me to think what a well-worn path seeking is. An ancient hymn from Egypt sings: "O great divine Soul who is in the Mysterious Dark, Come to me!" In an equally lyrical hymn to the Sumerian goddess Innana we hear: "I unfold your splendour in all the lands ... sweet is your praise." Setting out on this journey, or renewing it, we step in the footsteps of ancestors as old as humankind. Seeking is the stuff of our most ancient and deeply felt stories and myths. It is the purpose of religion and its meaning, even when religions and religious people seem sometimes to forget it. It makes sense of the most profound and unifying ethics to which the sacred draws our attention. It transcends culture and even time. It is also as personal as breath.

That joining of the personal and universal has never been more urgent. In twenty-first-century life our vision must simultaneously be personal *and* global. *How* we think, as well as what we think about, is essential to this picture. To look at this idea from another direction: *the challenges of our time are not only political and social; they are spiritual.*

Beyond all else, a seeking of the sacred reveals our essential interdependence. It may be "about" a relationship with God. It is undoubtedly about the ways we relate to one another. The most cursory understanding of the sacred shows me that I can't live or "save" myself at your expense. I can't and won't grow spiritually, morally or ethically while defiling or dehumanizing you or putting your life in danger. I cannot grow in understanding of what it means to be fully human while ignoring your fate, blaming you for it or trivializing it as your "karma."

The qualities needed to meet our most urgent social and environmental crises are the same as those we need in our communities and homes. They are the same as those we need to heal our personal suffering and lessen our confusion. Concern, connectedness, dignity, forgiveness, patience, tolerance, gratitude and an inclusive intelligence: this is what the world needs. This is what we need.

*All people are my brothers and sisters*
*and all things are my companions.*

The temptations of narrow, tribalistic "them and us" thinking are constantly with us. The dangers of such thinking, and the contempt and violence such thinking endorses, grow more evident. Yet human consciousness is capable of far more. *We* are capable of far more. My years of working with people as a psychotherapist and, more recently, as an interfaith minister with a large, diverse inner-city congregation convince me that we are ready to think about difference itself differently. We are ready to embrace the truth and fascination of our differences—and also to welcome and emphasize the yearnings that we share.

Seeing life itself as sacred—yours, mine, all of life—makes our differences far less frightening. More important, it makes sense of how *like* one another we are in our simplest and most profound longings. Whatever our culture, religion or language, we want food, shelter and good health. We want to be able to get up in the morning enthusiastically and sleep safely at night. We want health, safety and happiness for our loved ones. We want to know that our lives are purposeful and sometimes gracious. We want to feel part of something greater than ourselves. We want and need inspiration and meaning.

The more profound our longings, the more self-evidently universal they are. Sufi poet Kabir, one of the most joyful of teachers, helps us to understand this: "As the river gives itself into the ocean, what is inside me also moves inside you."

If this book has purpose and point, that is it. Everything would transform—insight, understanding, experiences and especially behavior—if only we could grasp that "what is inside me also moves inside you." "What is inside me" is sometimes called Being, soul, spirit, divine spark or seed, Source, Buddha nature, God or "that of God." Sometimes it is called meaning. Or love. Glimpsing that shakes up the familiar. It challenges the way we think about one another. It certainly challenges what we believe we can do to or ask of one another.

Acknowledging your gift of life as sacred doesn't mean I have to like you, agree with you or support your views. It doesn't mean that I have to lie down like a doormat for your feet. It doesn't mean that I should stand by passively or indifferently if you are harming yourself or others. It doesn't mean that I can afford to harm or diminish myself.

What it does mean is that I have no right to denigrate, hurt or kill you because you see the world and its problems differently from how I do. I have no right to crush your spirit to make myself feel bigger or more important. I have no right, either, to ignore or compound your suffering because it is taking place in a country far from my home, because your religion is not mine or because I loathe and despise your political or cultural ideology. Nor do I have the right to scorn or trample on my own precious, unique gift of life because it isn't measuring up to the plan I had for it.

~∾◌∽~

Whatever else the sacred is, it points to this: we are members of a single human family, marvelous and terrifying in its diversity. If we want to blink a couple of times and take this even half seriously, we have to dig deep. It must be *respect for all of life*. Understanding this, I must regard your gift of life as precious *whether or not I believe*

7

*you "deserve" this.* I must do you no harm and, moreover, I must wish you well *whether or not I believe you "deserve" it.* Like it or not, I see that our fates are linked.

This is the timeless ethical teaching at the heart of all the religions. It's what makes sense of the Golden Rule ("Do unto others as you would have them do to you." "See your Self in others and others in your Self."). To a great extent, everything else is embroidery.

"However many holy words you read," said the Buddha, more than two and a half thousand years ago, "however many holy words you speak, what good will they do you if you do not act on them?"

*Acting on them* is where my focus stays through much of this book: on the ethical implications of the sacred and how this affects our perceptions of who we are and what we are capable of becoming. This is not to leave out the transcendent, the ineffable and the holy. I believe it is to find it. For I suspect that it is only the sacred that we seek, yearn for and *desire* that is clean-sweeping enough to free us from the old and make the new realizable. Seeking the sacred, we are continuously being reborn to new awareness and to new life.

And yet, just like you, I live in what we pessimistically call "the real world." I know that as long as we are effectively conditioned into the kinds of divisive, defensive and aggressive thinking that the majority of the world's people regard as normal, this shift in perception may seem delusional. After all, the mighty institutions of religion themselves offer profound, unequivocal teachings about interdependence, loving-kindness, forgiveness, unity and compassion, yet all have a tragic history (in unequal amounts) of seeking power rather than transformation and conformity rather than compassion. We don't need to go further than the nightly news to see that far too often religions are cradles of violence rather than love. But what is just as true is that those same complex human institutions have also been the faithful preservers of the world's most magnificent (and undiluted) teachings on love. More wonderful, there have also always been brave men and women from all the religions who have determinedly lived life as sacred, sometimes under the most discouraging or dangerous circumstances.

～✦～

"The modern world is desacralized, that is why it is in crisis. The modern person must rediscover a deeper source of his [or her] own spiritual life."

To "re-sacralize" the world, as Carl Jung suggests, and to tend to what is alive, healing, tender and precious in this familiar material world, we must discover and rediscover the source and vitality of our own spirituality. And we must act on what we find, exactly as the Buddha urged in the quote on page 8. Acting on our highest ideals, we *embody* them and give them life. They also give us life and, dare I say it, they give us a life truly worth living.

Each time I choose the more loving direction, the kinder impulse, the most encouraging word; each time I choose to silence my complaint, my criticism or to deal with conflict nonviolently, each time I open more wholeheartedly to appreciate or express gratitude for what is around me; each time I offer help or comfort selflessly, or pause to reflect, give inner thanks or praise, or to align myself freshly with my finest impulses and self, I rediscover the source of my spiritual life—and I live it.

Religious, philosophical, psychological and spiritual writings offer countless theories about the sacred. But theories are rarely

transformative. We need to sense as well as think our way forward.
Our instincts and imagination must be engaged as well as our intellect
and heart. We must value and learn from our own experiences. We
need to surrender willingly and often to what is quiet within us. We
must know the source of our own spiritual life, however diversely
we name it. We must accept the resources and strengths it offers.
We must see holiness within it—and ourselves.

ھو

Basic to any existential or spiritual inquiry is the "who am I?"
question, and I pursue it in many ways through this book. It is
fundamental to how we perceive and perhaps even create what we
call our inner and outer worlds. Religion has itself become a choice
for vast numbers of us, not just *whether* to seek or believe but also
*what* to seek and believe.

I was surprised when one of my Catholic priest friends recently
told me that fewer people come to Mass regularly now that it is no
longer strictly required—and now that anxiety about "sin" itself has
moved into a supporting rather than a leading role. Were people
attending Mass out of fear in the past, rather than faith, love and
devotion? Clearly that's not universally the case. The Sunday before
he and I spoke I had been to Mass in a leafy suburb near my home
where the spacious church is packed four times each Sunday. (I also
attend services in other Christian denominations and a variety of
other spiritual settings, as well as leading my own spiritually inclusive
services and congregation. That story will emerge.)

Nonetheless, through your twenty-first-century gaze, it's safe
to assume that you see and interpret an infinitely more complex

world than the one your ancestors experienced. Never before have our choices been as extreme or diverse—and sometimes confusing. Never before have our personal choices had such impact on the world around us.

The contradictions in thinking about the sacred in this world are brilliantly exaggerated and exemplified by Sathnam Sanghera, a British journalist raised as a Sikh in a migrant Punjabi family living in Wolverhampton, a city in the West Midlands. On page two of his tragicomic family memoir, *If You Don't Know Me by Now*, Sanghera tells how as a Cambridge graduate and London journalist he stayed true to the strict tenets of middle-class London life, the first of which is: ". . . never confess to religiosity (you may as well confess to pedophilia)." A dozen pages later Sanghera is explaining the three strictest tenets of his parents' Sikh household, the first of which is: ". . . never confess to religious doubt (you may as well confess to pedophilia)."

⁓ↄ๏฿ↄↄ⁓

It is another and quite different British writer, Karen Armstrong, who points out in her typically exceptional book, *The Case for God*, that "Religion is a practical discipline that teaches us to discover new capacities of mind and heart."

That's not all religion is. And that's not all seeking is. Nonetheless, exploring the place religion has in your life, or discovering your most holy longings, you will weigh a range of teachings, assertions and "truths." How you understand those truths has traditionally been the business of religion. Today, it is increasingly your own business, even if you follow a traditional faith. I see that change as immensely hopeful. It puts the weight of conscience and personal responsibility where it belongs.

Karen Armstrong points to something similar when she writes that you will discover the truth—or lack of it—of religious teachings, "only if you translate these doctrines into ritual or ethical action."

That is exactly the journey that this book elaborates and affirms. Through the living of it you may even discover within yourself what Armstrong describes as a "knack" for religion—or the sacred. "People who acquired this knack," she writes, "discovered a transcendent dimension of life that was not simply an external reality 'out there' but was identical with the deepest levels of their being."

Armstrong's unequivocal linking of the transcendent dimensions with our deepest levels of being makes perfect sense to me. This steadies us, even in our darkest nights. I also like her use of the word "knack." There is something practical in it and also practiced. As I reread it I thought about how widely the term "spiritual practice" has come to be used in recent decades. *Practicing* our spirituality, we come to know it and ourselves in ways that will never be achieved when it is abstracted or theoretical. *Practicing*, we can afford to fail, to make many mistakes—and still go on. *Practicing*, we make it our own. It's this experience and discovery that is transformative. Yet, just like the sacred itself, spiritual practice and the yearning that drives it is also perplexing to articulate, never mind analyze. And those difficulties pale when we try to analyze and scrutinize the transcendent.

This last point is crucial. Rationalizing the transcendent, or valuing ideas about God far more fiercely than God, we run into the twin behemoths of atheism and fundamentalism.

Atheism is having its quite extensive moment in the sun. But as a blanket denial of the transcendent, it is relatively new. Historically "atheism" implied that the God in which you believe is not credible, rather than what we now understand by it: that believing in God is not credible. (And almost certainly signifies your weakness of intellect or character.) For centuries many Christians had no hesitation in calling Hindus, Taoists and Buddhists, for example, "heathens" or "atheists." Nothing could be further from the truth.

The "God" the so-called new atheists attack so vigorously has been dead for generations for many seekers, including me. That God may be alive and well for theistic fundamentalists, but there are strong historical and cultural reasons for this and far fewer spiritual ones. Meanwhile, I am with the Psalmist (104):

*Unnamable One, you are beyond simple knowing;*
*I praise you with unceasing wonder.*
*You are wrapped in light like a cloak.*
*You stretch out the sky like a curtain . . .*
*You walk on the wings of the wind . . .*
*. . . I will sing to you at every moment.*
*With every breath I will praise you.*
*May selfishness disappear from me.*
*May you shine always from my heart.*

I am with this teaching, too, from the ancient religion of the Jains: "Peace and universal love is the essence of the Gospel preached by all the Enlightened Ones. Let us forgive all creatures and let all creatures forgive me. Let me feel friendship toward all and bitterness to no one."

≈✧≈

Reverence, ethics, identity, teachings and stories, these all play such a rich and intrinsic part in bringing us into the sacred and revealing it. Telling our stories, listening to others' stories, we can't fail to become aware of the power of revelation in the mundane and everyday. The sacred is itself an experience of revelation: of *seeing* in a new way. It's like seeing four-dimensionally instead of three. With this come new levels of personal responsibility also. Again, that's no bad thing. Taking charge of our stories, interpretations, responses and behaviors is stabilizing and empowering. It doesn't solve all our problems. It doesn't eliminate the suffering that's part of human existence in such obvious and unequal measures. But it can certainly transform how we will view problems and relieve suffering. This is because at quite the same time even a hint of the sacred can give the most ordinary moments a transfiguring beauty.

> *Who can tell what miracles*
> *Love has in store for us*, asks Iqbal,
> *if only we can find the courage*
> *to become one with it?*

≈✧≈

Throughout this book I write about that power we have to choose to live lovingly and about "being good" as well as doing good (and certainly avoiding doing harm). The five major themes of the book—reverence, identity, love, "do no harm" and transformation—are particularly emphasized within their own sections, but flow throughout. The evidence is strong that living appreciatively and with a full-hearted engagement with life is the source of our greatest inward peace and happiness *whatever our outer circumstances*. It keeps others safe as well as our own selves. And it makes our seeking of the sacred meaningful as well as transformative. All of these themes, and the stories that exemplify them, give meaning and substance to that central insight.

Writing in *The Direct Path*, spiritual scholar Andrew Harvey expresses the sentiments that inspire such thinking. "It seems to me," he says, "that *all* the major religions have failed in one essential task—the reducing of human anxiety and aggression through the instruction of human beings in their essential divine nature."

To speak of our divine nature may already feel disquieting. To imagine that same divine nature (or our consciousness of it) reducing our human anxiety and aggression may seem like a pious folly. Or maybe it is easy enough for you to speak of the sacred, the divine, or even of our possible divine nature, but perhaps it is something else altogether to take this idea seriously enough to let it guide your perceptions, dreams, reflections and conduct?

Some lines in the Christian text Romans 8:5–6 make it clear that this urgency to integrate the sacred and the everyday is hardly new. Nor less urgent. "Those who live exclusively in earthly matter have a way of thinking which only understands the material; those who live in the spirit can also understand the spiritual. Materialistic thinking produces death, spiritual thinking engenders life and peace."

It is "spiritual thinking," and the actions that emerge from it, that literalism and religious one-upmanship miss by a mile. "Spiritual thinking" must relate to and reflect spiritual and ethical care. It has to come from the heart as well as the thoughtful mind to "engender life and peace."

In my own interfaith congregation there are many people who have been wounded by religion's claims. Two things stand out as particularly harmful. The first is when a religious tradition teaches fear more effectively than love—and conformity more effectively than compassion. The second is when a tradition fails, as Andrew Harvey put it, to instruct its adherents "in their essential divine nature."

Tell people how innately worthless they are and their feelings of spiritual entitlement will be impoverished. What we believe ourselves to be and what we identify with are essential determinants in the way we will see the world and respond to it. Throughout this book that returns as a central theme. What is far more exciting though is that *we are always more than our conditioning*. Throughout our lives we continue to come to crossroads moments. How and what we choose in each of those moments also creates us.

I cannot—and this book cannot—"give" you God or the sacred. (At least, I can't serve up the sacred like a dish of vegetables.) The best that I can do is affirm and accompany it and perhaps illuminate it. You alone can make the sacred real in your life. You alone can "translate" it and live it. Analogies with love and also poetry abound. Love and poetry must be *risked* if they are to be felt. The sacred is like that also. As these lines from the magnificently tender Chandogya Upanishad evoke, through the sacred alone you can discover the fullness of your nature.

> *In the city of the One is a secret dwelling that is the lotus of the heart.*
> *Within this dwelling is a space and within this space is the*
>    *fulfilment of all desire.*
> *What is within that space should be yearned for, longed for and realized.*

*As great as the infinity beyond is the space within the lotus of the*
    *heart.*
*Both heaven and earth are contained there.*
*Both fire and air, sun and moon, lightning and stars.*
*Everything is there. In that space in the heart . . .*

*This is the Self. Free from old age, death and grief.*
*Free from hunger. Free from thirst.*
*All longings fulfilled.*

In these pages I describe highly recognizable longings and experiences
lived out in ordinary lives. And I show that almost the first lesson that
the sacred reveals is that in the most "ordinary life" the extraordinary
is always present. Or, more accurately, that the ordinary (familiar)
and the extraordinary (less familiar), or the mundane and the holy,
weave a single fabric that we know as life.

In the section on identity I reflect explicitly on the power of
story, and throughout the book I use a multitude of personal stories,
including my own. I don't know of any better way to bring big
ideas to life than witnessing firsthand how they are being lived in a
whole variety of circumstances. I also offer a rich array of quotations
and teachings from some of the greatest teachers of the sacred who,
not coincidentally, are also some of humankind's greatest teachers
of love.

Of the many personal reflections the book offers, most came in
response to two questionnaires that I sent out partway through my
research and again toward the end, mainly to people already seriously

engaged with at least some of the questions that this book addresses. I offered my respondents a variety of questions to capture whatever was particularly resonating for them at this time. Most took this as a chance for considered reflection and answered just two or three questions in depth, exactly as I had hoped. From their responses, and from the many honest, courageous conversations that preceded and followed those questionnaires, a picture formed of a real variety of experience and interpretation of the sacred *and* of some tender, impressive commonalities.

Reflecting the likely experiences and personal histories of readers of this book, many of the people whose stories are in these pages feel free to engage with the spiritual or eternal dimensions of life without denigrating or abandoning the religious traditions, but also without being constrained by them. Many speak easily of God and with great love about their personal relationship with God. For others, the sacred search is vivid and desired but talk of God is not. For some, their home or chosen faith is essential for their spiritual sustenance and development. For others, seeking is itself an honorable path.

For most of the people whose stories I share, *seeking is primarily relational.* It is not for "Sunday best." It affects as well as makes sense of a life that is unreservedly concerned with questions of compassion and engagement. It lets them grow in appreciation and gratitude. It lets them face life's inevitable losses without obsessing or recoiling.

Seeking the sacred, we stir the mind and senses. We awaken heart, spirit and soul quite inevitably. We weave the temporal with the eternal. We discover and rediscover respect and reverence. We grow in our capacity for courage, forgiveness, delight and wonder.

We cherish the privileges of a shared existence, alive to all its dimensions. We open our hearts and minds to wonder, humility and awe.

I am wholeheartedly grateful to all those whose voices resonate on these pages: those I interviewed, those from whom I go on learning.

They reveal the sacred and make it real. *Thanks be.*

# REVERENCE

*All that is true,*
*All that is worthy of reverence,*
*All that is holy and good,*
*All that is lovely to look at and beautiful to hear,*
*All that has virtue and all that deserves praise:*
*Let this be the content of your thinking.*

Paul to the Philippians (c.5–67)

YEARS AGO, LONG BEFORE MY OWN search for the sacred was fully conscious, I was struggling to calm my racing mind. Like many others, I decided that it was high time to try meditation and yoga. A whole lot more years would pass before I began truly to comprehend how effortless meditation can be and how unnecessary and even obstructive "trying" is. But if I did not grasp the gentle art of meditation immediately, I did learn something else of true value.

In those early days, I had a teacher who offered a brief guided meditation at the end of each yoga class. While we sat cross-legged and not entirely still or comfortable on our thin foam mats, she would conclude the meditation by inviting us to view through the mind's eye "our whole selves."

It was a kind of blessing. As a young woman who felt very different on the inside from the ambitious, confident self I presented on the outside, this notion of the "whole self" soon became deeply affecting for me. Mind, body, spirit, thoughts, emotions, soul and whole self: *all sacred*. All one.

❧

We seek the sacred with everything that we are. Above everything this is an adventure that engages the instincts as much as the intellect; that is carried by imagination and vision; that leans on and develops a sensual appreciation of existence and being; that fascinates the mind and stirs the heart.

We undertake this journey as an individual choice. No one can seek (or experience) the sacred for us. Yet we invariably learn who we are and all that the sacred can be in the company of one another. That life-giving fluidity between individual and collective experience, between self and others, is crucial here. Our social and psychological maturity depends on our ever-developing capacity to be aware of one another: to be curious about what we share and interested in the ways we differ. This is no less true in our yearning for the sacred. In fact, it may be even more so because it is when we begin to understand the sacred that we also get a humbling, liberating vision of *who we all are*: who you truly are, who I truly am.

Into this insight alone, reverence emerges.

Far more than an attitude, more even than an experience of connection, reverence is a way of being that allows us to know awe, gratitude, delight and trust. Those are magnificent qualities and also transformative ones. Experiencing and learning them in the context of reverence, we cannot fail to become more passionately thankful for our own gift of life and far fiercer in defending and affirming what is most beautiful, consoling or compassionate.

Cultivating reverence as an idea and context allows us to recognize its subtle signs and languages more often and more appreciatively, as well as its rainbow-like extravagance. But even that conscious welcoming of reverence is never everything.

Reverence is also what lets us "catch chinks of a world beyond," as philosopher Huston Smith puts it in *Why Religion Matters*. Or perhaps it lets us discover that the world of beyond and spirit is right where we are. Or, in the words of Sufi poet Hafiz, that a "great palette of light has embraced this earth."

> *Is it true,* Hafiz asks, *that our destiny*
> *is to turn into Light Itself?*

More aware of reverence and more trusting of it, we may become easier in our moods, more trusting or expansive. And I love the idea that reverence is not always quiet and certainly not always solemn. In fact, I wonder if I can even suggest that irreverence is not the opposite of reverence. (I see the opposites of reverence as cynicism, nihilism, brutality and indifference.) Irreverence, by contrast, could be the playful or creative side of reverence. It's what fills our connections with curiosity, laughter, ecstasy and bliss. And in our most creative moments it's reverence as well as awe that allows the whole world to change as we stay still, even our eyes scarcely moving, yet perceiving something freshly and taking it deep within ourselves. Or it lets us express something in such a way that someone else is touched, moved, inspired or consoled. I have seen someone simply light a candle with such presence that the moment becomes reverent and unconditionally sacred.

In any moment of true communion there is reverence. And humility. So many of the personal recollections in this and all the other sections of the book affirm that. But I also love the idea that some of the holiest moments in our lives may be the least predictable. Experiencing reverence, we are not just whole but wholly present. Reverence is also a gift. Like the best gifts, it is often a surprise. And, like all sacred gifts, we need do nothing to deserve it.

Lying in bed one cold morning recently, reluctant to get up and start my day in any serious way, I was turning over the idea of reverence in my mind and suddenly remembered a shiny, very soft fabric called shot silk. I have no idea if it is still around, but when I was a child and it was still common for many people to make rather than buy their own clothes, this fabric fascinated me. It wasn't an expensive silk. In fact I think it was often used to line more expensive fabrics. But its magic came from the seemingly endless variety of colors that appeared when the fabric was moved. Turning it toward the light some of the colors would dominate. Turning it away from the light, a quite different look would emerge. It was literally "shot through" with an immense variety of threads that somehow didn't merge but took their turn to shine. I found it magical, inexplicable in its origins (how did they do that?) and marvelous in its effects.

As we seek the sacred, reverence quite naturally becomes part of our lives. So does a renewal of respect and gratitude. So does an awareness of connection and beauty. But not uniformly.

Recalling that memory of my child self experiencing such fascination and delight around a simple piece of fabric, I couldn't help but see an analogy with reverence, this immense quality unique to human beings that is infinitely diverse in its manifestations and moods, shot through with what brightens and illuminates, far more often subtle and implicit rather than "showy," yet changing for the better what we often call the very fabric of our lives.

~∽⌇∾~

There is modesty as well as discovery as we move toward understanding our deeper reaches. This need not be "everything," nor "all at once." Yet as we grow more confident in our sacred seeking, our sense of identity *changes*. What we identify *with* changes. What we believe life is *for* changes.

We don't become different people. Nor do we need to. It's our perspective that changes.

I suspect that we have all had that experience where we listen with attention to someone's story and the person in front of us literally transforms from someone we thought was easy to overlook to someone about whom we now genuinely care. Again, the person hasn't changed. What's changed is our knowledge and understanding of them. Our capacity for empathy and perhaps compassion is aroused, and in the presence of those qualities our sense of connectedness flourishes.

Perceiving a sacred, transcendental or holy dimension to life and to our own lives creates a change that is just as dramatic and usually far more universal. This is true even when our perceptions are hedged or tentative. What's more, as the sacred grows more real in our lives it shifts the way in which we more routinely see and interpret the world and other people, and respond to them. It also shifts the way we understand and treat our own selves and particularly those deep-down aspects of our own selves that feel most vulnerable.

We become less likely to put ourselves in danger. We become far less likely to put ourselves down or scold ourselves in the privacy of our own minds. We become less likely to experience those painful schisms between our inner and outer lives that were part of my adult years for so long and may be part of your inner experience also.

*Seeking* becomes a journey of healing as well as wholeness. As we see our own lives with greater appreciation, we become less dependent on the impossible goal of things always going well or (God help us) *our way*. Psychologically as well as spiritually we need to take in both hands a realistic understanding that we are not the center of every universe, that others will have needs as pressing as our own, that there is no relating without also sometimes compromising. We will learn that this is not weakness. It is strength.

As our view softens and broadens we also cease to see one another primarily in terms of status and utility, those particularly cruel agonies of our age ("Am I more important than you are?" "How useful could you be to me?" "Do either of us *matter*?"). Instead, we can afford to see the weaknesses as well as strengths that we have in common.

Experimenting with the idea that we belong, spiritually, to a single and infinitely diverse human family, the ideals of peace-making, kindness, concern, generosity and forgiveness make new sense. Reverence makes new sense. Cherishing what we perceive as awesome or precious makes new sense.

If we are lucky we will feel pushed to redefine our assumptions about independence, noticing how much we *receive* on a daily basis from others—and how much of our contentment depends on what we can *do* for others on a daily basis.

How we view ourselves will always make more difference to our spiritual and psychological well-being and happiness than any other factor. Academic studies, including Professor George Vaillant's remarkable forty-year study, *Adaptation to Life*, and his later book, *Spiritual Evolution*, show that unequivocally. But we know it, too, from the simplest observations of our own lives and the lives of the people around us.

Seeing ourselves as spiritual beings (however loosely we define that) gives us the confidence to develop our capacities for engagement and for altruism, to be stimulated and provoked as we connect with other people in their wondrous complexity, honing our spiritual resources and values and living them out. It also gives us the confidence to forgive life and ourselves when things do not go to plan. This priceless view and the confidence that comes with it need not depend on a formal religious affiliation (though it might include it); it depends on identity, values, outlook and attitude.

Claiming our confidence from the inside out, some of the loneliness, helplessness and isolation that drive so much contemporary pain can fall away. Where pain continues, we can meet it more truthfully and ably. We can bring thoughtfulness and compassion to it rather than fear or contempt. We can ask ourselves what might help. We can let ourselves be more alert to inspiration and guidance.

As so many stories in this book will show, inspiration pours into our lives in all kinds of ways. These are rarely entirely predictable. We can "notice" that with greater interest and trust. Doing so, we will soothe ourselves. We will *receive* more comfortably, with less anxiety, confusion or resentment. We will remain more open to other people and more sensitive to their reality. We will build confidence in our inner world and in our capacities of reflection, imagination and instinct. We will trust the *presence* of the sacred in our lives and the inner processes that seeking unfolds and allows. We will feel more attuned to the world of the senses, more alive, less hectic or driven.

In that frame of mind, we will be less afraid of our pain and far more trusting of ourselves.

A lovely example comes from Clare Coburn, formerly a teacher and now an academic and storyteller living in Western Australia. Her reflection illustrates that essential *forwarding* or opening up which is needed to receive the gifts of insight and inspiration that reflect and carry the sacred.

Clare says, "I remember a particularly bleak time when I was unable to trust life. I felt depressed and absolutely unable to take in anything positive. In my work life, I was being both controlling and acting the martyr, foolishly unable to reveal my vulnerabilities and doubts to anyone whilst working with lots of challenges. I knew I was really down when I went on a long walk in mountainous country. I walked up a hill and sat overlooking a moody landscape. Clouds moved rapidly overhead so grayness and sunshine alternated.

"As I sat eating some tasteless sandwich I had brought with me, I was suddenly surrounded by butterflies—hundreds of them. It should have felt like I was on the set of some South American magical realist film, yet I was frozen inside and couldn't take in all this remarkable beauty. Despite my lack of feeling at the time, it was a turning point.

"Around that time, someone advised me to get back to writing and I began to keep 'morning pages' again, a practice Julia Cameron recommends [in *The Artist's Way*]. One night, a few months later, staying with a friend, I knew I had to leave my job and my relief was immediate.

"Looking back, those butterflies seem like a kind of omen. I had a similar omen recently where I was visited by ladybugs on an almost daily basis for about a week until I made another spirit-nurturing decision and they have ceased to visit or, at least, I have stopped seeing them. I have a suspicion we receive such reminders all the time and are simply not aware that these small miracles are compelling us to move and grow."

∽⦿∾

There have been times in my own life when my sense of the sacred and, even more particularly, my spiritual practices of meditation, prayer, study and journaling have been especially open, vulnerable or fierce. I am quite sure that I have been far more needy than usual of spiritual comfort in those periods but also more sensitive and aware of what is so continuously available to me. They have largely been tough times, occasionally desperate, and I would not wish to have any version of them in my life again. But I must also acknowledge with profound gratitude what poured forth within me and—or so it seemed—*for* me at those times. Without the sacred and a glimpse of my place within it, I truly do not know how I would have got through my own darkest and most mystifying passages and learned to see them as part of life but not all of it.

The visionary poet Rainer Maria Rilke puts it best. He speaks of a vision of life and of the sacred that's vast and fearless enough to encompass beauty *and* terror: "Let everything happen . . ." he writes, because Rilke knows and you and I also know that everything *will* happen, including death. And it is in how we think about that "everything" that our seeking of the sacred becomes truly transformative.

Perhaps this means relieving rather than denying suffering, or obsessing about it.

Perhaps it means pausing long enough to take in the holy in the most ordinary as well as the extraordinary.

Perhaps it means perceiving the ordinary and the extraordinary as one.

Listening closely to people in all kinds of situations for many years, hearing their stories, sharing their secrets and witnessing their changes in perception and well-being, I can say that the most significantly transformative experience any of us will have is to recognize the value of our own existence. It is this that will change for the better our inner stability and our outer behaviors.

This insight illuminates our connections to others ("My life has intrinsic value. So does yours."). It also relieves us of the illusion that we must create our lives entirely alone. We are responsible for our lives, but we are not isolated. That recognition—and its consequences—is essential to any claim of spiritual maturity. It can rescue us from helplessness and self-absorption. It can wake us up to our power to create and sustain a way of living that has intrinsic meaning regardless of the applause that may—or may not—be coming our way.

This can literally transform our view of ourselves and of one another.

There are few more moving expressions of how awesome such a change can be than in John Newton's hymn "Amazing Grace," where we hear: "I once was lost, but now am found, *was blind, but now I see.*"

What's more, as our spiritual evolution continues, so we continue to see anew and afresh.

SACRED SEEKING AND SEEING CAN—perhaps must—affect us at all levels of being and particularly in our ways of relating. It is here that our favorite ideas about the "spiritual" can be both challenged and refined. It's also here that we learn how much constancy and presence of mind it takes to live compassionately and appreciatively and to keep one another safe.

I want to share the simple, clarifying way that my friend Jolyon Bromley expressed this to me. With a relatively intense appreciation of the sacred he explains, "In general terms what is important to me is 'presence,' a sense of connection to loving, creative forces which are essentially ineffable. The knowing is important but the sensing and the *being* are more important. I'd like to think I'm in constant communion. When I feel lost or alone it is because I have put my attention somewhere else and I'm called to shift my focus to reconnect. The higher self, the Cosmic Self, is always there to reconnect. This is a great source of stability, strength and peace in my life. I live with a wonderful sense of blessing. How can I be so fortunate?"

But, as Jolyon explains, the "blessing" of the sacred doesn't end there. He is a tertiary teacher and liturgist, and says, "The other side to this is a necessity to work constructively with whatever or whoever crosses my path. Not to be content in my own little world but to be involved with others, with issues which are important in shaping the kind of world we live in. Therefore I feel drawn particularly to environment issues, concerns about poverty and social justice—which are all connected. There is no one way I experience the transcendent: through Nature, meditation and prayer, music and the arts, friendship and deep rapport with people to give a name to some."

It's with real relief that most of us will discover how this lifelong pilgrimage is never "about" our own selves only. It is not about the relentless burdens of getting ahead (though it may soften those burdens). It is not about a life that is constantly going our way. It is not about getting our youth prolonged, our pockets filled, our merry or comfortable way of life privileged above all others. In fact, many of the most convincing stories of inner transformation show very clearly that sometimes it is in the face of *not* getting what we most wanted, or what we believed we had to have, that we are freed most effectively to live from a steady heart and mind rather than a fragile ego.

There is real comfort in that. I know I am not alone in feeling not just intimidated but sometimes tyrannized by the emphasis in some contemporary spiritual teachings that every moment can be (and the implication is *should* be) a "wonderful moment."

Some moments are plainly not wonderful. To add to our suffering in those moments by blaming ourselves for not thinking sufficiently positively or abundantly is never helpful. What we can discover is that it is possible to heal our hearts and minds gently and persistently. And that we can bring compassion and trust to such times rather than self-blame or despair. To do that is to sacralize the difficult as well as the serene moments that are characteristic of every human life. To do that is to remain constant to the sacred.

Sometimes it takes a breakdown of the familiar to re-evaluate what we already have and *who we already are*. As Jolyon described it, it may take a time of feeling "lost or alone" to push us to reconnect with our inner world and spirit. Experiencing that this is possible, especially in times of confusion or grief, is truly priceless. It brings a sense of being and belonging. It offers a steadying truth that lets us live from our strengths.

~⊶⊶~

That we never explore, discover or live "the sacred" for our own sake only is central to my personal credo and this book. Two profound teachings support the urgency of thinking inclusively.

The first comes from George Fox, seventeenth-century cofounder of the Religious Society of Friends (Quakers), a religious rebel who believed in the then-radical possibility that people could have a direct relationship with God, unmediated by clergy. He was also convinced that there was "that of God [soul, divine spark] in everyone," *unconditionally*.

"Unconditionality" is spirituality's (and our own) biggest test and I return to it many times in these pages. Here, it is the unconditionality of the early Quakers' conviction that challenges our usual patterns of viewing some people as friends and others as enemies (and acting accordingly), or seeing some lives as of value and others as valueless.

It's that unconditionality which gives rise to the famous Quaker testimonies of "spirituality in action," including peacemaking, equality, simplicity and integrity.

The second teaching is just as significant. It comes from Paramahansa Yogananda, perhaps the most influential of Hindu teachers in the West, who died in California in 1952. He taught: "Only spiritual consciousness—realization of God's presence in oneself and in every other living being—can save the world. I see no chance for peace without it. Begin with yourself. There is no time to waste."

The need captured by Yogananda to "save the world"—and ourselves—has only increased. Our world has never been as crowded. Our weapons have never been as dangerous. Our hatreds and prejudices are literally unaffordable. Yet, in so many spheres, our spiritual ignorance goes unchallenged.

War remains an institutionally and politically approved "solution" to social conflict. Injustice flourishes and is frequently rewarded. Billions of our fellow human beings live without basic physical necessities. Bullies define themselves as victims or martyrs. Ten million children die each year before the age of five because of preventable disease or starvation. And in rich countries millions of people express through their addictions or despair a bleak starvation of the soul.

Guiding and even urging me on in this writing has been Jung's key insight that I also discussed in this book's introduction: "The modern world is desacralized, that is why it is in crisis."

I see the challenge of re-sacralizing the world as our most urgent, affecting in every way those other more familiar world challenges of climate change, inequality, poverty and starvation, religious and ideological persecutions, mass migrations and war.

Making the world sacred—or, more precisely, *making our view of the world sacred* and acting accordingly—certainly cannot be left to governments, corporations or major institutions, even religious ones. Religious institutions are themselves far too deeply implicated in the problems to relieve them effectively. This is a quiet but passionate revolution that can only be achieved by individuals—*in the company of one another*. It means thinking as well as perceiving with reverence and often with humility. It means thinking *inclusively*, taking for granted that what is most important to us is also important to others.

Each of us can be responsible for the changes in attitude and behavior that are now imperative. Some of those changes will be wildly inconvenient. Some will be enhancing, entrancing and liberating.

Whatever it takes to see our lives as sacred—and to regard the world beyond our own selves also as holy and precious *and to act accordingly*—arouses and speaks to our highest levels of personal power and responsibility. This is reverence not as pious hope or nice idea but as action. What's more, such a call is utterly congruent with this precise historical and social moment. Millions are playing their part. And they are discovering what their part is, however tentative or unobserved. For, as Jung also pointed out, this shift in consciousness and deed must begin with how we think about our own lives *and* the way our lives illimitably and inevitably connect.

Our understanding of ourselves as individuals and as part of a greater whole makes this an exhilarating time—at least for many. We have means of communication and of accessing information that just years ago belonged in science-fiction novels. (I typed my first book on a typewriter. Already that seems much like trying to get somewhere by horse and cart.) Turning on our electronic "windows" to the globe we can literally see the plight of others wherever they are. Increasing global consciousness teaches us that we share each other's fate with unprecedented intimacy.

This intimacy is itself a challenge. We dare not ever say, "I didn't know." Praying for a kinder world is not enough. We must become kindness. We must live it. And when we fail to live it we must have the courage and the grace to start again. But there is another ingredient here also that makes me deeply hopeful. For the first time in human history we not only share a threatened future—and are beginning to comprehend that it is, indeed, *shared*—we also share an unprecedented spiritual inheritance.

Wherever we are, and virtually whatever our circumstances, if we choose to do so we can explore, study and learn to live the highest, most compassionate and most transformative teachings of all the great world philosophies and faiths. Without demanding or compromising a religious affiliation, we can discover, absorb and live the finest teachings the world has known. From the East and from the West, from the North and South, from religions that define themselves as theistic and those that are immanent and transcendent, those teachings, prayers, scriptures, revelations are ours to seek: the most encouraging, sublime teachings on living the sacred.

RELIGION IN ALL ITS VAST VARIETY weaves in and out of this story of sacred seeking. Yet for many people religion is not essential to it. In *Beyond the Post-Modern Mind* philosopher Huston Smith talks about religion's "scope" in these terms: "Religion began in the individual's direct relationship with the transhistorical and ultimate—God by whatsoever name. From this inviolate starting point and continuing center it has proceeded to shoulder, successively, concern for interpersonal relationships and society's institutions and structures. To live up to its calling, it must now add to these agendas concern for other species and life's sustaining environment."

In the West not just religion but belief itself is increasingly experienced as a matter of choice. It contributes to most people's sense of identity. In some lives it is primary. But rarely is it fixed. Just as we no longer automatically take up our father's profession or raise our children exactly as our mother did, so most of us no longer automatically profess the "faith of our fathers [and mothers]" as our forebears did. Or we may share the same faith, but interpret and live it quite differently. The spectrum of belief has never been greater. The impact of belief has never been more critical.

I am powerfully aware that I am writing and you are reading in a world that is increasingly religiously fractured. Simultaneously it is stridently post-religious for many, yet resurgently and sometimes dangerously pre-modernist for others. Statistical evidence, as well as the nightly news, tells us that religion or spirituality remains a primary force in the lives of the majority of the world's people. It also tells us that the variety of experience and opinion has never been greater.

The paradoxes and extremes of twenty-first-century living create a dynamic context where our values can be tested and strengthened, our ideologies and favored explanations challenged, our highest values affirmed and our deepest and most holy identity forged, fractured or discovered.

The rhetoric of our beliefs, though, is always secondary to how we live. "Believing" in love as a value, and perhaps also in a God of love, while living unlovingly, is progressively less convincing. The rapid integration of psychological insights with spiritual seeking and understanding has been one of the key markers of the spiritual upheaval and evolution of the last half century. And its impact still has far to run.

In our most spontaneous moments, in our most intimate and accepting relationships, in our moments of greatest tension or frustration and perhaps also in our times of most confronting loneliness, the reality of what we think about other people and ourselves, and the degree to which we value this gift of life, will inevitably emerge.

"Whatever someone does there will be fruits of that action" is not a new saying. It comes from the historical Buddha two and a half thousand years ago, and if it seems familiar that is because it so strongly echoes "By their deeds [fruits] you will know them."

The saying isn't new. But our comprehension of its sentiments has a real chance of growing less guilt-stained and more profound.

Actions, and attention to actions, are center-stage here. What we tell ourselves may possibly set the compass for our existence. It may determine our attitudes. It may let us sleep well at night (or keep us awake). *How we live*, though, has the greater and more immediate power to shape who and what we are becoming—and what "deeds" and "fruits" we leave behind as we go.

It is within this context of unprecedented information as well as choice, personal responsibility and diversity that we find ourselves seeking the sacred. We find ourselves yearning for moments of inward connection; for the stopping of time and the meeting with eternity that deep reverence brings; for a sense of trust in times of terror; for unspoken communion; for awe and holiness; for intimate connection with something greater than ourselves; for a sense that this transitory life is not all there is; for a love for ourselves and others that can heal our insufficiency; for a joy in living that authentically honors it.

❦

Ours is a time unlike any other in spiritual and religious history. The grip of religious authoritarianism has been loosened in many countries by education and democracy. We might sometimes be reluctant to think for ourselves but we are free to do so. We are also free to question our beliefs as well as the very notion of what "belief" is. And religious and atheistic fundamentalisms aside, our tolerance for people cherishing beliefs that are quite different from our own is generally far greater than it was even a generation or two ago.

As a familiar example, in my own childhood in 1950s New Zealand it was common for conscientious religious people to avoid others not of a different religion or no religion but of a different Christian denomination or a different branch within the same denomination, and *to feel entitled to condemn them.*

It was also common for people to modify their behavior (or not) on the basis of what might arguably follow this life rather than for the sake of treasuring this life and relishing this life and doing what we can for no greater reason than *because we can.*

How contrary this is to the teachings of Jesus himself and his earliest followers. In his letter to the Corinthians (1 Corinthians 10:31), the early Christian, Paul, urges seekers in the troubled city of Corinth—and us—to: "Do everything in such a way that the divine can be revealed through it."

Paul might equally have said: *Do everything in such a way that the divine can be revealed through you.* For me, this is the essence of sacred living, revealing a confidence that the mysterious divine or transcendent can reveal itself through us, that we can step up to a manner of living that is not simply reverent and awe-filled but "divinely expressive."

Doing that, as humanly and as imperfectly as we probably will, we can be wholeheartedly mindful that Spirit (however you think about that) lives in and through us, and in and through the world around us. In twenty-first-century life more of us than ever are free to seek the sacred and to express the sacred not from fear or compulsion but with a passion for inquiry and meaning, as well as love.

These lines come from the Oracle of Sumiyoshi in the ancient Shinto tradition to magnify this thought.

*I have no bodily existence.*
*Universal kindness is my godly body.*
*I have no physical power.*
*Steadfastness is my strength.*
*I have no spiritual knowledge other than what is given by Wisdom.*
*I have no power other than the exercise of gentleness.*

~~~

Choice is critical in seeking. It wakes up both our will and our capacity for conscious discernment. Yet choice (or free will) may not be the first thing we consider when our minds turn toward the sacred. As someone who had to learn catechism answers by rote through my school years—chanting them much as we did our times tables—and who had to recite a daily proclamation of faith without questioning a single word or sentiment within it, even placing the words "choice" and "sacred" in intimate proximity is liberating.

And something else makes our appreciation of choice richer still. Or maybe just a little more ambiguous.

A person's belief system may be quite vague, for example, yet still their seeking can feel utterly compelling. Rather than "choosing," it may seem as though they have no choice but to seek, so deep is that urgency within them. There are few more eloquent expressions of this than in the opening lines of the glorious Psalm 42, one of my personal favorites.

*As a deer longs for flowing streams, so my soul longs for you,*
  *O God.*
*My soul thirsts for God, for the living God.*
*When shall I come and behold the face of God?*
*My tears have been my food by night and by day.*
*While people ask me: "Where is your God?"*

This is not an either/or situation.

We may feel inwardly called or pushed to seek the sacred *and* still be aware of the privileges and responsibilities of constant choosing.

We may, more pointedly still, feel called to the ineffable mystery and source, the One who yearns for relatedness as we do. This is the divine One who, in the words of the Islamic *hadith* (sacred saying), "wants to be known." ("I was a hidden treasure and I wanted to be known.") And yet remain uncertain.

The yearning is real. I am sure of that. A sense of "call" or inner yearning is real. I am also sure of that. *And* our essential sense of freedom and choice remains critical.

⤙⤚

When fear ceases to be a factor and choice can be realized, we may never entirely know why one child out of several in a family is intensely religious while the others are indifferent to religion and spirituality, or even hostile.

Temperament, personal and social experiences, intellectual interests, passions, talents, values: these are hints, but they never add up to a complete answer.

Why is one of us "drawn" to Buddhism or to a contemporary guru, for instance, while another of us with more or less the same spiritual interests and appetites returns after years away to our parents' faith of Judaism or Sikhism, though perhaps practicing it rather more intensely than our forebears—or much less?

Did I *choose*, for example, an interfaith path with a passion for the teachings of the world's mystics—or did that path choose me? Did I feel the pull of its invitation because it is intellectually satisfying, emotionally compelling and convincingly sacred? Because it is practical in the ways it guides me to live, as well as inspirational? Because it is uncompromisingly ethical: nonviolent without exception? Because it brings so much responsibility back to me (where I believe it belongs)? Because it gives me a direct path, connection to or experience of the transcendent? *Because it leaves no one out?*

As with any formative relationship, there is always mystery about "fit." Fate, luck, grace: they are all ways to describe what we can't fully understand.

Coexistent with that, and not in the least undermining of it, is the reality that whatever our path or inner pilgrimage *we are still constantly making choices.* And we need the clarity and constancy to recognize them as choices—and make them our own.

Omar is a chef. He is also the father of five little children. His Syrian-born parents had a religiously mixed marriage. His mother had been raised Muslim in a liberal family and his father, who is still living, is Coptic Christian (Syriac Orthodox).

"Choosing your religion was pretty normal in our family," Omar told me. "Choosing not to have a religion was maybe a bit less welcome, but my folks have been astonishingly relaxed with my sisters as well as with myself. Their mantra became, 'We only want you to be happy!'"

Becoming a father five times over has had a huge effect on Omar's spiritual journey and particularly on how he perceives himself.

"We are adamant that we can teach our kids to be really good people without taking up a formal religion as such. My wife's family are very relaxed Muslims but she has never been interested in religion at all. To tell you the truth, she has quite an allergy to organized religion and I can't bear the word 'spirituality,' although for me marriage and being a dad is the most spiritual and precious aspect of my entire life. For me relationship and connection are everything and I am grateful every day.

"For me and my wife 'reverence' would certainly be found in the way we think about our family, how we get together, have extended family coming and going in our home, treat our neighbors, my workmates at the restaurant. All that. Those are daily choices that I can't afford to make in a lazy way. I learned to be decent and loving from my parents and I am honestly not sure how much religion had to do with it. More than anything, I want our kids to learn to be just as loving from us. That's my biggest ambition, to raise good kids. I know I can't control everything that happens by any means, which makes me that much more passionate about 'choosing' where and when I can. We say little prayers together. We talk about people respectfully. I'm quietly confident. So is my wife. I like that."

❧

*You do not see the world as it is; you see the world as you are.* "Choosing" drives the journey of awareness. It's what the Buddhists call "coming awake." What this adds up to is that we will never "see" what is outside our awareness no matter how many people are standing on the sidelines, shouting and pointing. We have to *see* and understand. We have to *see* and choose for ourselves.

The capacity to choose at least some of our behavior and responses is one of the marvels of conscious human existence; it may even be the greatest. Without it, we are slaves to sentiment, ruled by our impulses and reactions as well as our past limitations.

A striking quotation from English writer and philosopher C. S. Lewis supports this idea. In *Mere Christianity* he writes, ". . . every time you make a choice you are turning that central part of you, the part of you that chooses, into something a little different from what it was before. And taking your life as a whole, with all your innumerable choices, all your life you are slowly turning this central thing into either a heavenly creature or into a hellish creature."

Two and a half thousand years earlier, the historical Buddha was saying something remarkably similar. "Mind is the forerunner of all actions. All deeds are led by the mind, created by the mind. We are what we think. All that we are arises with our thoughts. With our thoughts we make the world. Speak or act with an impure [confused] mind, and trouble will follow you like the wheel follows the ox that draws the cart . . . Speak or act with a pure [clear] mind and happiness will follow you, like your shadow, unshakable."

OUR DRAMATIC MOMENTS OF *SEEING* MAY seem like an epiphany. That's when we perceive and comprehend a situation quite differently from moments before and *feel less limited*. Sometimes these epiphanies resemble moments of synchronicity when events and perception collide in such a way that new conclusions or insights seem inevitable. Sometimes they are more like that "bolt from the blue" that seems to come from outside our own selves and in totally unexpected ways.

John Williams's story describes this phenomenon, and it's particularly telling that he was not a conscious spiritual seeker but a "very busy and stressed executive" in his mid-forties when he went to a local Sydney suburban church to listen to a piano recital in which his young son was taking part. John remembers the occasion vividly.

"As I sat in the church, somewhat bored, I was transfixed by a banner on the church wall. It was a depiction of the Holy Trinity, with the words underneath '*God Is Here.*' I sensed clearly an 'inner voice' saying to me, 'John, this is your home, I want you here!'

"I have been attending that church from the following Sunday up to today, eighteen years later! It transformed my life. I now know that this is called an apocalyptic experience, when God breaks through our normal senses and 'speaks' to us in a direct way. It is not uncommon and the authenticity of the experience is demonstrated by the way it changes a person's life."

John now describes his religious identity as "Christian, not in a fundamentalist way but in a pluralistic way in that I believe God can have a personal relationship with any person, no matter what their faith tradition. God is for me the sustaining Being for all of life and of the entire universe. Our being as humans exists in God and is sustained by God."

Of course I was interested to know whether this experience of revelation and inner authority has continued for John. He told me, "Prayer, meditation and reflection are all important for me, and very similar. I feel God 'speak' in the circumstances of life, when I am intent on hearing God's voice."

Seeking the sacred, we may be particularly open to inner revelations. We may even feel needy of them. We may also be particularly vulnerable to being influenced by them. Yet how do we know that we are hearing from "God," our Higher Self, our "small, quiet voice within," our own inner wisdom—or our wishes and delusions?

Perhaps it is safest to say that we rarely can know with complete certainty. In an age when rather too many people feel confident to read the mind of God and report back what they find to the rest of us, it becomes ever more necessary to test our inspirations and insights for unconditional and inclusive kindness.

Freedom of inquiry is as much a virtue around spiritual matters as any other. Not all sacred experiences are easily described. Nor do all make conventional "sense." Self-importance, sentimentality, portentousness can all be mistaken for reverence.

That makes it more and not less necessary to ask whether what we are receiving and taking seriously is genuinely nourishing; whether it is unifying or divisive; whether it is harrowing or healing. We should also feel free to ask: "Who's benefiting here?" Dogmatic, authoritative, pompous or self-important insights are rarely "divine" in my view; they are not even respectful. John's insight, by contrast, was decidedly healing and stabilizing for him. And it has continued to be so.

We could have many more such moments. And perhaps we need them. These are "teaching" moments that lead us into knowledge in quite different ways from our usual everyday analyses and information gathering. "We commonly do not perceive the world of Spirit," writes contemporary American theologian Marcus Borg in *The God We Never Knew*. "Although we are spatially close to God (for we are in God) we are epistemologically distant: our senses are geared to knowing only one level of reality—namely the world of matter and energy, time and space . . . we humans are like the Brazilian amphibian fish whose eyes have two lenses, one for seeing under the water and one for seeing above the water. But most of us most of the time have cataracts on our second lens."

A moment of unexpected grace or insight may hurtle us beyond the limitations of our own defenses. Sometimes it is awe itself that takes away our breath and then restores it. At those times "choosing" may seem barely to be part of the picture, yet how we interpret our experiences—how we *choose* to interpret them—continues to define them. It also continues to shape our most fundamental sense of being.

The epiphany moments that interfaith minister Heather Roan Robbins has experienced have also been powerful and transformative. Now living "next to the reservation of the Turtle Mountain Band of Chippewa Indians on the Canadian border with the United States," Heather remembers that series of moments vividly.

"A visit to a Full Moon meditation as a teenager at the Alice Bailey trust, in a roomful of experienced meditators, I felt that quick and profound depth of meditation I have only rarely been able to get back to on my own.

"Coming back to a high Episcopal church after many years in Buddhism and paganism and feeling, anew, the power and validity of the risen Christ, the empathy for my sorrows—in a way I had not felt when I walked away from Christianity early on.

"A weeklong pagan retreat with [writer and spiritual teacher] Starhawk in the mountains, enacting a form of [the Sumerian goddess] Innana's journey.

"The blessing of a hospital chaplain who prayed for me after surgery and the blinding healing light that exploded in my head when she anointed my forehead.

"Magical experiences around the death of both parents, which let me feel the continuity of souls and the spiritual support that waits for us all."

Heather's experiences in "locating the sacred and holy" are also vivid in her memory and strongly reflect my own. Heather says, "I feel it wherever three or more come together to dwell in the presence, or with healing intent, no matter what the [faith] path.

I feel it in the rhythms of science, when reverently shared, which weave together a portrait of wholeness: implied if still mysterious unified field theory, the awe of interconnection in cell biology, parapsychology and quantum physics."

Consciously or unconsciously Heather is echoing one of the most beautiful of the sayings attributed to Jesus: "When two or three gather in my name, there am I in your midst."

~~~~~

The twin capacities to *see* and to *choose* both our interpretations and actions within a context of reverence are dependent primarily on at least some degree of openness. This, in turn, depends on the subtle qualities of inner confidence and self-respect, characteristics that arise not from status, success or riches but from discovering that we are *capable* of seeing the bigger picture, capable of discerning, choosing and of *choosing well*. It may also come from a degree of humility that is itself freeing.

*Seeing* and *choosing* rescue us from the myths of our own help-lessness—or the delusion that tells us we have only our credentials and achievements on which to depend. Seeing and choosing let us know that we are capable of using our minds wisely *and* that we are capable of recognizing, learning from and getting over our mistakes. This is realistic. It is also compassionate, because as long as we are terrified of making mistakes we will live with intolerable fear and anxiety. We will also live at a distance from our sacred selves.

Seeking and choosing are not just essential to the sacred journey: this *is* the sacred journey. Jungian analyst and writer Jean Shinoda

Bolen suggests, "If we are spiritual beings on a human path rather than human beings who may be on a spiritual path then life is not only a journey but a pilgrimage or quest as well." What else but this would be potent enough to challenge the widespread notion that each of us is a victim of our own past, enslaved by our shortcomings, and condemned to repeat our own or even our parents' ignorance and failings?

Whose hand is on the tiller in your life?

In which direction is the compass of your life pointing?

Is your heart as well as your mind open to follow in that direction?

These are liberating questions. Taken even a little seriously, they could free us from replaying some of our most exhausted dramas on an endless loop. After all, what else but a developing confidence in our capacity to live with greater presence and consciousness would let us transcend as well as transform the everyday markers of success, wealth, status and achievement on which we more usually depend?

I am reminded again of the words of Paul: "Do everything in such a way that the divine can be revealed through it."

As crucial for us, as we learn to live with greater confidence in the sacred and with less anxiety about the self, is the chance to turn the teaching around in yet another direction: "Do everything in such a way that you can *discover* the divine [the sacred] through it."

A compelling echo of Paul's teaching occurs in writings collected as *The Wedding of Body and Soul* from the supremely loving twentieth-century Sufi teacher Hazrat Inayat Khan. Here, too, is an explicitly encouraging reminder of the power of choice and its centrality in the life of a spiritual seeker.

Inayat Khan wrote, "The Divine Presence shines equally upon everyone, yet it is our own personal choice whether or not we reflect that divine light into the world. If one does not allow the various attributes of Divine Presence to flow freely into the world, then one finds that daily life is filled with the conditions that arise when those attributes are obscured. For example, if we block the divine flow of loving-kindness, then we experience anger. Or, if we block the divine flow of compassion into this world, then we experience hatred. Oh dear friend, please look at your own life, and realize ..."

*Realizing,* I'm struck by a memory of how saddened I felt when I was told of a man in his sixties who spent much of the morning before his late-afternoon death checking the value of his stocks while his family sat beside his hospital bed. Perhaps it was his way of denying his fear of death. Perhaps if he was well enough to be thinking about financial decisions he was unable to comprehend how near death was. I have no way of knowing what was in his mind or heart. What I do know is that for many people those everyday markers or currencies of wealth, success or power are not everything, and that in some of the most challenging moments in our lives they may be revealed as less than nothing.

Because they are so familiarly alluring, however, sometimes it takes a truly painful loss or an extended period of suffering for someone to realize that even the best temporal gifts are, indeed, temporal, and that even while we have them they won't necessarily satisfy the holiest yearnings of the human spirit.

Sometimes exceptional success also brings that level of insight, especially when someone's goals are met, their dreams realized, and still they feel agitated, bored, craving or empty. In 1924 the poet Rainer Maria Rilke wrote in a letter to a friend: "However extensive the external world may be ... it hardly bears comparison with the dimensions, *the depth-dimensions*, of our inner being, which has no need even of the vastness of the universe to be itself all but illimitable . . ."

Perception of "the depth-dimensions of our inner being" is another way to talk about reverence or maybe wonder. The Bengali poet Rabindranath Tagore expresses something similar when he says, with mesmerizing bluntness: "Our true life lies at great depth within us."

Great hungers as well as great peace arise from those depths, from "the depth-dimensions of our inner being." It is in our depths that differences between us become increasingly irrelevant. It is in our depths that we know ourselves to be at one with all souls. It is from our depths that we yearn and seek. "I am so thirsty for God strong and living. When will I see the face of God?" cried Bruno, eleventh-century founder of the Roman Catholic religious order the Carthusians.

"I am so thirsty for God strong and living. When will I see the face of God?"

Hungers and thirsts are elemental in physical life. That is true in spiritual life also.

When those desires are frustrated, it becomes tempting to dance more frantically in the shallows, to pursue increasing levels of risk or excitement, to chase what is most sensational or distracting, to cultivate rage or outrage, to accelerate our own self-righteousness, to lust for applause or to fall into the troughs of cynicism, passivity or meaninglessness.

It takes a quite different kind of courage to name those yearnings as spiritual and to meet them. Or, more precisely, to allow them *to be met*.

Whatever our minds are fixated with, or turned toward, grows increasingly real in our lives and ever more compelling. That was the theme I developed in my book *Forgiveness and Other Acts of Love*. Choice is again central. Give a great chunk of your waking thoughts over to your anxieties, sense of injustice or, worse, your bitterness or hatred, and the toxicity of those emotions will flood your mind and life.

This is tragically predictable. So is the fact that the emotions still being generated long after an event (sometimes months or years after) will often be far uglier and more corrosive than whatever was triggered by the event itself. We see this in international and civic matters. We see it close to home. An alternative response is possible.

Almost all of us are capable of shifting our thoughts away from what will harm us toward what will heal and uplift us. This requires awareness and the conscious exercise of choice, but the rewards are tremendous. As we more consciously and confidently "reverence" life and our gift of life, gradually some of the intensity of our pain will recede. And something marvelous will take its place.

What we gain is not just a revitalizing burst of personal power but also a deeper and more confident sense of ourselves, and of the strengths we are free to call upon. This is self-encouragement at its most potent. It can literally shift our perspective on ourselves as well as the situation. It can certainly save us from some of the agonies of helplessness. If we are grieving it may allow us to be more fully present to our grief, rather than fearing or resenting that we may be overwhelmed by it. I believe this happens in part because we are calling on the strengths of spirit—with as much entitlement as we can muster. And also because we are avowing our connections

to the flow of human and possibly divine inspiration—again, w
as much entitlement as we can muster.

The values I chose for my healing focus when writing *Forgiven*
included forgiveness, courage, tolerance, restraint and generosity. B
our repertoire for choosing is huge.

Calling upon our spiritual strengths to support us is a conscio
process that I have learned to trust unreservedly. It is not an avoidanc
of pain. It meets the truth of our situation without obscuring that
truth through accelerating anxiety about how well (or badly) we
are coping. It is the transformational theme of most of the personal
accounts I have chosen to include here. It is the practical expression
of an unshakable reverence for life. It is what secures a spiritually
focused life that is not necessarily explicitly one of religious faith. It is
the primary way to skirt the ego's self-referential anxieties and draw
with trust from a deeper place that "belongs" to us all *unconditionally.*

This insight, and my faithful practice of it, literally saved me from
fear and brokenness over several harrowing years. It demonstrates the
most basic lesson of consciousness: that we can *notice* the direction in
which our thoughts, dreams and ideas are most constantly turning
and, when they are not taking us in a positive direction, *we can do
something about it*. Central to this is noticing that our choices have
consequences way beyond our own lives and concerns.

What could be more obvious? What could be more easily overlooked? We are not isolated little rafts bobbing about on the high
seas and occasionally colliding with or clinging to another raft. We
are, as so many spiritual teachers have pointed out, spiritual beings
on a complex, contradictory human journey: capable of finding
meaning and inevitably interconnected.

It is such a lovely paradox that even the most rudimentary eking of the sacred takes us inward to discover our "great depths" t frees us from the tyrannies of self-absorption and self-focus. I am minded of British writer Karen Armstrong's thought that I shared the introduction. People who acquired the "knack" for religion for spiritual self-inquiry, she claimed, "discovered a transcendent mension of life that was not simply an external reality 'out there' ut was identical with the deepest levels of their being."

That union of the immanent and the transcendent is essential for many in their understanding of the sacred. It allows them to know: *my life has depth and meaning. I am part of something infinite.* However we articulate a similar insight, it makes us far less frightened of the suffering, uncertainties and losses that are part of being mortal. It *grounds* us even while it elevates and inspires us. And it most usefully forces us to rethink our notions of separateness. Sitting for a moment with this idea, we see it's barely possible to grow in confidence about the strengths and stability we ourselves can call upon without growing in awareness that these are the sacred inner inheritance *of all living beings*.

This means seeing those potentials within our own selves mirrored in others—*without exception.*

THE SACRED MOMENTS THAT CONNECT US most deeply
to life *and* let us value life most deeply are always found *within* life
and are not divorced from it. It is liberating as well as realistic to
acknowledge this. They may be moments of solemn or exquisite
ritual. They may equally be moments when you are splashing the
baby in the bath or rolling up your sleeves to help a stranger. This
idea is richly developed by Constance FitzGerald, a Baltimore
Carmelite nun, when she writes, "Our experience of God and our
spirituality must emerge from our concrete, historical situation and
must return to that situation to feed it and enliven it."

*Enlivened*, the situation will be changed—and so will the participants. An awareness of the sacred may be momentary. But it also
changes and enlivens the moments that follow.

*A transformed moment, a transformed consciousness—and person—cannot
become "the same" again.* Allowing ourselves to be conscious of the
depths within life and ourselves, we draw from and gain a degree
of stability and trust that even the highest levels of psychological
health will rarely give. This comes out of the twin experiences of

connectedness and relatedness that for millions do not necessarily depend upon a personal relationship with God but do allow for a sensed, experienced, personal connection with the infinite Whole that exceeds words, concepts and descriptions.

Sometimes it is a meditation practice that supports this kind of inner stability. Meditation is one of the most effective ways to experience firsthand that we are more than our thoughts, instincts or emotions. Sometimes it is learning to deepen our experience of self through prayer, reflection, reading or writing a journal that is most supportive. Or as in Omar's account earlier of teaching and of *being* goodness to his children, partner, neighbors and workmates, it may be doing our usual chores with conscious willingness, engagement and mindfulness: transforming the way we think about them—as well as the way we think about ourselves.

The common factor here is being willingly present. *Present*, we are far less likely to be bored or distracted, even when what we are doing must be repeated many hundreds or thousands of times (making a meal, sweeping, cleaning up, tending our garden, walking to the bus stop, singing the baby to sleep).

*Present*, we are also accountable to one another and to ourselves. We are awake.

There's nothing heavy in what I am describing. On the contrary, when we feel steady within ourselves we can afford to be extremely lighthearted. The *ir*reverence I praised earlier comes back into focus. I have never given a retreat, for example, where our capacity to be deeply present to the sacred within and without, and inarguably reverent, was not matched by our capacity in other moments to be hilariously and sometimes very loudly joyful. We may spend far more time turning inward than usual when on retreat, but when we gather socially around abundant meals or in moments of celebration, it is with delight as well as acceptance and interest.

～✦✧✦～

A reverence for life, and the inclusive appreciation for life that comes with that, need not be dependent upon an explicitly spiritual outlook or on religious affiliation. Sometimes specifically religious ritual releases our capacities for reverence; sometimes it stultifies them.

That's made particularly clear for me in these reflections from Igor Kukushkin, who lives in Riga, capital of Latvia, and was the Russian translator of one of my own books. (I rarely get to "meet" my translators even by e-mail so this was very special.)

Igor was born in Leningrad ten years after the end of the Second World War. His father was an officer in the Soviet army and the family lived in many places, including Sverdlovsk and also the Kaliningrad district, as well as the German Democratic Republic (DDR). For many years of his life, "the church was officially separated from the state."

Igor continues: "Like millions of other children, I was brought up in atheist surroundings [although with the ideology of communism]. I studied the history of the world's major religions though. I read both Testaments [Old and New], Buddhist sources, translated video lectures by Krishnamurti and Osho. But I ought to add that whatever insights I had from my religious readings, it always was a purely intellectual experience.

"Funny thing is, my mom told me that when I was a baby my granny—who lived through her whole life in a small town on the Volga River [in Russia]—asked a Russian Orthodox priest to baptize me, which he did at her home. So one might say that technically I am Christian, belonging to the Russian Orthodox church, but this is a joke, of course, as I am a nonbeliever. Almost all religious sources of major religions contain dogmatic statements which safeguard the 'Big Truth' of this particular religion and in many cases these statements are rather militant. These dogmatic statements can do much harm, history showed it so many times, when they are used to brainwash uneducated or illiterate people or when some people willingly cling to them believing they can justify their intolerance of 'infidels.' This problem is religious and psychological. It is also an educational one.

"I translate from English and teach the English language. At fifty-four, I still prefer Mark Twain's *Huckleberry Finn* to any religious book because each time I read Twain I realize that, yes, we are spiritual beings, *though not necessarily religious ones*. Glimpses of beauty and harmony in life always help me to overcome difficulties. They are always there, you only have to look for them: city pigeons basking in autumn sun in the grass, the dance of snowflakes in winter air, thousands of tiny bright stars in the night. But the most valuable support always comes from people around you. Nothing can beat human concern and this is always revitalizing and unique.

"We are human—and our humanity is our precious gift. So I suppose for me kindness and human life are words standing closest in meaning to the words 'holy' and 'sacred.' I think Life in its infinite possibilities and complexity is just one profound, never-ending Mystery. It is like a beautiful flower and I suppose the best relationship a human being can have with a flower is to care for, grow and cherish it."

It is as we gain familiarity with our spiritual resources, and most particularly with our capacity to care consistently, that we will most effectively be freed from the twin tyrannies of insecurity and self-absorption. *Who am I?* becomes a less daunting question. Meeting the world from a place of trust, energy and excitement becomes newly possible.

A magnificent verse comes to us from Shams of Tabriz, the mentor so adored by the renowned Sufi poet Rumi. It is recorded in the *Maqalat* (Conversations) and offers us a perfumed road home.

What is the utmost end of need?
*Finding what has no needs.*
What is the utmost end of seeking?
*Finding what is sought.*
What is the utmost end of the sought?
*Finding the seeker.*

Georgia Carr captures the directness of this experience. She is a musician, composer and singer who has created many musical interpretations of the greatest poets of divine love, including Rumi. Georgia says, "I experience God as a verb not a noun. In the intimacy of every breath my Beloved is breathing itself through me. In the still darkness of the night and in the glory of the dawning light, I am never alone. Behind every life experience the True Teacher is there, inviting me to bring even more of myself into the healing power of love. I feel myself to be part of this great Being of Love which accompanies me through the difficult challenges of life, constantly inspires my heart in song, and ignites my spirit in unity with all."

Perhaps you will read what I have just written and regard Georgia's vision of her own life, as well as the intimacy and trust it expresses, as unusual or unusually fortunate. What is unmistakable, though, is her contagious reverence for life. It's a reverence that demands a degree of humility but rewards with an immersion in a spiritual reality that is palpable in Georgia's music and thinking.

It's true, of course, that the religious and spiritual freedoms I am pointing to can be complicated. They support the kind of self-awareness that the ancient Greeks pointed to unequivocally: "Know thyself." They prevent us from making the kinds of excuses to ourselves that keep us immature and helpless as we look around for others who know more about our lives than we do or whom we can blame for what is not going to plan. They make us stand up. They make us grow up. That's their song of freedom. Choice becomes ours even in the most severely outwardly restricted circumstances.

They can also, however, induce a sense of self-blame when our feelings don't match our best intentions. At those times we need to bring compassion to our setbacks, and especially to the uncomfortable feelings that come with them. We need to look at our own selves through the "eyes of the Beloved," as the mystics put it. And we need to harness our stubbornness here, our tenacity and persistence. It is impossible to feel reverence for ourselves or for our gift of life—or for life—when we are flooded with insecurity. Those feelings may only become worse when we beat ourselves up for having them or feel rage when someone directly or indirectly brings to our attention another possibility.

Two things help. The first is very simple. Our inner changes are not always "convenient" to outer timetables. We can't and we do not always move right along at a pace that others would like and we also might desire. We may need to grieve, mourn, regret intensely. But we can do so without blaming ourselves for our feelings or telling ourselves that *this is all we will feel until our own death comes.* Despair is indescribably frightening. Whatever our circumstances, we can save ourselves that.

The second point is just as uncluttered. It is that when we feel spiritually as well as psychologically adrift or bereft we need to and we can ask ourselves what support would most benefit us.

We need to hold fiercely to the consciousness that *we are not alone.* Inner abandonment feeds despair. Sacred teachings for some of us and prayer, a spiritual community for others, a support group, honest journal writing, a relationship with God or the inner divine, however tentative: these are all ways of knowing ourselves from a place of plenty rather than depletion. And they all involve some reaching out as well as reaching in.

AS OUR REVERENCE FOR LIFE DEEPENS and grows more familiar, and as we *use* our gift of life rather than believing it is using us, our respect for our own lives becomes more secure. This happens quite naturally. A teaching from Shintoism captures this for me: "That mind which gives life to all people, throughout the world, is the very mind which nourishes me."

Could it be clearer? Sacred "nourishment" is available to all. The divine "mind" is mind to all. We are in it; it is in us. Seeking has source as well as direction. And its welcome is universal and unconditional. This is the kind of teaching you would want to wrap yourself up in at night so that it could imbue your dreams.

The challenge to take up this depth of encouragement in a meaningful way is fourfold: to feel and identify a spiritual thirst or hunger; to awaken the will needed to reach out (or surrender); to discern and partake of what is most nourishing; to embody and live it.

This process releases our capacities for wisdom, as well as hope and compassion. I am inclined to think that anyone who has opened up a book called *Seeking the Sacred* may feel at least a little of that spiritual thirst. Perhaps the act of reading is already an expression of the need to reach out or surrender. That leaves two steps only: to discover what is most personally nourishing and meaningful, and to bring that to life through your own choices and experiences.

Just as ancient as the Shinto teaching are these lavish words of praise for Wisdom herself from the Wisdom of Solomon (7:7, 10, 11): "I prayed and understanding was given to me. I called on God and the spirit of wisdom came to me . . . I loved her above health and beauty and I chose to have her rather than light, because her radiance never ceases. All good things came to me along with her, and in her hands uncounted wealth."

How do we breathe life into those words rather than simply reading them? How do we allow them to breathe new life into us? How do we grasp the notion of an unceasing radiance, translating and transforming it so that it is dynamic, provocative, even troublesome, rather than merely "beautiful?" How do we seek and claim our portion of "uncounted wealth?"

Are we up to that?

Sometimes when I am teaching I hear myself saying with considerable passion that we are not spiritually ambitious enough. Only days ago I said it again in the old inner-city church where I lead spiritually inclusive services and meditation, thinking then also about what I was writing here. For nearly two hundred years people have taken their hopes and needs with them to that particular church. In many ways, we walk in their footsteps. We seek the sacred. We seek reverence. We seek meaning and reassurance that our lives matter. *And* we allow ourselves to be inhibited if not by what we are seeking, then by thoughts of our own inadequacy.

*We limit our capacities to seek, rather than allowing seeking itself to transform the ways in which we see ourselves and one another.*

Fear of our own longings is part of it. We learn early to contain our passions—even to be ashamed of them. Our distractibility is also part of it. Old habits of insufficiency or unworthiness also linger for many, whispering to us that to live "spiritually" is pretentious, overly precious or possible only for the saintly few. We are trapped, often, by the very emotions that effectively awaken the heart.

~⚬~

Living with an open heart is certainly easier to describe (and encourage) than to achieve. Anxious self-absorption, along with the defensive and sometimes offensive behaviors that self-absorption drives, is at epidemic levels in the West. We are drowning in an ocean of self. Education and economic privilege don't change it. Counseling or psychotherapy often makes less difference than it should. Competitiveness and ceaseless one-upmanship are rampant. Individuals and, increasingly, institutions are vastly distracted from their sacred potential by their refusal to take responsibility for their actions or even to acknowledge the effect of those actions. Instead, the culture of blaming others grows more pervasive, as does justifying wrongdoing rather than making amends.

Religious beliefs self-evidently don't always save us from this. Justifications of violence in the name of religion are heartbreakingly common. But a "spiritual perspective," with or without religious beliefs, also does not and cannot provide any guarantee of self-responsibility or care.

Unconstrained egoism and self-interest is always a danger in spiritual or quasi-spiritual movements. In fact egoism can be especially dangerous in spiritual groups or movements because it may be more shadowy and covert than elsewhere. People may be truly adept at praying fervently, preaching or teaching eloquently, sitting in meditation for many hours, serving up "pure" food, chanting exquisitely or offering service to people they don't know or live alongside, and just as adept at crossing psychological or sexual boundaries to get their own needs met.

Wrongly understood and used, almost any spiritual practice or attitude can inflate us. Only when wisely lived can it strengthen and connect us.

Sentimentality may also get in the way of authentic spiritual seeking. It may even stand in for it. We see this depressingly exemplified in contemporary books and articles or television programs that claim to be about spirituality or to be spiritually driven yet focus on a very narrow version of self-interest, sometimes in quite outrageously shallow ways. In a world that already worships material wealth and personal ambition rather than kindness, fairness or justice, this too can be perilously distancing from our sacred potential.

However slight, any shift in perception to a more inclusive and respectful vision is always significant—and never for our own sakes only. At the very least it means we will find ourselves less anxiously needy or psychologically defended. With that, we will be less judgmental or harsh with other people and far less inclined to exploit them. We will certainly be far more interested in thinking about the effects of our choices and attitudes. And we will be increasingly confident that no one is responsible for those choices other than our own self.

∼✺∼

Whatever our circumstances, we need to find ways to remind ourselves that from a spiritual perspective personal good and common good are never separate. In fact, I would go so far as to say that our spiritual maturity depends upon our capacity to see our personal "good" (well-being, emotional and moral health and happiness) as irretrievably linked with the common good (how our choices affect and influence and collectively create what we call "community").

No one wants to miss any chance to feel "good." Depression and anxiety have reached plague proportions in the West. "Feeling good" may easily seem like the necessary antidote to that. As a craved state of existence, however, it can congeal into self-absorption all too easily. What's more, a world entirely focused on our own selves is always far too small to be uplifting.

Please don't misunderstand me. I am not proposing a new cult of suffering or martyrdom. I grew up with plenty of that in my later childhood and know its shadow side intimately. But the pendulum of expectation has swung far in the other direction. Many people experience grief, loss and suffering, even disappointment or frustration as a personal affront, adding outrage or self-pity to what are anyway difficult emotions to bear and navigate. That undermines their confidence and their courage. What's more, in that state of mind it is impossible to care wisely and compassionately when others suffer.

"I prayed and understanding was given to me. I called on God and the spirit of wisdom came to me . . . her radiance never ceases. All good things came to me along with her, and in her hands uncounted wealth."

Taking my hands off the keyboard, turning my office chair toward the window and sitting still for several minutes, open and present to "unceasing radiance," I experience the stretch between the ancient and the immediate as an essential part of this journey.

Seeking the sacred, we yearn for what is most sublime in human experience. And we yearn for seeing the ordinary in newly appreciative ways. Our yearning takes us far as well as deep. It also settles on the nearby. It raises questions and cannot always answer them. It confounds linear thinking. It teaches patience. It reveals the tenderness and beauty that are intrinsic to a meaningful existence. But it must be something more than personal comfort or "feel-good" moments that we seek; more even than compassion or kindness.

As we discover and rediscover inspiration and meaning we must give them new life, letting them challenge all of our presumptions. A moment of surrender or reflection, as refreshing as the purest water, lets me know that when I read the dazzling poetry and scriptures that have survived sometimes for several thousand years, *I am receiving something priceless.* What's more, I do not have to be worthy to receive it or even ready. Worthy/not worthy are irrelevant concepts here. I have only to lift up my eyes or look inward.

"I called on God and the spirit of wisdom came to me ..." In these moments of again consciously reverencing life I feel such closeness to whoever wrote those timeless words as well as to those who treasured them enough to preserve them, memorizing them and singing, chanting or praying them for hundreds of years before they could be written down.

From every culture and within every culture, inspiration is *here* for the taking. And yet as wonderful as those inspirations are, my sense is strong that there will never be a more effective teacher in our lives than our own lived, complicated everyday experiences or, more precisely, than our conscious reflections upon those experiences: the stories we inwardly create about them, and from them.

I love this example from interfaith minister Dennis Swartz, who has been practicing the spiritual philosophy of Science of Mind for twenty-five years. His spiritual life has combined with what he calls his "worldly" life in Washington, D.C., for at least that long.

"Most of the time I look for the spiritual reasons behind what's happening in the present," he tells me. And this supports Dennis in ways that are not always accessible to analysis but make a significant difference to his inner stability and confidence.

Dennis continues: "Some of my 'worldly' challenges I've been able to overcome in time through use of my spiritual principles, while some are still a work in progress. The greatest lesson I've learned from all this is that life is a spiral *upward*, not a spiral downward. I may find myself in the same old situations but on closer examination most times I get a little different perspective and understanding on causes behind them. What's happening in my life is not so much *about* me as it is *for* me. It's another opportunity to gain a deeper awareness of just what I'm made of."

It takes tremendous courage to consider that whatever is unwelcome in our lives is not happening to us but possibly *for* us. I don't see the universe (or "God") as directly intentional or interventionist. That's right outside my belief system and my experience, although I frequently pray for guidance, support, insight, comfort and relief. But I do see that virtually whatever happens that is serious enough to shake us to our bones, we can in time retrieve some wisdom from it. This is not necessarily *why* it happened, although when something has come about because of our carelessness or lack of attention it is good to face that and be clear.

We give ourselves a priceless gift when we open to the highest, most refining levels of inspiration that are available to us. Music, nature, the abundance of wisdom from the world's spiritual traditions, other people's hard-won insights and kindness, a freshness of view, prayer and reading: all of that can be miraculously inspiring.

At the very same time, we can discover how much there is to gain from the events and experiences *unfolding in our own lives*. We can learn from our mistakes, triumphs and disappointments, from our pettiness and our greatness. How and what we learn, what prejudices we will reinforce or explode, what new levels of self-responsibility and care for others we will achieve, will depend entirely on the context within which we are seeking our answers. This, in turn, will depend on who we believe ourselves to be, as well as what we believe we are capable of becoming.

Another deeply encouraging example comes from Sue, a calm, generous woman in her sixties whose life has been anything but easy. Married young, the mother of four adult children, a former pastoral care worker and now a grandmother, hers has been a life that has often taken her to extremely raw places, particularly in relation to one of her children who has had years of severe mental illness. Yet Sue's resilience is fundamental now to her sense of self. And what that resilience depends on is a hard-won knowledge of what she frequently describes as "God's faithfulness."

Sue explains, "God for me has become over a period of many years of searching my best 'friend.'"

Does Sue have faith in a transcendent Being? This question is irrelevant. She explains that, for her, "God is 'dwelling in my heart!' I know our Dearest Heart is there because I have been able to be led over the past thirty-seven years into a new life of love and forgiveness that I never, ever knew existed. At the age of sixty-four I now feel for the first time in my life so deeply happy and joyful in the knowledge that no matter how hard life can be, and it has been very hard for me at times, that there is a way through it all that leads to a loving outcome, one that I often could never have envisaged if I had just relied on my own judgment.

"I run to that 'mystery'—I cling to that 'mystery' and I begin to know that 'mystery'—through every brother and sister who crosses my path. I know when I am miserable, frustrated and sad that I need to sit and reflect on *how I got there*. Usually when I retrace my steps and reflect with our Beloved Mystery a thought will come from nowhere to help me understand and encourage me to stretch beyond my boundaries and act upon it. It's an awesome thing to look back and see the intricate way, that amazing patience of the Spirit in helping me and waiting for me to 'choose once again!'"

Sue's journey toward this depth of understanding and peace of mind has been a long one. She explains, "I was a baptized Anglican with nonpracticing but very 'loving' parents. We never went to church and when I asked my father once what churches were for—probably at about the age of four—he said they were for baptisms, marriages and funerals.

"I chose Catholicism early in my married life after a horrific tragedy that affected our family deeply. A neighbor's child drowned in our backyard swimming pool. We were not at home but the child broke through an old lattice fence and was drowned. And he was there for hours. This was not something we could have prevented but the death of this child was more than I could bear. I can remember yelling out, 'Oh God, Oh God,' and feeling surprised within myself that I was calling out God's name. I hadn't actually acknowledged that there was a God for many years. I had decided that God didn't exist after my mother died suddenly from a brain hemorrhage when I was fifteen. Six years later I experienced the sudden death of my best friend who was murdered in a premeditated shooting by a person she had worked with. As far as I was concerned these two people had been such beautiful good people and I couldn't believe in a God that allowed these sudden deaths. That, for me, was unforgivable.

"When I look back on it Roman Catholicism started me on a journey of forgiveness. The Church ministered to me for many years and I have a great respect for her—like the respect I have for my mother. Like the Church, my mother fed and cared for me for the first fifteen years of my life in so many ways: the physical and the spiritual do intertwine. I became an avid Mass attendee and all my children went with me whether they liked it or not until they were old enough to make their own decisions.

"Reading the Bible, the lives of the saints and spiritual books, and being helped and shepherded by many wonderful priests and friends, led me to this time in my life where I feel loved and free in my own being and know beyond a shadow of a doubt that I am a part of God and so is everyone else on this planet. I believe God wants us to know that we can head toward our healing and wholeness in this life no matter how hopeless the situation looks and feels.

"To be able to experience and get a glimpse of what true forgiveness is really about goes way beyond words. It just needs to be lived. We all know deep within when a heavy burden has been lifted off us and the 'peace that surpasses all understanding' returns.

"These days being a universal Catholic feels a comfortable description of where I fit. I am very happy to attend the ritual of Mass when I feel I want to partake but I now know in my life I can and often am in the dear Heart of God in my thoughts in an instant. I have been supported by [twentieth-century 'revealed' text] *A Course in Miracles* for years now and am so happy to know there are so many ways to commune with the Heart/Mind of God which then gives me the guidance I constantly need to love and forgive myself and all the other wonderful human beings that I have been given the grace to journey along with."

Listening to Sue, and to many other people's stories, I am repeatedly reminded that to see our lives as sacred is literally life-saving. It can take time for this thought to become personally meaningful. Often we will endure times of confusion and perhaps despair before even a glimpse of such confidence dawns. When it does, it creates the quietest and most lovely revolution.

EVEN THE MOST OBLIQUE CALL TO the sacred urges us to regard our lives with respect and hope *whatever our external circumstances*. It shows how naturally love can become our primary expectation *and* identity, our point of reference, light and guide. It shows us that love loosens the bonds of self-absorption. Love makes it unnecessary and then repugnant consciously to hurt or demean other people. Love makes it possible to be expansive, inclusive and generous. Love also makes it possible to worry less and trust a great deal more.

Many people are hesitant or afraid of seeking new meanings for love. They may be especially afraid of the implications of loving and wholeheartedly accepting themselves. That motif comes up often when I talk to people about their spiritual development. But true love is liberating. What's more, it is impossible to seek the sacred, to seek to live more lovingly, and to exclude our own familiar, imperfect selves.

It's not abstractions about love but our moment-by-moment *living more lovingly* that will teach us what love is. This means restraining some habits (anger, frustration, self-pity, helplessness, impatience, intolerance, selfishness, criticism, sarcasm, resentment . . . the list is long). It means consciously and actively cultivating other habits (thoughtfulness, a willingness to give the benefit of the doubt, encouragement, taking pleasure in others' successes, good humor, generosity, forgiveness . . . that list is also long).

This is a lifetime change. After all, we don't usually manage to identify as a spiritual being—complete with spiritual resources and strengths—in a single moment. When that does happen, we might be seriously tempted to call it enlightenment! Most of us take a far curlier route to seeing more clearly and living more lightly and lovingly.

This time, *our* time, is marked by cynicism and individualism, by greed, injustice and unsettling restlessness. Yet its freedoms are fresh and precious. We live in a time of perpetual questioning, not least about what it means to be human. That freedom is a jewel. Under the protection of this jewel, understanding can become the developing, organic process it surely is. Understanding can be reborn each day in the light of what we never cease to learn. In the English language we speak sometimes of things being "*dead* certain." It's a chilling phrase and too often an accurate one. This is never more true than in the context of religion or religious zealotry.

While formal religion remains an inspiration to kinder and more engaged living for billions, for others it is reason enough to cultivate prejudice, to close minds, to banish, exile, punish; to promote self-righteousness of the most deadly kind; to kill as well as die. Alongside those extremes of belief and disbelief, religion is also, for countless millions, irrelevant or despised.

Those shifting sets of extremes—*dead* certainty about religion or spirit (for or against), or cynicism, indifference or horror—may appear to be the religious markers of this age.

Yet those are not the only voices to be heard. The stories that I have listened to over years convince me that many contemporary seekers would cheerfully say that the world's religions have a profound value—*and* that they are human institutions capable of tragic failings. This doesn't mean that we can no longer learn from them. On the contrary, as with all our relationships, we have a great deal to learn from those failings in both practice and interpretation.

I am confident that there are serious spiritual seekers prepared to live with ambiguities and questions and to embrace them, while also wholeheartedly welcoming the illuminations and gifts sacred to our moment and our time. Increasingly I meet people for whom seeking is itself a path. And questions of doctrine or any kind of monopoly on truth are entirely secondary to discovering *how best to live right now*.

Nigel Marsh isn't "typical" of this cohort. For one thing, he is an accomplished author and motivational speaker and an exceptionally successful advertising executive on the global stage. But I do feel that he speaks for many when he describes why, despite having no belief at all in a personal "God," he keeps going back to Meeting for Worship with the Religious Society of Friends (Quakers)—and as a young man at a British university chose to study theology rather than any other discipline.

"Although I have no faith I attend Quaker meetings (when the demands of four young kids allows). I keep going back for a number of reasons. In no particular order, the first is I secretly, and vaguely, hope that attendance in some way increases my chances of one day actually believing! Secondly, I come away from each session feeling a slightly better person, motivated to be a slightly better person and determined to look for the best in other people. Thirdly, I enjoy the hour of worship itself—an oasis of calm in what is otherwise a rather busy life. Fourthly, they don't require me to pretend that I believe anything. Lastly, it helps me focus on the stuff that matters as opposed to the stuff that we think matters."

To a great extent, seeking the sacred is all about seeking "the stuff that matters." And what will let us know that we also "matter." This is a markedly twenty-first-century position, speaking out of and exploring a terrain where personal responsibility is highly valued and where the complex processes of inner transformation are honored. It also acknowledges the inner fragility to which we are all subject. And it creates a terrain where a reverence for life itself becomes sacred.

*～ひ～*

After a lifetime of religious and spiritual exploration and experience, I increasingly treasure the chance to worship, pray, sing or meditate with anyone genuinely seeking to touch or express the sublime in their lives. And going to places of pilgrimage or worship, I am aware that I rarely know exactly what to expect.

An event that happened years ago wonderfully exemplifies this and remains pivotal in my memory. My two children are now in their mid-twenties. Then they were barely at school and I was rarely free to respond spontaneously to invitations. But late one afternoon, as I was thinking about nothing more serious than what I would prepare for dinner, a friend called to ask if I would like to go to a small gathering that same evening for the oracle of the Dalai Lama. The oracle is a revered monk in the Tibetan tradition who happened to be visiting my home city of Sydney for a few days. At this time His Holiness the Dalai Lama was himself widely known and loved but nowhere near the spiritual supernova he has become (not at his own wish, I suspect).

Despite my years of interest in meditation and Eastern teachings and practices, I knew nothing at all about this monk who, in a state of trance, guides or advises His Holiness on spiritual matters. But as preoccupied as I was, something pulled me toward that event. I got myself ready and went.

In my mind's eye, there were fewer than fifty people in that modest upstairs room hastily decorated by local Tibetan Buddhist practitioners. Perhaps there were fewer than thirty. We sat in meditative silence for a time and then the oracle gave a talk. I don't understand Tibetan. His English was extremely limited. The translator's English was also limited. I have no idea what the oracle said, but what I do remember as vividly as if it were yesterday was the exceptional atmosphere of that exquisite occasion.

In the monk's presence I felt a boundless expression of loving-kindness, openness, harmony and inclusion. Those spiritual qualities radiated from him and touched and opened me in a rare and unexpected way and, I suspect, everyone else who was present.

This was not something I had in any way anticipated. I could not have "created" the experience imaginatively. Had I been able to do so, I would have done it again many times. I could not even have "desired" it because, although I have been fortunate to be in the presence before (and since) of some outstandingly learned and devoted spiritual practitioners, this went far beyond anything I had previously experienced or could have sought.

The overwhelming impression I had then and for many days afterward was that I had been "woken up" to the presence of the Holy Spirit—a presence that can be likened to the sun: always there (can only be "there") but sometimes shrouded behind clouds, in this case, the "clouds" of my everyday doubts and distractions.

Does it seem confusing that I might believe I felt the presence of the Holy Spirit or the spirit of holiness (*Ruha d-Qudsha*, in Aramaic)—familiar, though in different ways, to Jews and Christians—in the presence of a highly esteemed Tibetan Buddhist monk?

In part this is an issue of language. Someone else might speak of the monk's "Bodhicitta" qualities: the radiance that comes from unconditional loving-kindness and compassion. Yet another person might avoid any religious terminology and simply say how miraculous it felt to be in the presence of such a loving man. It is, however, also the case that contemporary Zen Buddhist monk and writer Thich Nhat Hanh freely speaks of the Holy Spirit as the "energy sent by God" and likens a moment of receiving this "energy" to a moment of authentic mindfulness.

In one of his many teaching books, *Living Buddha, Living Christ*, Thich Nhat Hanh writes: "To me, mindfulness is very much like the Holy Spirit. Both are agents of healing. When you have mindfulness, you have love and understanding, you see more deeply, and you can heal the wounds in your own mind ... [I feel] all of us have the seed of the Holy Spirit in us, the capacity of healing, transforming and loving."

As with any authentically sacred experience, the time that I spent in the presence of the oracle transcended his or any particular religious teaching. The clarity and intensity the monk radiated confounded all speculations. And it was made much more precious because it was so completely unexpected. With so few comprehensible words, it had nothing to do with depth of scholarship or the usual meanings of "brilliance." Nor was it something that one might routinely find in local temples or spiritual centers, Buddhist or any other kind.

What I experienced took place in an unprepossessing room in an unremarkable building in a fairly rundown part of the city. There were no trappings of ritual to stir the imagination. Before and since I have been at far more dramatic ceremonies, including highly ritualized empowerments given by His Holiness the Dalai Lama himself. The evening I am describing could not have been more humble nor more transformative. For days afterward I felt I was living a joyful spiritual cliché. My feet were not touching the ground yet I remember noticing that I was feeling exceptionally "grounded," allowing me to be in rare and welcome alignment with my then excessively busy and demanding external life and the profound spiritual longings of my inner world.

⁓ৎৣ৶ৎ

A more recent occasion demonstrates in a far less dramatic way how different "different" religious experiences can be—and, again, how unpredictable. And perhaps this anecdote has a special value, too, because it comes much closer to what most of us are likely to find.

This time I was visiting one of the smaller Hawaiian Islands for a week's lovely holiday with my closest friend, who is as fascinated by religion and as inspired by spirituality as I am. We had scanned the island for religious "opportunities" and decided to go to two Christian services on the only Sunday morning we had there. Our hopes were high for the first service. We had been charmed by the picture-book look of the place—white clapboard building, tall steeple—and a delightfully warm welcome on the noticeboard outside. Those hopes were quickly dashed, however, as we were harangued along with the rest of the tiny congregation about our miserable state of sinful existence, the only solution to which was to take a tragically limited view of Jesus Christ into the center of our lives. There was "religion" in plenty. What was entirely missing was the gentling presence of the sacred.

With plummeting expectations we turned up to the second service and found ourselves literally brought to tears by the genuineness of the experience, by the palpable sense of holiness and holy spirit as well as community, by the humility and kindness and insights that were so abundantly in evidence in the young priest, especially, but also in the large, varied congregation that spilled out beyond the vast open-sided church to the sturdy benches outside.

EXPERIENCE, INTUITION AND THAT mysterious but unmistakable quality of "presence" are all vital aspects of our seeking. They are also vital to our understanding of reverence. Yet each is also highly subjective and in continuous flux. Noticing from time to time what motivates us, as well as what satisfies or disappoints us, we can learn much about what it is that we are longing for. We can also learn a great deal about what sustains us.

Kim Cunio is an exceptionally talented musician and composer with whom I have worked closely during recent years. We have come to know each other well as we have pushed through crazy deadlines to create work together that would adequately express our shared passion for music, poetry and, above all, spirituality.

Music is a remarkably powerful tool for creating as well as understanding transcendent experience. In the space of a few notes it can enhance our most profound needs for reverence as well as for the consolations of presence.

The power music and poetry potentially have to "translate" the sacred and our yearnings for it goes way beyond culture. This is particularly well understood by Kim who, in his own words, "was born Jewish, into quite a devout Eastern family: a mixture of Baghdadi [Sephardic Jewish] and Burmese/Indian culture." All of this has been of tremendous benefit to him.

"I received great nourishment from Judaism as a child [and] it did not bother me that the synagogue was a place of relatively little spirituality because my father had a great deal of it, and therefore the synagogue could be a place for play. I heard my father speak the *Sh'mah Yisrael* prayer to me every night of my childhood till I was at least five. I cannot thank him enough for this. But as a teenager I knew that I would struggle to be a literal Jew. Indeed, one of the nicest things about being born into that path is the fact that no one cares if you believe as long as you identify with the culture."

In his twenties Kim spent a good deal of time with Buddhist teachers. In his late twenties, he "discovered the wonders of a Hindu yogic path and a part of me came home." Now he senses that he has a commitment to a more universal and inclusive transcendent mysticism and says, "I love pretty well all religious ritual. I regularly attend a meditation group, take retreats every year, go to interfaith services and still go to the synagogue on occasions and particularly for religious festivals. My favorite [religious events] are musical spiritual events as I love to fuse my love of music with my love of the divine. I see the faiths like a family: some are a bit nutty, some are cosmic, and some are really good at helping to keep me grounded. Ultimately they are my nonphysical companions on the road to self-awareness and one day I will be alone again, as I started."

Kim regards himself as a "God-lover" and regards life itself as a "divine inheritance." As he told me, "I had about ten years, my Buddhist phase, where I still believed intently in God but was content to do spiritual practices without the names of God on my lips. I guess I substituted 'Buddha nature,' or 'enlightened self,' for much of what God has always symbolized for me. This was very good as it encouraged me to take responsibility for my own mind."

Kim also explains with a real lightness of heart his capacity to be present to the mystery where the names or descriptions of God matter far less than yearning, seeking and experience. "God is both theistic and non-theistic to me now. That is the great bit: beyond duality. As a child I had no doubt of a beautiful presence and I was always attracted to the mysteries, and the greatest mystery is from where our consciousness comes.

"At some point I surrendered and said, 'I will have faith in something I cannot intellectually understand,' and from that point many experiences came, some very subtle and some very strong. Within this was a definite dictate to purify my life so I could have and interpret these experiences with greater joy and clarity.

"Of course everything is a mystery.

"Our dearest friends are like volcanoes ready to surprise us as they surprise themselves. Our own minds are barely known to most of us. I certainly have not fully charted mine. Children sometimes do this very well, as long as they are not constantly distracted outside themselves, as do many people who have their own version of dreaming. A mystery is simply something we cannot 'know,' and personally I am quite happy not to know everything. An orange is still an orange regardless of whether I know its chemical compound, its history, all the people who have grown it, etc. And even with that knowledge I will not truly know even one orange. All I can do is abandon myself to an orange when I see it and taste as much of it as possible when I eat. That is how I relate to the mysteries."

Kim turned forty recently. Like many contemporary seekers, he sees mysticism as inherently anarchic—refusing conformity and "discipline" in a worldly sense—yet demanding an inner discipline combined with an active engagement with the world that rapidly develops an unconditional reverence for the mystery of life and the mysteries within life, as well as trust and bliss.

◈⟋⟍⟍⟍

Driving home some months ago from the same Saturday morning meditation class that Kim attends, with my mind filled with thoughts about God and the passion of our search for God and the sacred, I turned on the radio in my car and found myself listening with fascination to the voice of renowned Canadian architect and former University of California academic Christopher Alexander.

Alexander's eloquent views about architecture, and an authentic form of creativity *grounded in actual place rather than in theories about place*, were themselves captivating enough. And they wonderfully echoed what I hope to achieve here: an affirmation of spirituality grounded in attitude, values and behavior.

But what grabbed my attention as I drove and listened was Alexander's simple, moving description of how he tackles problems when confronted by a decision where there is only a slim margin of choice: where, in essence, either choice could be right.

The example he gave was that he might need to choose between two kinds of pillars: the slender pillars would be more elegant but the heavier pillars would be sturdier. How should he compare and choose between elegance and sturdiness?

While he spoke I found myself quite automatically scanning my own mind for points of reference, as Alexander clearly intended his listeners to do. I had to ask myself how *I* value sturdiness. Or elegance. And how I value them in relation to one another.

What made this fascinating is that it seemed to be a three-dimensional puzzle. Or perhaps an aesthetic one. But all those usual measures and considerations collapsed instantly when Alexander said, "I ask myself which would be the gift I would like to give to God."

Earlier on that same morning, over bowls of black rice, fruit and coconut milk, members of our meditation class had wondered aloud whether it is possible ever to talk meaningfully *about* God without opening to the experience *of* God. There had been something of a consensus about how personal and distinct, yet universal, such experiences of "God" usually are, even when people are keen to avoid the old metaphors and symbols we associate with God.

Is it possible to have a life-changing, intimate connection with God without casting God in one of "his" traditional roles?

Can "seeking" be unshackled from dogma and "belief" in the conventional sense while remaining intrinsically reverent, even holy?

Heading home through the rain, hearing Christopher Alexander speak as directly as the meditators at breakfast had, was like being given a gift myself. Unexpected, delightful, satisfying: as all great gifts are.

Christopher Alexander then went on to point out—and again I was identifying strongly—how many of the decisions we make are self-focused. I believe he meant that we make decisions to do something as well as we can, and *also to reassure ourselves*. In other words, we may be seeking less to reassure ourselves that what we are doing is all right than that *we ourselves are "all right."* This acute need for reassurance explains why we can feel so violently attacked or insulted when someone criticizes our decisions or even casually or indifferently questions them.

By contrast, using his sense of what it means to offer a "gift to God" as his measure, Alexander the architect—who described himself as someone raised as a Roman Catholic who now rarely goes to church—felt that he was able to move his personality self out of the way, bring his sense of God into the foreground and put his own ego and its attendant anxieties into the background.

This sounds as simple as a lullaby.

As I recall those listening moments and write about them, I can feel myself newly lulled. Nonetheless, in the context of thinking about the "God" to whom one is or would be making the gift or offering, the waters darken.

I might well wish, for example, to offer the writing of this book as a gift to God. If I were in a Buddhist frame of mind I might wish to express a hope or prayer that whatever "merit" this book may generate would not be for my benefit only but for the benefit of all living beings as we raise each other up.

That kind of dedication is not at all foreign to me. In my years in Catholic schools I wrote AMDG on the top of each right-hand page of my school exercise books, offering up my paltry schoolgirl efforts *ad majorem dei gloriam*: to the greater glory of God. And the influence of such intentions continues to fascinate me. Do they do something more than focus the mind or set a compass for the heart?

My schoolgirl dedication was like a mantra, a word far in the future for my adolescent self. It was a rhythmic reminder written in ink and across my consciousness to bring an awareness of God into my daily activities. God, after all, doesn't need "greater glory." The need is not God's but ours. Nonetheless, any routine like this creates a flow of positive intentions and itself becomes an invaluable act of consciousness.

In a way that is remarkably similar to Alexander's question to himself—"Which would be the gift I would like to give to God?"—it creates and enacts reverence.

It also arouses a sense of choice and consciousness. What motivates us to do what we do? How does it influence us? How does it align us with what we most value?

Those small acts of dedication surely have some effect on what is created. They will also significantly affect the person doing the creating.

IN FREEING OUR MINDS FOR REVERENCE, it is helpful to remember that it was the Greek philosopher Plato who urged "contemplation of the eternal, beautiful and good"—spiritually transformative qualities connecting us to and perhaps arising from an unseen world beyond our familiar senses. "Concerning these things [ultimate truth]," wrote Plato, "there is not, nor will there be any treatise written by me. For they do not at all admit of being expounded in writing as do objects of other studies … Only after long, arduous conversance with the matter itself … a light suddenly breaks upon the soul as from a kindled flame, and once born keeps alive of itself."

Hundreds of years later Paul, the man often described as "the first Christian," wrote a letter to the Philippians (4:8). It includes these lines:

*All that is true,*
*All that is worthy of reverence,*
*All that is good and holy,*

*All that is lovely to look at and beautiful to hear,*
*All that has virtue and all that deserves praise:*
*Let this be the content of your thinking.*

Come forward more than one and a half thousand years or so to meet a twentieth-century German theologian called Rudolf Otto who died in 1937. Otto wrote a book called *The Idea of the Holy* that is certainly not reader-friendly by today's standards. However, it is deeply affirming to those of us risking intimacy with the sacred. In Otto we have a writer who wants us to know awe. Who wants us to disentangle the utilitarian from the sublime, and moral obligation from the numinous and holy. This is a writer who knows what reverence is and how inevitable it is when *a light suddenly breaks upon the soul as from a kindled flame.*

In the decades since Otto's death, I suspect we have become more and not less awkward with the holy—though no less in need of it. As the old metaphors for God have weakened and faded for many, we may also have become lonelier for God.

When it comes to the holy, we are easily discomfited. *How could an intelligent person believe . . . speak of . . . or seek?* In this highly judgmental context, theories about religion are fine. Experiences, longings, desire for the divine are not fine. Defensive responses become unsurprising.

It's in *The Idea of the Holy* that Otto makes a key point about the difficulties we continue to have in affirming what may be most profound and meaningful in human existence. "The most remarkable characteristic of Plato's thought," he writes, "is that he himself finds science and philosophy too narrow to comprise the whole of man's mental life ... No one has enunciated more definitively than this master-thinker that *God transcends all reason*, in the sense that He is beyond the powers of our conceiving, not merely beyond our powers of comprehension. 'Therefore is it' "—and now Otto is directly quoting Plato—" 'an impossible task both to discover the creator and father of this whole universe and to publish the discovery of him in words for all to understand.' "

Freeing ourselves from the literal and the linear should not strip our lives and imagination of richness; it should add to it. Perhaps contemporary theologian Marcus Borg helps us out a little when he uses the terms "God," sacred or Spirit interchangeably. And he makes this clearer when he writes in *The God We Never Knew*, "By 'concept of God,' I simply mean what we have in mind when we use the word *God*. All of us have some concept of God, whether vague or precise and whether we are believers or non-believers."

Borg himself thinks of God as "the encompassing Spirit," not separate from the universe but a "nonmaterial layer or level or *dimension of reality* all around us."

This is the same dimension of reality that mystics understand as love.

The abbess, scientist, healer, composer, mystic and writer Hildegard of Bingen, who died in 1179, brings us this presence. These words were revealed to Hildegard in one of the many visions that began when she was less than three years old and continued to the end of her long life:

*I, God, am in your midst.*
*Whoever knows me can never fail.*

*Not in the heights. Nor in the depths.*
*Nor in the breadths.*
For I am Love,
*Which the vast expanses of ignorance will never still.*

Invigorated by love we can face our inner constrictions and defenses bravely. In the language of spirituality: the lover of the divine surrenders to love from the divine. Death and fear recede. Meaning is transformed.

Here we have a true all-or-nothing situation. Here we come to the crux of this book. We are either *all* spiritual beings having a human experience, as twentieth-century writer and priest Pierre Teilhard de Chardin memorably put it, or none of us is. We either *all* have a soul or are a soul, all have Buddha nature or are Buddha nature, are all made in the image of the One—or *none of us is.*

This is the ultimate equal opportunity. Beyond tribes, cultures, religions, beliefs, passions, ideas we are a single spiritual family. Or, I would suggest, there is no "spiritual."

༺ঙৃৎ঵ঽ༻

Lived consciously, our seeking of the sacred will liberate us from helplessness. It will connect us with greater interest not to people only but also to the magnificent, sometimes treacherous elemental world on which we depend. It will make the world newly wondrous even while it lets us see what needs attention—and what needs to be left in peace. Tenderness and appreciation for our own lives can grow from this, whatever the sorrows that are an inevitable part of human existence. And reverence can also grow.

A reverence for existence is infinitely precious. It is liberating and it is humbling. But even that inner stability and confidence, and the peace of mind it brings, is less goal than sustenance on a complex journey of seeking—to which each one of us is unconditionally invited.

# IDENTITY

*Our birth is but a sleep and a forgetting:*
*the Soul that rises with us, our life's Star,*
*Hath had elsewhere its setting,*
*And cometh from afar.*
*Not in entire forgetfulness*
*And not in utter nakedness*
*but trailing clouds of glory do we come,*
*from God, who is our home.*

William Wordsworth (1770–1850)

OPENING TO THE SACRED, WE TRANSFORM our vision of ourselves. We might redefine our answers to that primary existential question, "Who am I?" We might add a less familiar question: "What am I?"

Identity and also what we identify *with* jostle here in a tiny space. How does the "I am" statement end for you? *I am a . . .*

As I write this I am wondering what your response would be if I could sit with you and ask, Do you identify primarily with your nationality? Or is it your culture, gender, religion that comes first to mind? Is it your values or achievements? Do you first see yourself through your human relationships? Or your lack of them? Or perhaps your work identity rises above all else? Or is it an addiction, illness or betrayal that dominates your *I am . . .*?

And, if we were to go on sitting together, perhaps you would let me also ask whether it is possible for you to take all those attachments and identifications very seriously indeed *and* also see yourself as a spiritual being whose very life is sacred?

I can't prove the sacredness of your life or mine. Where I can be entirely confident is that *how* we think about life and *how* we regard all other life forms on our planet is driven by what we believe and the stories or narratives we tell ourselves. And that this inevitably determines the quality of our existence.

~~~

Identity emerges through a confluence of stories. Whatever our culture or circumstances, we live in a thicket of stories. These stories enlarge or contract our sense of the possible. They strengthen us and keep us safe. They can also put us (and others) in mortal danger.

Almost all of us have a primal "story" that inspires our way of being or justifies our reasons for keeping our life small. Often we are barely aware of how formative this story is. Perhaps at the age of fifty you are still a "neglected child." Perhaps at the age of fifteen your guiding story is one of determined idealism. Perhaps your story is of being lost; or found. Whatever that story, it will be hypnotic in its power, opening your eyes to some possibilities, closing them to others.

Culture and religion remain potent. Your story may be that only fools and the needy cling to religion. It may be that God loves you infinitely and unconditionally. Or that you are a helpless sinner and must beg and plead for a wrathful God's grace and forgiveness. Or that you have created this life through choices in an infinite number of previous lifetimes. Or that there is no intrinsic meaning to life and that with your last breath the party is over.

Stories may be spoken or unspoken, shared or deeply private, yet still be transformative. Repeated often, or existing on the cusp of awareness, they create and drive an inescapable dimension of human consciousness. They teach us how to be human. They teach us what "being human" could mean. So great is the power of story that we are less affected by what happens to us than by how it conforms to our expectations and how we explain it to ourselves. "Making sense of things" is a uniquely human capacity. And it drives our being and becoming.

Identity as well as being are shaped by multiple versions of story: dreams, symbols, metaphors, imagination; the weaving of the public with the private; through others telling us who we are or should be; through the discoveries we make and how we reflect on them. We literally become the embodiment of the stories that ring most convincingly within us. Learning who and what we are, we "author" our own lives. We stumble forward. We make presumptions. We read our minds. We change our minds.

A compelling illustration comes from Eboo Patel's outstanding memoir, *Acts of Faith*. Patel is an Oxford-educated American Muslim of Indian origin and founder of the Chicago-based Interfaith Youth Core. He writes: "In college, I had understood identity as a box to lock myself in and a bat to bludgeon America with. I was seduced by the notion that we belonged to a tribe based on the identity of our birth, that our loyalty rested exclusively with the tribe, and that one day my tribe of dark-skinned third world people would rise over our white oppressors."

Many factors changed Patel's mind (literally, his ways of thinking). Primary among them were the writings of the legendary twentieth-century author James Baldwin. A brilliant African-American who lived for many years as an outsider, even in relatively cosmopolitan Paris, Baldwin was an influence on my younger self also. His experiences and courage touched me deeply and I recall reading his books like a hungry person in my late teens and early twenties. It was with exceptional interest that I read these lines from Eboo Patel about Baldwin and the power of identity:

"Here was a black man who had been chased out of restaurants because he had the temerity to ask for a cup of coffee from the front counter, rejecting separatism in favor of the hope of pluralism, a society where people from different backgrounds worked together, protected one another, sought to achieve something more meaningful for all. Here was a man who viewed identity as a bridge to the possibility of pluralism."

James Baldwin refused the identity thrust upon him in what was then a radically unjust, racially intolerant and disunited United States. Eboo Patel discovered his chosen identity—chosen in part in response to his external circumstances—to be equally limited and in need of spiritual as well as psychological evolution.

✦

We may spend a lifetime without questioning who and what we believe—or who and what we believe ourselves to be. If we are more fortunate we may over time question almost everything. I can't emphasize too strongly how important this kind of self-creation is, and the self-responsibility that ideally accompanies it. If I don't feel responsible for the kind of person I am, how can I possibly take mature responsibility for everything I do?

The "right to question" is basic to any version of freedom. So is our right to be "ourselves" and to discover for ourselves just what this means at each and every stage of our personal and social development.

As someone who is deeply affected by poet Rainer Maria Rilke's plea to "live your questions now," I am thrilled by the privilege of being alive in a time when we can question virtually everything. Buddhist writer Stephen Batchelor in fact goes as far as to suggest that "our very existence declares itself to us as a question."

In the same book, *The Faith to Doubt*, Batchelor also warns, however: "Once we find something to believe in, it is easy to forget the original question."

A capacity to interrogate, explore and experiment is the bright side of our complex "individuality." It lets us know that we can and often must find things out for ourselves. It is also vital to achieving our human and spiritual potential.

This doesn't mean that we will always find or even need answers. "Answers" are often nothing more than a temporary salve for the itch of our anxieties, after all. The point of asking questions is surely less to discover answers than it is to live in a state of mature engagement with the questions that matter most.

Like so many other contemporary seekers, I remain deeply suspicious of any system, religious or otherwise, that discourages questions, argument, investigation and doubt or—heaven help us—forbids them. A closed system is always a danger, not least to itself. Its members risk becoming authoritarian or cowed. A Zen teaching sums this up wonderfully, as Zen teachings often do:

*Great doubt: great awakening.*
*Little doubt: little awakening.*
*No doubt: no awakening.*

OUR INNER STORIES BEGIN WITH OUR first experiences of self-reflection, probably before we are conscious of "self." With their inevitable omissions, repetitions and embellishments, with their tragic features and comic ones, their illuminations and shadows, those innermost stories are every bit as important in creating who we are as the more familiar markers of temperament, gender, race, culture, education, parenting and social class. They describe our most personal vision of what life is and what gives it meaning. *They tell us who we are—or should become.* And, as we live them out, they demonstrate to others who and what we believe ourselves to be.

A spiritual teaching on this comes from Sufi teacher Hazrat Inayat Khan: "Man is the picture or reflection of his imagination. He [and she] is as large as he thinks himself, as great as he thinks himself, as small as he thinks himself to be. If he thinks he is incapable, he remains incapable; if he thinks himself foolish, he will be foolish and will remain foolish; if he thinks himself wise, he will be wise and become wiser every moment ... Whatever is impressed on man's soul, with that the soul becomes endowed, and that the soul will become."

Some of what is "impressed on [the] soul" and imagination—through the conscious and unconscious realms of the mind—is domestic, subjective and personal. Some of it comes from what we could call meta- or collective stories that describe "life" to us.

Religious teachings, ideologies and philosophies as well as cultural assumptions and customs are highly significant here. These meta-stories could be likened to the air we breathe: we take them in as often unknowingly as knowingly. And we take in the complex issues they present around gender, race, social class, age, success and status and, of course, the meaning and purpose of existence.

They create the context within which we are continuously evaluating our experiences and creating our expectations. They create the circumstances in which you are teasing out for yourself the ideas I am presenting in this book. They influence how we will engage with life. And they support—or impede—a trust in the sacredness of life.

I am not ignoring the psychological factors that also affect us. But those factors routinely grab our attention (and I have certainly paid them close attention in other books I have written). What I am emphasizing here is an intertwined, dynamic process whereby we breathe in certain aspects of an infinitely complex "story" of what life is and means, of what our own personal life is and means, and breathe (and live) that story out.

For millions, religious identity *is* religion, particularly when elements of defensiveness creep in. Sometimes the "story" that creates and sustains a religious identity is more important to a person than their relationship to or with God. In other words, *being* a Jew, Christian, Buddhist, Muslim or Hindu may be more important than praying and believing as someone of that faith is assumed to do. This may be emphasized when religious identity connects you to some people and separates you from others. Chandler Burr's novel, *You or Someone Like You*, takes this as a central theme and plays it out within an increasingly tense "mixed" marriage, in that case between a Jew and non-Jew.

In my childhood, few people in the Catholic world hesitated to use the description "*non*-Catholic" for all those "others." I know of Protestant Christians who still today talk of "Christians" and "Catholics," or of the "saved" and "not-saved"; of Mormons who refer to all non-Mormons as "Gentiles"; of an Australian boy raised in Australia by his Indian parents who have made it quite clear they would never accept a non-Indian, non-Sikh, non-medical-doctor bride. The list goes on.

What I am emphasizing here is the power of story in the creation of identity, and its effects on the lives of people from a range of faith backgrounds who see their religious affiliation as more tribal than creedal. When any version of religious apartheid dominates, the call to love becomes faint or inaudible. God as source and inspiration of love may barely be in the picture. Indeed, when religious affiliation is extreme—and no religion is exempt here—"God" is often reduced to a bit part, wheeled onstage to bolster the outrageous claims on which prejudice feeds.

How else to understand that someone can believe they are serving or pleasing their God by dehumanizing, killing, starving, enslaving or going to war against their fellow human beings while someone else will risk their own health, security and relationships to care tirelessly for complete strangers—serving that same God?

How else to explain, as Dr. Viktor Frankl attempted in all his books but with exceptional clarity in his supreme *Man's Search for*

*Meaning*, that in the worst of situations (and his "worst" were the death camps of the Holocaust) some people will discover within themselves unprecedented depths of dignity and compassion while others will find only rage, revenge, cannibalistic self-interest or despair?

Identity cannot be distinguished from what we identify *with*. Nor can it be separated from our most personal sense of being and meaning.

Yes, there are psychological "reasons." There are also spiritual ones.

⁓ᘐᕓᘗᕒ⁓

In the most ordinary of circumstances an absence of love, joy, tolerance and plain good humor leave powerful traces on how people see themselves and value their own existence. Perhaps I am struck by these "ordinary" examples because of my own conviction that it is in such experiences that the sacred is found—or lost.

Donna is a passionate, highly competent woman now in her fifties. I am touched by how clearly she catches the sad trail of this, and especially the inevitable confusion caused when religious people claim to worship and adore a God of love, yet treat others—or themselves—with violence or contempt. Looking back from an adulthood lived mainly in the United States to her childhood in the straitlaced New Zealand of the early 1960s, Donna remembers how "Mrs. Fricker" particularly exemplified the lack of love and joy, generosity and simple kindness that she came to associate with religion.

"Mrs. Fricker was a pillar of the Methodist church I grew up in from age two," Donna remembers. "She seemed to be an unkind, ferocious person, especially to little children. To an eight-year-old 'good girl' who thought church/God/Jesus was all about love, this was disorienting.

"At age fifteen, freed from the parental contract to attend this church anymore, I visited a different church in our village each Sunday, my heart touched by the Baptist singing and the Presbyterian boys. All I knew was Christian and confusion: 'Do as I say not as I do.' For example, my family found it impossible to fathom that our new Jewish neighbors did not celebrate Christmas. They were ridiculed along with anything and anyone else that differed from our righteous, superior ways.

"The judgmental, bigoted environment of my youth fanned the inborn passion that set me apart from my family: a profound acceptance of all and an abiding faith in the wholeness and rightness of all that is. Amidst the tedious, confusing, disjointed, compulsory churchgoing, the monthly communion services were the precious highlight because they touched some aspect of my being in a way that satisfied me. Those services were extra long as each adult went to kneel at the rail at the front of the church to receive communion. I loved this long process: the organ playing quietly; the minister in full regalia offering over and over in his sonorous voice the body and blood of Jesus. The atmosphere of beauty and reverence reached beyond my mind and restless young body deep into the soul."

Donna's instinct about what her soul and self needed, despite the careless bigotry around her, was critical to the person she has allowed, encouraged and sometimes pushed herself to become: someone who has "a profound acceptance of all and an abiding faith in the wholeness and rightness of all that is."

Today, decades later, Donna's kindness, humor and vitality, and especially her remarkable inner strength, testify to her having survived

Mrs. Fricker and those like her, but not easily. Donna left New Zealand for the United States in her twenties and tells me that it was not until she was in her thirties that she woke up to what she calls "living life."

"Previously I had existed as *surely a good girl should*," she says. But the changes she needed to make to achieve a freer way of living took years to recognize and achieve.

This doesn't surprise me. My own experience is that any significant change to our inner sense of self or identity defies simplistic expectations. Sometimes it takes "forever"; sometimes it is so instant it seems as though it has already happened. That continuum and the paradoxes it represents was rather how it was for Donna.

"I totally rejected the concept of the God I grew up with and for a long period could not even utter the 'G' word. I am grateful for what I name *grace*: an energy beyond mind, beyond cause and effect, beyond conditioning that offers me the frame that I am, at essence, a spiritual being. As far back as my memory goes I have felt safe (a spiritual safety) and a deep knowing that *all is well*, that all is in perfect order. This does not mean that I have not ached and felt challenged and tormented and experienced deep despair. But somehow there is this untouched 'witness' of deep, unshakable faith that is very much in my awareness. In more recent years the relationship has developed to be almost constant. This relationship does not prevent my reactive humanness but it has evolved to offer real-time perspective and detachment from what previously would have been heart-stopping drama and soul-destroying wounding."

Part of Donna's "soul-destroying wounding" was the toxic mix of attitudes so freely expressed by Mrs. Fricker. Yet however grim the "Mrs. Frickers" outside ourselves may be (and are), they are far less of a worry than the "Mrs. Frickers" who take up a more permanent kind of occupancy in our own minds.

This is another way of talking about the super-ego, or the darker side of our crucial conscience. Conscience is something we need. Without it, we are dangerous. We need to be capable of admitting to being wrong when we are wrong; capable of asking for forgiveness and making reparations when we have done wrong; and we need to be capable of feeling shame as well as guilt, without losing ourselves in those feelings.

Discernment is our great friend here. This means learning to look at the consequences of our attitudes and actions rather than at our own justifications or excuses for them. It means *listening in to our own stories*. And allowing ourselves to be guided by what is most healing and least harmful.

Guilt, remorse and shame have had very bad press in recent years, and with good reason. Those who would get most benefit from feeling these complex emotions are perhaps least likely to accept them. Worse, these potent emotions have been manipulated for generations to belittle or punish others, or to establish a hierarchy of power that is rotten to its core. But that does not mean that we should make ourselves incapable of feeling remorse and sorrow if we are wrong, and especially if we have harmed others or ourselves.

A strong identity and sense of self allows us to see a situation truthfully and learn from it. It is not only religions or religious people who feel entitled to condemn, dehumanize, punish and even kill from a place of ruthless self-righteousness. But when this is done in the name of religion or the sacred, it becomes a travesty of love.

THE TWIN PROCESSES OF SEEKING AND transformation call to us from the most ancient myths as well as the world's religions. Seeking the sacred, we hear and sometimes heed those calls and we do so in multiple ways. Yet there is a familiar note also that crosses cultural and religious borders, speaking clearly to what we share. Those precious, common calls to the sacred invite us to pay close, mindful attention to the way we think about ourselves and to who and what we believe we are. This is not to bring our attention incessantly or obsessively back to ourselves. On the contrary, it is (again) because *how we think about ourselves will emerge loud and clear through the way we think about and treat other people.*

(How we think about God, and particularly what we believe God is or perhaps what the meaning of life is, will also emerge loud and clear through how we think about and treat other people, and I return to that vital theme many times in these pages.)

Indeed, because it so inevitably reflects in our behaviors, how we think about ourselves has to be our first and most persistent sacred investigation.

What would it take to see your own life as sacred?

Where and how is "goodness" reflected in your choices?

Do you see yourself as a source of encouragement for others?

Are you willing to assume responsibility for your life—without conditions?

On what basis do you judge the value of others' lives?

What is your life for?

John Allison is a poet and former teacher who, in his own words, lives "amidst the tall trees of the Dandenong Ranges east of Melbourne." John is someone I have "met" through the magical connections that writing and reading allow. After my book on Rilke was published he contacted me—just in time for me to ask him, in turn, what he believes his spiritual identity and story to be. He told me, "Seeing myself as 'a spiritual being' is an ongoing developmental path. From late adolescence I was convinced of the reality of reincarnation, and that remains so. This implies awareness of a core entity that evolves throughout lives, and thus my present life has meaning and purpose. There are times when this is evident. But there are other times when nothing seems certain—this is suitably humbling.

"An important corollary is that others also must be spiritual beings, and so are also to be respected. It is a task of social imagination to perceive this, and to realize that there must be meaning and purpose in their lives, in their behavior."

John's confidence that he is a spiritual being has emerged at least in part from living through the deaths of his sister (when he was nine) and his best friend (when he was fifteen). Both deaths were accidents and left behind an awful mix of grief and incomprehension. Yet, as John explains, "Something else resulted from these deaths. I became contemplative in late adolescence and a more peace-filled, knowing, spiritual self has gradually coalesced around this inwardness. I still persist in using the word 'ego' (in its Latinate sense of 'I am') for this self, but since my forties I've recognized this self/ego is both presence and emptiness: a space I choose to inhabit and, if not, a limited identity of habit and reaction occupies that space—resulting in difficulties."

In *Walking Out of Another World*, one of John's own books, I found an exceptional description of himself at three: exceptional because his sense memories are so strong, exceptional also because they so lavishly demonstrate that the more wholeheartedly we can engage *into* (not just *with*) life, the more clearly its depths are revealed to us and become us. That richness speaks so vividly to me of the sacred: *more* life, not less; *more* engagement and texture, not less.

Here is John recalling his three-year-old self who is noticing: "the lanolin musk of a pile of woolsacks; odours of thick oil and creosote oozing from rusted drums against the back wall of the barn . . . the fussing, clucking chooks in their fenced run; the *cawdling* of magpies, the sudden barking of sheepdogs . . . There are earlier memories, but this is my first experience, as I walked from gate to yard to shed to barn, of mood."

Then, much later in the same book, John shares this moment of quiet jubilation: "Sometimes, walking in the world, I am stopped by wonder. It is astonishing to be alive."

Identity that reflects and connects us to a religion or religious faith is never homogenous. Often, though, we behave and react as though it is or should be, especially in relation to those we call "others." As a painful example I increasingly hear generalizations being thrown around about Muslims, with scant regard for the fact that more than a billion people living in virtually every country in the world, speaking many languages and exposed to a huge range of educational and cultural conditioning could hardly add up to a single "type." Equally, a minority of Muslims are quick to condemn the rest of the world as "infidels" and to condone limitations on women that are at best abusive and at worst life-threatening.

All such stereotyping is irrational and dangerous. It's also commonplace. What else is it but stereotyping, for example, when convinced atheists feel free to condemn the intelligence and common sense of all believers?

Sam Harris is a clever, persuasive writer. But what are we to make of these sentiments that appear quite early in his best-selling *The End of Faith*? "Nothing that a Christian and a Muslim can say to each other will render their beliefs mutually vulnerable to discourse, because the very tenets of their faith have immunized them against the power of conversation."

There are currently about two billion Christians and a further billion and a half (or so) Muslims sharing life on this planet. Perhaps there are far more. Even if there are far less it is fair to suggest that innumerable formidable factors have played a part in making each of them who they are. Those same complex factors have *made each of us who we are.*

With this in mind, it becomes easy to suggest that some and perhaps many millions of Christians and Muslims have *not* been effectively "immunized against the power of conversation" and may indeed be "conversing" richly and productively even as I write or you read. And not with adherents of the "other" faith(s) only, but also with those who believe differently and variously within their own vast and vastly diverse faith families.

Zuleyha Keskin is a young Muslim, a pharmacist and mother living in Sydney who is devout *and* engaged actively in interfaith activity. She is able to say, "I am certain of God's existence and presence at all times even if I am not always conscious of His existence and presence. My reflections on my surroundings and on myself have brought me to this conclusion. God's existence is like breathing; when I am conscious of my breathing, I know it is there. But I also know that my breathing will be there when I am not conscious of it."

The depth of her beliefs and the security of her religious identity allow rather than disallow Zuleyha to engage fruitfully with people of other faiths. Nonetheless, whatever story we tell ourselves about what religion is will also markedly determine what we will perceive as well as experience.

Another example is shared by Yulianto Lukito, a Buddhist born in Indonesia, the world's most populous Muslim country, and now living in Sydney. Known to his friends as Sin Sin, he studied Buddhism at primary school but then "took it for granted." At eighteen he decided "to look back at the religion I was familiar with, which is Buddhism, and treat it as my spiritual guidance with a willingness to understand it more deeply on a personal level."

To Sin Sin, "Being religious is not necessarily the same as being spiritual. To me, spirituality is very personal. It's about looking within and understanding how our own mind works. We need to learn to accept who we are, our negativity, our defilements and, with an open heart, we shouldn't be afraid to face the reality of our negative aspects.

"By acknowledging these, we can then direct our heart and mind to virtues and transform the negativity into something positive. Spirituality is an ongoing process and it's not just about our destination. Every day and every moment is a precious spiritual moment. It's a matter of how we see the world around us. This is a constant challenge for me."

The causes and effects of "how we see the world around us," as Sin Sin puts it, are particularly well worth thinking about when cultural examples of religious toxicity abound and when people's difficulties with religion can seem so overwhelming that it becomes hard to remember the good that religions point to, and also achieve.

The "story" of religion is itself immensely powerful. So are the stories of and within the religions. Some of those stories are uplifting in ways that are unparalleled in secular philosophy. Some lead to gross oversimplifications and to stereotyping of the most dehumanizing and violent kinds.

STEREOTYPING IS THE SHADOW SIDE OF identity. It tells you who you are—even and especially when this has no resonance whatsoever with your inner sense of meaning. It insults your humanity and depends for its power on a painfully familiar capacity to reduce complex human beings to a few derisory adjectives.

We are all capable of such thinking, no matter how tolerant we believe ourselves to be. Decades after I knew better I can still hear myself passing outrageously self-righteous comments about people who are driving social injustices on the world stage, or people who have injured friends or members of my family. Generating some compassion for the cruel and unjust—particularly when they are powerful—is one of the toughest challenges of a spiritually focused life. So is avoiding making excuses for them. Or for our own narrow-minded, condemnatory thinking.

We need to know that it always harms our own sense of self when we reduce "the other" to little more than an object of our contempt. Such behavior demonstrates a brutal ignorance of the subtle and even the gross complexities of each individual's unfolding situation, and of spiritual claims that in our vast and often uncomfortable diversity we are a single family.

Identifying the harm that such attitudes and behaviors cause, we have no better teacher than our own awareness. We, too, are capable of acting in these ways. We, too, know at first-hand the pain we feel if we are discounted, dismissed or belittled.

How we think about ourselves and what we believe we are capable of being will largely determine what kind of person we are becoming—and also what kind of *people* we are collectively becoming. Those twin processes are indistinguishable. Affirming an inclusive spiritual perspective will support us in a healthy refusal to fit into the prison of someone else's stereotyping. It will also help us to challenge and tame our own reductive thinking.

The contemporary philosopher George Steiner has written a provocative critique of those tough "Who am I?" and "Who are *we*?" questions. In his example, they are illuminated by the creation of the State of Israel in 1948. Steiner focuses on Israel and he raises equally timely questions about what we can and should expect of "religious" people—perhaps including our own selves.

"Israel," Steiner writes in "Zion" in *My Unwritten Books*, "marks both an ancient and an unprecedented miracle in Jewish destiny, in the possibilities of Jewish survival. But in order to be, Israel has had to regenerate capacities and values dormant since the Book of Joshua. It has had to cultivate, to glorify, military skills and ruthlessness. The internal cost has been considerable ...

"Essentially powerless for some two thousand years, the Jew in exile, in his ghettos, amid the equivocal tolerance of gentile societies, was in no position to persecute other human beings. They could not, whatever their just cause, torture, humiliate, deport other men and women. This was the Jew's singular nobility, a nobility which seems to me far greater than any other. I hold it as axiomatic that *anyone who tortures another human being, be it under compelling political, military necessity, that anyone who systematically humiliates or makes homeless another man, woman or child, forfeits the core of their own humanity* . . .

"The State [of Israel] lives behind walls. It is armed to the teeth. It knows racism. In short: it has made of Jews *ordinary men*."

꘎ꕤ

The failure of many religious people to live wisely and well feeds our casual judgments of others and is widely canvassed. In the case of Israel, the situation is more complex still as many people who are ardently Jewish (inside and outside the State of Israel) do not identify as religious. Being Jewish is central to their "story"; being religious is not. And those who are religious identify with this in a brilliantly *untidy* variety of ways, as in every other religious grouping.

Yet if we take 'religious people' as a category for a moment—and that gives us far more people globally than not—something striking emerges: the rage and outrage so many of us feel when religious people become, as Steiner expressed it, "ordinary men" (and women).

In the same essay Steiner argues for the impossibility of living up to religious ideals. "The normal man and woman pays lip service; they do not, they cannot live their works and days in this blinding light. This failing, however, nurtures fierce psychological resentment."

I want to challenge Steiner's view that we cannot live up to our religious and spiritual ideals. I believe that we can if and when those ideals are themselves nourishing, inclusive and self-accepting: *when they express the sacred rather than the ideological.* And yet it is indisputable that in the name of religion (and God) "religious" women and men live out the shocking worst of their human capacities as well as the sublime and inspiring best.

So is it not possible to suggest that *against much evidence* we go on expecting something different and *better* from those who believe or seek?

And perhaps also of ourselves?

~~~~~

The highest religious ideals are also the least adorned. A wonderful story demonstrates this. As the story goes, the first-century teacher Rabbi Hillel the Pharisee was asked to sum up the instructions of the Torah (the first five books of the Hebrew Bible) while standing on one leg. "What is hateful to you, do not do to your neighbor," he said. "That is the whole of the Torah. The rest is commentary. Go and learn it."

Seeing all human beings as "neighbors" is the spiritual demand here, along with responsibility for everything we do. No qualifiers, no excuses. Two vital qualities are needed: imagination and empathy. I write about this much more extensively later in this book. Enough to say here that healing hearts and minds, bringing happiness to others, lifting their spirits and our own, sharing what we have, regretting our mistakes and doing something about them, we would, with imagination, kindness and intelligence on our side, bring the kingdom of heaven to earth.

Heading in that direction—and why not?—edicts and ethics will, however, take us only so far. Context matters. *How we see ourselves matters.* Something less tangible must take us further. It's another wise man, Rabbi Abraham Isaac Kook, who died in 1935, who illuminates that holiest of possibilities.

*There is one whose soul expands*
*until it extends beyond the border of Israel,*
*singing the song of* humanity.
*In the glory of the entire human race,*
*in the glory of the human form,*
*his spirit spreads,*
*aspiring to the goal of humankind, envisioning its consummation . . .*
*Then there is one who expands even further*
*until he unites with all existence, with all creatures,*
*with all worlds,*
*singing a song with them all.*
*There is one who ascends with all these songs*
*in unison—the song of the soul, the song of the nation,*
*the song of humanity,*
*the song of the cosmos   resounding together, blending in harmony,*
     *circulating the sap of life,*
*the sound of holy joy.*

A SACRED VISION OF *WHO WE ARE* shifts our parameters of being. It can soften and even blunt the edges of our prejudices, envies, scorn and competitiveness. At a personal level, it can redefine status for us and lessen our terrors of failure. It can make our gender expectations and biases less troubling as we more readily accept someone in their human complexity as well as their sacred depth. It can make our differences less abrasive as we begin to comprehend that each of us *is more than our thoughts*, more than our instincts and emotions, more than our allegiances.

As we make those discoveries for ourselves—little by little learning to perceive and interpret life more inclusively and generously—it also changes the way we think about the sacred.

This seems to me to be very well understood by Amrita. The daughter and sister of medical doctors, she is a graceful, talented woman who chose medical research rather than medical practice, and has had an exceptionally successful academic career. At the outer levels of identity and status, her life has been satisfying and rewarding. But, like so many people whose stories are shared here, those hard-won outer successes have not been enough.

Amrita explains, "It may seem odd for a person trained as a scientist to have a relationship with mystery. Being a curious soul I enjoy the process of analytical thinking and investigation not only in my work but also in daily life. It is the notion of 'wonderment' that captivates me initially, whether it is an observation or experience. I am open to appreciate the experience before I decide to examine it further and don't at all feel a conflict when something occurs that is a complete mystery. When too much effort is expended on trying to reason and thus validate a mystery the essence of the experience is lost for me.

"My early childhood was in Asia and it was in this rich environment that I initially observed a range of spiritual practices. Although I was brought up in the Christian faith and attended church as well as Sunday school I remember being very curious about other religious practices. I did not realize until my adult years as to how much attention I had paid to these observations. I progressively felt that I was simply going through the motions of occasionally attending church but not connecting in a spiritual sense. I yet admired my grandmother's deep faith in God and devotion to the practice of Christianity. What always remained with me throughout my life is the concept of goodness in intent. I paid less attention to dogmatic notions in religious practice and more attention to sincerity in intent."

Hearing Amrita say this I felt such a strong connection to her capacity to accept what is mysterious (as distinct from what is available to analysis). I also felt in tune with that quite vital distinction she is insisting upon that if the sacred is to be successfully integrated into our lives, rather than being regarded as an ornament to them, then "goodness in intent" and action trump ideology every time.

How someone behaves will "betray" with great accuracy their inner sense of self and identity—and often also what they identify *with*.

Behavior is far more telling than what someone claims to believe. This doesn't deny the weight of belief. It reinforces it, because when someone believes one way and acts another it is fair to assume that their beliefs are rhetorical rather than authentic. And rhetorical beliefs cannot transform us.

Amrita prizes what she continues to learn about the sacred from her own experiences. "My spiritual connection with nature was beautifully experienced recently in the presence of Native American Indians who were potters [Amrita is also a passionate potter]. Early morning was greeted with an offering of corn in their prayer bowls to the gods for appreciation of earth, the water from the river, material from nature they will use for making and firing their pots. In conversation throughout the day they will speak of aspects of nature with such spiritual reverence. It was not weighed down with heavy solemnity but spoken of as though it was a guardian, a friend, a family member. It was like music to my ears.

"I have arrived at a spiritual freedom that I had been seeking."

❧

Whatever the sacred is, it is not separate from our most apparently inconsequential moments. It is not separate from our familiar selves. It is certainly not separate from those inner and outer stories that we absorb as inevitably as a sponge absorbs water.

The sacred, the holy is integral to who we are. We are not talking here of soul divorced from body, of "holy days" marked out from other days, of a chosen few and an unchosen many. The realities of interdependence are themselves sacred truths. "Look through the eyes of the Beloved," Rumi urges. "You will see the Beloved everywhere."

*How* we connect with others is the most sacred of our spiritual practices. It is the most challenging and the most refining. Choosing gratitude, kindness, good humor, tolerance and self-respect—in the presence of your doubts—you will find and create opportunities to express them in your life and to applaud and encourage them in other people.

"Story" remains vivid. What we identify *with* will inevitably grow stronger in our consciousness and our entire existence. Perceiving life through the lens of the sacred makes it impossible to behave as though our actions are free of consequences for others or ourselves; they are not. As we discover the nature of what we share, those discoveries will connect us more reliably to others. We will experience our connections with decreasing possession and increasing reward. Quite inevitably this will also connect us more reliably to the sacred depths within and beyond ourselves.

Crucial to that shift is regarding our own difficulties with good humor and lightness. I felt such recognition when Mary Ann told me during a brief intense conversation that after many years of expensive self-development courses and even longer as a meditator she was finally giving up taking her identity cues from what she imagined others think about her. Instead, she is taking her cues from her own sense that her life is intrinsically valuable. What's more, she has immediately noted a positive change in the way that people are responding to her. This seems to be as true in her working life at a major financial institution as it is among her friends and family.

Mary Ann explains: "I'm convinced that people take their cues from whether we have respect for ourselves or not. As long as I was regarding myself as deficient I was inviting people to treat me like that. I felt confident to *say* that I regarded myself as a spiritual being but in actual fact I was seeing myself through the wide-angle lens of my neuroses and demonstrated a constant lack of self-love and self-respect that surely conveyed itself to other people."

Mary Ann's liberating shift in perspective is something I recognize from my own life. Like so many people addicted to constant work I always have a string of plausible reasons why I am driving myself so hard. It was not until I was writing my earlier book *Choosing Happiness*, and reflecting on the work I was doing with people with terminal illness, that I faced the most fundamental reason of all for my own overwork. I finally saw how obedient I was to the belief that I must justify my very existence by doing work that is of social benefit and *doing it constantly*. My unconscious driving belief was that unless I was looking after my children or hard at work, and unless my work was of measurable benefit to others, my life had little value.

Even now, I can feel how persuasive that argument is. I can also feel myself wanting to emphasize to you the privilege of doing work that is of value to others. But the truth is that this can be done and will be done just as effectively when we can see life as a gift—perhaps a divine gift—not solely valued for what we are "doing" with it. "Contributing" can also be done at a slower pace—and is even sometimes best achieved by "doing" very little at all. For me, the paradigm shift was between identifying with conditional love or unconditional love. Conditional love lets me love my life (and myself) when I am giving or doing "enough." Unconditional love lets me love and value my life. Period.

~༄༅~

As you recognize who and what you *already* are, what strengths and resources you *already* have, what experiences and knowledge you have *already* acquired, you will radically enhance your inward security and confidence. This will let you face your inevitable challenges with quiet confidence and let you look outward in ways that are genuinely empathic, ethical and supportive.

Awareness of the intrinsic value of your life helps you identify with your strengths and resourcefulness rather than your shortcomings. You can enjoy your sweet moments of achievement and completion rather than hovering over whatever disappointments or setbacks life is currently dishing up. You may redefine how you understand and seek "success."

This kind of confidence and sense of sufficiency need not be confused with overweening self-regard. That's almost always defensive and easily punctured. A sense of sufficiency and confidence, by contrast, is born from and also expresses trust and love, two profound spiritual qualities.

Your inner critic and mine—much like Donna's unforgettable "Mrs. Fricker" earlier—knows little or nothing about sufficiency. On the contrary, she (or he) may mistake "sufficiency" for bigheadedness, for being "spoiled," smug or self-satisfied. Inner critics might vary their messages between criticisms, warnings, whining, bullying or belittling, but are unlikely ever to be spacious, kind, light or forgiving, or to remind us of the preciousness of this fleeting life, the preciousness of our own lives and the capacities we have to meet even the most difficult moments with courage and hope.

The stories that pour through us as we sleep and while we are awake are laden with emotion and value judgments, conscious and unconscious expectations and a wild bouquet of projections.

*Who am I? What am I? What* consequences *does my self-understanding or self-image have?* These are essential questions when it comes to identity, but it is impossible to consider them fruitfully without also understanding the force of those known and hidden expectations, assumptions and projections. They will take us forward or keep us in tiny cages. They will make lovers of life out of us; they will keep us embittered. And they will emerge quite inevitably through our attitudes, choices and behaviors.

Two quite recent anecdotes illustrate this, each one vivid and moving because they emerge and land so close to home. In the first instance, I was out shopping with my friend Charlotte. We were trying on clothes in a city discount outlet and particularly enjoying it because for once we had the time to relax on a lovely Sunday when neither of us was working.

The saleswoman managing the shop was about our age. She became quite talkative as we each chose and bought something. Then, as we were leaving, she asked if we would like to join her company's mailing list. Charlotte agreed and when she gave the woman her details—including her date of birth—the woman began to ask her some fairly personal questions. By this point I was quite uncomfortable and went back to the car. A few minutes later Charlotte joined me, with tears in her eyes.

For weeks she had been discussing with her closest friends, including me, giving up her tiny city apartment and buying a small house in the country. What she needs, she believes, is more space and especially a garden. But the upheaval would be costly and her journey to work would be longer so she was feeling confused about her own desires.

Within seconds of my leaving the shop, Charlotte told me, the saleswoman looked at her and said, "Do you have a garden where you are living? I sense you need a garden."

Make of this what you will. What Charlotte made of it is summed up in her few words: "What a push from the angels!"

Charlotte's "inner story" is one that allows for and welcomes the possibility of guidance from what she calls the "unseen." Someone else might interpret the saleswoman's words as a coincidence or as timely or synchronistic, or might dismiss them altogether as intrusive and irrelevant. Expectation and interpretation are crucial here. That means that the *content* of this otherwise trivial story matters far less than the *context* in which Charlotte heard and interpreted it.

(Should I add that within a month Charlotte had found a small house with a garden that, in Charlotte's words, "simply fell into my lap?")

My second example is less happy but perhaps reflects even more dramatically how our crucial sense of inner possibility is liberated or restricted by those inner, subjective stories that we may believe are hidden—but rarely are.

This time I was sitting with a group of friends over an early dinner as we listened with concern, and not for the first time, to an intelligent woman in her late forties repeat the many reasons why she could not make a much-needed change in her life circumstances. Yvonne—as I will call her—is a physiotherapist who is living in an extended-family situation with family members who disrespect and abuse her. She has been living with these people for a dozen or more years and has been complaining about living with them for most of that time.

Yvonne isn't particularly well off but certainly has enough money to live independently. As she spoke, describing scenarios that are intolerable by any measure, several people tried to encourage her by offering plausible, practical suggestions for change as well as cogent reasons why she deserves to move out of harm's way. Yet, as each person spoke, Yvonne came back with deeply felt arguments about why change isn't possible. More strikingly still, as the conversation progressed she became increasingly undermined and helpless.

At one crucial point this competent and often witty woman said, "I can't come up with clever answers. I only know what my feelings are."

This was undoubtedly a frustrating response to her would-be helpers. Nonetheless, it was honest. Yvonne's inner story paralyzes even her capacity to imagine effective change and, like any one of us, Yvonne will never achieve what she cannot first imagine. How Yvonne views and values herself emerges from a lifetime's worth of emotional patterns *reinforced by* that hypnotic story of inner helplessness.

Yvonne doesn't need "clever answers." She needs an inner shift in how she describes to herself who and what she is. Her crisis seems to be one of self-confidence. And it is that. But more than that, it is a spiritual crisis of identity and *being*.

LIKE SO MANY OF THE STORIES in this book, my own story of seeking is simultaneously unique and familiar. I was born into a nominally Anglican family in New Zealand at a time when Catholics were from Venus and Protestants were from Mars. And all other religions were so far out in outer space that, other than Jews, they could not be taken seriously.

Those were the "good old days" when Catholics could go to hell for eating a meat pie on Friday and Protestants could go to hell for singing pop songs or dancing unless they were already preordained to go to heaven. (This made things quite confusing if you were also trying to factor in free will.)

Catholics and Protestants met on Planet Earth, but rarely happily. My own parents—both university-educated teachers—were not religious. They had been raised as Anglicans and my father's widowed mother was genuinely devout, but I suspect my parents saw to it that my early experience of religion was minimal. In fact, my strong sense is that, like many intellectuals in the post–Second World War period, my father, and perhaps my mother also, regarded religion as something irrational and likely to die out as education and improved social circumstances brought greater justice to earth, thereby eliminating the need for people to cultivate the sad delusion that they would receive such justice in that illusory place called "heaven."

When I was eight, my adored mother died. She had been ill with cancer for nearly two years. She had probably been dying for most of that time yet when her death came one week before Christmas it was sudden and she didn't have a chance to leave a special note or say goodbye to her two daughters. She was thirty-eight.

Within months of her death my father became a Roman Catholic. He "took instructions" in that faith, to the horror of most of his nonbelieving friends. In the process of being "received into the church" he was formally rebaptized, dismaying his mother who felt more insulted by the assumption that his previous Anglican christening hadn't "counted" than by his previous broad contempt for religion in all its (Christian) forms.

Following my father's conversion, in every possible way my life and that of my older sister totally changed.

We went from Mars to Venus and became Roman Catholics too. This change was inseparable from all the other unwelcome changes that marked and followed the death of my mother. Predictably, it was profoundly disturbing. Nonetheless, there was also excitement associated with the drama of our "conversion" and, as a little girl in desperate need of distraction, I suspect I liked that.

What I could not bear at that or any later time was other people's pity. To be a motherless child was so bleak for me that I could not bear to see any version of that reflected on other people's faces. I quickly learned to deflect even the smallest signs of gravity, and discovered firsthand what an effective mask it was to be "funny" and precocious.

"Standing out" by embracing Catholicism was opportunity for drama of a different kind. I liked the newly ordained red-haired and rather nervous curate who "instructed" my sister and me in a small room in the local presbytery where he lived with an aged senior priest. I was eager to please him and noticed with fascination how unavoidably he blushed when my clever twelve-year-old sister asked surprising questions. Our curate was a good, earnest man and I have no doubt that he believed that he was doing these two motherless girls a profound spiritual favor, making it possible for us to become part of "our Holy Mother the Church."

In his eyes, and perhaps soon in ours, he was giving us the only certain chance for salvation. How could we possibly have said no? But there was another factor complicating this turn toward religion also.

My father, at the time of his conversion, was in his late thirties. He was a talented and clever but wounded and difficult man, and not only because he was grieving the loss of his first wife. I can distinctly remember, at less than ten, hoping, and then intensely praying, that his newfound religion would make him a happier person. Those prayers are my first conscious memory of hope in the transformational power of religious faith.

Looking back, I can barely imagine how the circumstances of my "conversion" could have been more dramatic. As though that were not enough, the Roman Catholic Church itself was then insular, self-righteous, superstitious, obsessed with sin and sacrifice, and arrogant in its judgments and denunciations of the non-Catholic world from which I had come. This created a highly charged atmosphere that permeated and distorted my most private thoughts.

In the second year of our existence in the strange new world of Catholicism and Catholic schools, and less than three years after my mother had died, I was ordered out of one school and sent to another far less distinguished school (in fact, not distinguished at all) for misbehavior so mild that it should not have turned a hair. But harsh judgments were the order of the day and there were to be no allowances made for anyone who did not fully appreciate the need for abject and *grateful* conformity.

Yet as confusing and hurtful as those events were, they are not the whole story. There was in that intense Catholic world also kindness, community, laughter, excellent music, a fine education despite huge numbers of students and overstretched, exhausted teachers (almost all of them nuns in a semi-enclosed, rigid order). There was an aesthetic appreciation of Catholicism's intellectual traditions and high art as well as glimpses of its intricate and challenging theology.

There was much craziness in those depths, but they were *depths*.

More crucially still, there was the alluring emotional power of belief—or faith—carried to me through words and instructions and especially through the power of mystery and symbol.

*I go unto the altar of God.*

*To God who gives joy to my youth.*

*To God* . . . Sometimes I was sure that I knelt at the altar of God. Sometimes I felt at least some joy in the presence of that God. And although I could not have articulated this, I relished the fidelity to the symbolic and ineffable that gave and continues to give Catholicism a profundity and richness vast enough to meet the hungers of seekers over generations. It's this that has allowed the Church to survive as a vehicle of the sacred, despite its long and well-documented institutional shadow.

My childhood is long gone and so is the world in which I lived. The country I grew up in and left at the age of twenty is a different place. To a considerable extent, the Catholic Church is itself a different "place." And I am a significantly different person. Crucial to those differences is how religious identity and belief are understood and embodied.

Did I *believe* in a loving God, all those years ago?

Or did I believe with greater conviction in the God who could penetrate my thoughts and would judge them, leaving me nowhere to hide?

As little Catholic scholars we learned our catechism by rote. Who made the world? *God made the world.* Who is God? *God is our Father in heaven, Creator and Lord of all things.*

Did I believe that? Or any of the other creedal teachings from original sin to Christ's virgin birth to the then-essential Christian teachings on atonement: that Christ became a blood sacrifice in response to and as savior of the continuing sins of the world?

Did I believe I was a sinner in imminent need of salvation? Was that my spiritual identity?

I probably did. It probably was.

And what about the special merit of prayers on saints' days, or of prayers prayed in particular ways? Praying with arms painfully outstretched, as Christ's own arms were stretched on the cross, was apparently especially helpful to the poor souls in purgatory (a temporary version of hell) who could not come to their own aid but were waiting in desperation for a fourteen-year-old in her little bedroom in suburban New Zealand to stop thinking about herself and start thinking about their fate instead.

Did I believe that? Did I believe in a God subject to that kind of plea-bargaining? I suspect the answer is again yes.

Writing this, I realize the extent to which I am still haunted by traces of that time: guilt that I may not be doing "enough" for others and guilt more generally. Whatever I did or did not believe, the emotional effects of those rituals and relationships, those customs and teachings were profound.

⁓✤⁓

That this is a familiar story does not make it less painful for each individual person who lives it. I believe that it is inexcusably abusive to teach a young child that they are a "sinner," rather than that they are a spiritual being who is a unique expression of love.

Lorraine Whiteley is a teacher, partner and mother of two adult sons. With her characteristic precision and care, Lorraine now describes God as "the loving intelligence that pervades the universe." She adds, "I *observe* this loving intelligence in the magnificence of the natural world and the many wonders of the physical universe. I *experience* this loving intelligence as the drive to grow and develop and become more fully myself."

The nourishment that Lorraine gets from this relationship was palpable as we talked. But as with most of us this is not absolute or constant and it was clear that Lorraine's perceptions of this benign source and influence, and the effect this has on her self-perception and identity, were once very different.

As Lorraine told me, "Originally 'God' for me was a being with a personality who was interested in control. Very much like my parents, God liked people who were polite and who thanked Him for what He did for them. Also like my parents He could be angry, judging and rejecting.

"I could understand such a God, but my conflict arose with the teaching that God is also loving. I could never really see where the loving came into practice. In my Anglican Sunday school, God had sent His son Jesus to die for me, because I was a sinner. That wasn't very loving toward Jesus was it? Poor Jesus had to suffer because God's law required it. If He was God, why didn't He change the law? I could see the inconsistencies in the teachings I received and I tried to force the teachings into a sensible personal philosophy. When the conflict became too great, I just walked away. But there was an enormous sense of loss involved in seeing through the gaps in my religion; loss of certainty, loss of community, loss of belonging, loss of the sense of security provided by faith in the God who would look after me."

When I questioned Lorraine more closely around these core issues of identity within a spiritual context she emphasized, "What I needed to recover from were ingrained beliefs about my *inherent lack of value*.

"Growing up reciting the litany of sinfulness and insignificance led to a sense of personal worthlessness and guilt. With hindsight, I can see that what most helped in my recovery was that which I now define as my experience of God; that is, the call toward understanding and knowing myself. What is recovery but moving away from adherence to constricting, life-denying ideas and toward a sense of personal worth and the freedom to choose one's own ways of seeing?

"It takes courage to do this and commitment to the process. And [now] I think even these qualities are gifts from God. It all seems very much to have been 'guided' by an intelligent hand, and that hand is what I call God."

This doesn't mean that the God in which Lorraine believes is the interventionist figure of her childhood and mine.

Lorraine explains, "I cannot be asking my 'Heavenly Father' to provide me with things I want or need, as I learned to do as a child. I can't be asking God to intervene on my behalf. If I need the weather to be fine tomorrow for my picnic, what about my neighbor who needs rain for her garden? How will God decide? It's all too silly really. So I actually don't know how to pray anymore for that basic assistance, or who to pray to. Or why God would be interested in such banalities.

"I seem, however, to *experience God in prayer as an answerer of my questions.* I very often simply raise a question that has been bothering me, and an answer comes, sometimes straightaway, in that I hear the answer in my mind quite clearly. Or it comes soon after in a conversation, or book or a passing remark that delivers just the next thing I need to know that helps shape my developing understanding of whatever it is I'm wondering about (my spiritual questions, of which there are many).

"So I would probably characterize my relationship with God as a teacher/student relationship. I don't experience transcendent feelings of unconditional love, or acceptance or forgiveness or anything else really on the emotional level. But intellectually God is totally there for me. And I know at that level at least I am never alone."

IDENTITY IS ALWAYS A MIX OF the conditioned and the chosen. The balance of that mix can veer wildly. We may consider ourselves at greater liberty to choose now than at any time in human history. Yet this may still be more complex than we think.

At the 2009 Parliament of World's Religions held in Melbourne a colorful swami from India got up to declare passionately that children worldwide are raised in spiritual slavery, brainwashed in religious dogma long before they have any chance to discover what it could possibly mean to think for themselves.

Their religious identity, he argued, is forged at a time of vulnerability. Whether the child grows into an adult who can "choose," and whether this is done in good or bad faith is, in his view, irrelevant. Harm is done.

He himself had been raised in pre-partition India as a Brahmin (the highest caste). Even as a tiny child he would have to undergo elaborate cleansing rituals if someone of a lower caste inadvertently touched him. His most intimate sense of identity, and the way in which he perceived and responded to others, was entirely determined by the religious beliefs of the powerful adults in his life.

In reaction to this "slavery" in the midst of privilege, his entire life has been spent not just rebelling against the rules of his upbringing but "atoning," working for social justice and particularly caring for and speaking up for children suffering from religious dogmatism imposed on them by adults.

Hilary Star is a tertiary lecturer and interfaith minister and the daughter of devout, courageous Protestant missionary parents who lived and worked for many years in Japan. She recalls a childhood in Japan, New Zealand and Australia that was essentially caring but was also highly authoritarian both at church and at home. Like most deeply religious parents, Hilary's mother and father would never have questioned their right to insist that their children diligently mirror their religious identity and worldview.

Hilary explains, "Having been raised with a fundamental belief that I am a sinner, all the ramifications of that contributed to my feeling a sense of unworthiness, of never being able to measure up. Mine was a fundamental Baptist family with a very strong message of a God who was powerful and holy and loving, but also judgmental. Hell was a reality. So was God's anger and judgment. I experienced the church community also as judging and harsh with very specific rules about how people were to identify and behave. My inner experience in response to that was to feel unworthy and fearful of God.

"My personal sense of identity as an adolescent and young woman was that I could only please God by being the person my parents wanted me to be. That is, someone who lived a life as they did, who believed what they believed, and who made choices they agreed with.

I remember family mealtimes where Dad would strongly correct us if we made any statement or comment that did not align with his beliefs and understanding of people. I feel I have spent most of my life seeking to meet approval and recognition from God (from my parents—inextricably linked).

"I remember the first time I felt consciously present to myself, Hilary, a person distinct from that consciousness and identity so influenced by my parents and church. It was following a Buddhist silence retreat with Sister Annabel Laity from Plum Village in France where [Zen monk and peace activist] Thich Nhat Hanh lives and works. At that retreat I felt for the first time a sense of a loving self, distinct and yet connected to others. I felt able to understand myself deeply as having a unique journey in life and having a self that could observe, understand, and make choices without being judged or deemed 'bad.' I felt I could grow and extend my understanding of myself and others in a fresh way, open to learning from others without fear and with curiosity about what they believed and experienced in their lives. For the first time also I was feeling released from the heavy weight of responsibility that I needed to 'convert' them to Christianity.

"Many years later, with a wonderful spiritual counselor's guidance, I wrote two lists, one of God as I had experienced God in my younger years, the other the God I was beginning to experience myself. This was an amazing step in awareness for me, to begin to claim my experience had some validity, acknowledging and realizing that I did believe in a different God to the one I had known through the church and my family."

So how had that change happened?

Hilary continues, "For me a lot of change in my view of God began through my experience of Buddhist teachings. Learning to meditate and find peace within myself enabled me to move past the constant voice of self-criticism that blocked any view of a loving, caring Divine Spirit.

"What also helped was that about twenty-five years ago a new teaching came in an Anglican study group I belonged to. There for the first time I heard about love being at the core of us. This seemed such a radical idea but over the years since many experiences have led me to understand us as human beings so differently from that original sin perspective. The greatest change in my sense of identity is realizing I have a 'greater mind' available to me, a growing sense of relationship with 'that of God' within/as part of me, and both of these [concepts] provide me with an understanding and experience of identity where I have a choice between my ego/personality/'I' perception to one of spaciousness linking me to Divine wisdom and knowing."

Hilary's story is close to that of another friend. This is a woman who also grew up in a well-intentioned but very strict and controlling Baptist family, and as a young adult moved to an explicitly Pentecostal church.

She has described to me how for years she would feel the most extreme tension and anxiety when in the company of someone who was not "born again," waiting for the moment when she could and indeed must raise the possibility of speaking to that person about Christ—and about taking Christ into their life and heart.

She would literally be shaking sometimes, not because she was a zealot, as you might imagine, but because she was and is extraordinarily kind. Believing utterly in a God of judgment and a literal doctrine of salvation, it was unbearable for her to withhold from that person what may be their only chance to be saved.

And if they were not saved—within my friend's highly specific framework of beliefs—then they were not only lost in this world but would suffer horribly in the next one *throughout eternity*.

To save the "not-saved" is an awesome, terrible responsibility. Far more terrible, at least from my perspective, was that the God in whom my kind and merciful friend then believed was *capable* of behaving in this brutal and unyielding way. "This is your chance. Take it—or risk the fires of hell for that unimaginable time we call 'forever.'"

In the presence of such a God, how is love learned—or achieved?

The desire of actively religious parents that their children will share their religious identity as well as their beliefs can overwhelm almost every other consideration in even the most affectionate families. When this doesn't happen, and an adult child makes independent choices that are markedly different from those of their family, it can break hearts in ways that can seem particularly tragic. The parents may feel profoundly disrespected. They may fear for the fate of the soul of their child. They may also feel that they have failed in their most sacred duty: to keep their child close to God. When religious people believe that theirs is the only "right way" to God—or believe that God thinks so—the situation can become intolerable.

These imperatives can make it extremely difficult for the adult "child"—who is not a child other than in their parents' eyes—to discover and realize their own inner identity. Sometimes this is possible only when the adult child's convictions at least match those of their parents. But "possible" does not make it easy.

Daya is a mathematician now in her forties. She grew up in a close family and spent many years in India and Britain before coming to live in Australia. Her spiritual journey has been a complex one, but I think it is fair to say that the power of yearning within her was such that when it was not met or satisfied in the religion of her birth and culture she felt literally compelled to look elsewhere.

Daya's impulses took her away from a religious perspective that was less precise to something far more precise: from devotion to a "mystery" to a consciously experienced relationship with God. A journey in the other direction is perhaps more familiar now, at least in the West (away from a strict religious identity and idea of God to something less dogmatic and more inclusive). But that was certainly not what Daya was seeking.

She explains, "I was brought up in a strict religion—which I absolutely loved. I loved the lifestyle. I loved the daily early morning mantra and 'rotating the rosary' prayers. I loved the principles and I loved God. I'm not sure where this deep love for God came from but I've always had it. However, I recall the concept of God was never very clear and there came a time when a space appeared in my life in which questions started to emerge such as: 'Who and where is God?' 'Can He hear me?' and 'Why and what am I doing?'

"No answers came from any of my practices. I realized that I was sustaining a relationship with a mystery and the lack of direct answers just started to cause increasing amounts of heartache and sorrow. I realized that I couldn't sustain a relationship with a 'Being' [so far] 'out there.' I really needed to know and feel God personally. Moreover, this relationship absolutely had to be reciprocal—questions answered—and the heart, my heart had to be healed."

MY OWN INTENSE YEARS WITHIN THE Catholic faith from the age of nine woke me up, spiritually speaking, and substantially formed me. The unambiguous spirituality of the Mass, the hours of adoration of the Blessed Sacrament to remind worshippers of the intimacy and wonder of the divine becoming human, the three-times-daily bells of the Angelus, the constancy of prayer, the rituals that marked each part of each day as a series of new opportunities for remembrance of God, the unswerving conviction that we live in the presence of the unseen and the miraculous and that our inner lives have greater depth and vitality than our outer lives: all of this worked on me.

That world of provincial Catholicism was psychologically bereft and superstitious, but I know that living within it—and with it living in me—I *felt* the power of the sacred.

One of my most vivid memories of adolescence is of observing a teacher I knew well, a young nun, lost in blissful contemplation during our long solemn High Masses. She appeared, as I watched her, to be literally transfigured from the clever, too often harsh teacher we knew in the classroom. Staring, I learned secondhand that the soul is the source of our deepest yearnings and that "feelings" are merely vehicles for the soul's urging. For me, this was an immense moment of spiritual realization. And I was an eager witness. In my mind's eye I can see her clearly still. I can also see my confused, curious adolescent self. Sister Mary St. B. is lost in awe—and my fourteen- or fifteen-year-old self is observing her, transfixed.

Yet, like so many, my personal spiritual story swings between extremes. The suffering I experienced over the death of my mother (mirroring the anguish felt by my sister), and the absence of an easy or healing relationship with either my father or his second wife, as well as an introverted nature hiding behind my loud, distracting self, made me intensely vulnerable to Catholicism's obsessive emphasis on suffering. I would go so far as to say that this emphasis was often idolatrous. Ghoulish stories of suffering and martyrdom, ceaseless retellings of Christ's agonies, betrayals, humiliations, beating, crucifixion and death, the looming presence of crucifixes in every church and room at school and on the habits of the nuns, along with explicit urgings to add suffering to our lives through penances and self-sacrifices, combined to elevate suffering over every other human experience.

The first of Buddhism's Four Noble Truths is also the "truth of suffering." Crucially, however, the three subsequent noble truths offer a way out of and beyond suffering. They show how much of our suffering is caused by our own ignorance and obstinacy. And they offer a path to "resurrection" (self-realization or enlightenment) that relies upon eight steps (the "Eightfold Path").

Those "steps"—based in ethics but transcending simplistic notions of "good behavior"—lead to an increasing awareness of who we are spiritually *right now* and what we are capable of being. They achieve this through accelerating our understanding of what the mind is, beyond its cognitive functions. (Who is choosing?) With particular skill they teach through experience the essence of our interdependence and inter-being, increasing our capacity to care about the effects of our choices on other people as well as ourselves.

I have condensed this vast philosophy unforgivably, but hope it is clear that from this perspective we "save" ourselves (from ignorance and unnecessary suffering) in large part through understanding two cojoined principles. The first is that from a physical or material perspective everything is transitory. The second is that from a spiritual perspective everything is interconnected (including my life and yours, and what we call life and death).

This emphasis on *a way of living* that reduces unnecessary suffering and takes us toward greater happiness makes it more and not less ironic as well as tragic that it is the agonizing suffering of Christ and his followers, and not the mystical event of Christ's resurrection, that takes center stage within Christendom, ruling the consciousness of millions of souls, emptying them of joy and utterly determining how they will see themselves and one another.

"Healing," writes Thomas Moore in *The Soul's Religion*, "is of the essence of spirituality, and all real healing is spiritual." What's more, "A spiritual point of view allows us to appreciate the source of our illnesses and the means of their healing, both of which arise . . . from the same place."

In my early years of intense Catholicism, not healing but suffering was the primary narrative. *And it should not have been.* The most elementary understanding of the wisdom story of Jesus shows that it is not his suffering and death but his resurrection that promises that we, too, can *heal our view of ourselves and of what life is.* This is what literalizes a triumph of love over fear and of the eternal over the temporal. This is what promises that the divine, the sacred will be found in our suffering but is not bound by it—and nor are we. *This* is an ecstatic noble truth. But in my long-ago childhood, it entirely passed me by.

❧

At the age of sixteen I left school and home to study law (in a deeply unfocused and inefficient way) while also working as a law clerk and living with girls who were about as careless of their future as I was of mine. Less than a year later, I had given up on Christianity and believed it had given up on me. The rigidity and, perhaps even more, the constant guilt and shaming in part drove me away. I was also giving up on parents—both the temporal and the heavenly kind.

Leaving Catholicism behind, Protestantism did not seem an option. It was clear to me that Catholics in those pre-ecumenical days reserved a greater degree of pity or contempt for Protestant "non-Catholics" than they did for nonbelievers or followers of other faiths. (The converse was just as true.) That partisanship was hard to shake.

For years I rarely prayed. I rarely turned inward to the presence of Mystery. I rarely evoked the help of angels, one of my favorite practices from childhood. Yet I remained convinced that this brief life was not and could not be "everything."

Remembering the dreams and intense anxieties that marked those busy, ambitious and extroverted years I suspect I saw my inner world as a place of sorrow and insufficiency. Years of analytic therapy did little to repair that. (In fact, with no context for introducing me to my spiritual strengths or resources, it protracted my suffering rather than relieving it.) Through those years, however, I remained entranced by other people's religious convictions and curious about their attachments. I envied "people of faith" and was often drawn to them. I wanted some of what they had. If I saw a spiritual talk advertised, I would attend. If someone offered to take me to church, temple or synagogue, I would go. If I found a memoir or biography of a religious person, I would read it. But I saw myself as an outsider, looking in.

Spirituality was more than an identity. It was a home.

I could see that. Yet I remained homeless.


Gradually, politics came to fill those spaces of longing. Politics in my late twenties and early thirties was as passionate as religion could be and much more pleasurable. I felt in tune with the people who were similarly engaged. I admired them and felt affirmed and encouraged by them. It became easy to say that I was a feminist or peace activist. That was an identity that was as comfortable as the clothes I wore to declare it. Family allegiances were forged, broken and remade between peers. From a political rather than religious perspective, the "wrongdoing" that caused so much pain and suffering in the world was not mine; it was only mine to recognize and challenge. This gave me some relief from the feelings of insufficiency and shame that I associated with religion and with my own deepest self. The world clearly needed fixing and I could be part of that. It seemed so much more credible and far nobler than "fixing" myself.

⌘

I had left New Zealand as soon as I had saved enough money to do so. I was just twenty. My goal was to live for some time in Israel, a country I had idealized for its socialist experiments as well as for the profundity of what I perceived as its citizens' unique religious suffering.

The months I spent in Israel were intense and confronting. I traveled widely but lived near Beersheba in the Negev desert, and saw close by the suffering of the Bedouin people, the suffering of the people of Gaza and also the celebration, fears and defensiveness of the many cultural groups who collectively make up the Jewish Israelis. I lost forever my innocent illusions that "right" can be one-sided.

The people I lived with were mainly from South America and while they were not strictly religious, they kept a kosher kitchen and observed the Sabbath faithfully. The strongest memory I have of those *kibbutzniks* is of their indifference. Wide-eyed boys and girls came and went. One to them was much like another.

Watching from the sidelines I could observe, nevertheless, how integrated religious observance is within the interstices of Jewish daily life. And that fascinated me. It would be years before I would fully understand that belief and creed matter far less in Judaism than observances or religious practice. I have grown to love this aspect of religious life and especially how it gives priority to what is personally accountable, without diminishing the transcendental dimensions that underpin it.

Some of this is made clearer by Kim Gotlieb, a man of great warmth who has lived in Sydney for years but—like me—was born in Wellington, New Zealand, where he grew up in an Orthodox Jewish family.

For Kim, "Rituals are profoundly important in shaping the spiritual path and a necessary rudder to deal with the vicissitudes of life's unfolding. There is a teaching in Judaism which says, 'We will do and we will listen.' That speaks to me about the need to surrender to a practice in order to find out whether it can work for me. While there is very little linear evidence that my Jewish practice brings me closer to G-d, I have to accept that I do the practice and I feel closer to G-d."

Kim's simple statement of commitment and awareness of presence reminds me so strongly of Jewish mystic Moses Cardoveros, who wrote, "Each of us emerges from *Ein Sof* (The Unnameable One) and is included in it. We live through its dissemination. It is the perpetuation of existence."

The possibility of an inclusive, authentically soul-driven identity emerges here. "Each of us emerges from *Ein Sof* (The Unnameable One) and is included in it." As part of his morning ritual, Kim recites a beautiful affirmation based on the prayer for putting on a *tallit* (Jewish prayer shawl): "Blessed is the Source out of which all being has emerged."

Kim emphasizes why this is so important. "This [affirmation] links me to a story which proscribes that I wear *tzitzit* (fringes) to remind me that I am a vessel for the Divine Light, with an obligation to live a holy life. It is like a gong that endeavors to align my energies with the higher vibrations of spiritual ascendance, which include purity and right action in a landscape of peace and love. This helps me to deal with the range of earthly experiences which unfold in my day—both relational and internal/emotional which can have an energy that wants to draw me down to more base expressions of my humanity."

The structures of Jewish life have remained crucial to Kim through his personal changes and development. He explains this. "I am almost formulaic in constructing a life myth which includes a relationship with the mystery which is unknown except for the knowledge that it must have a considerable effect on the unfolding nature of my own process and the world in which I live.

"I attend religious services at least four times a week: Monday and Thursday mornings at 6:45, Friday at 6 p.m. and Saturday at 9 a.m. More, of course, when there are Jewish festivals. I rarely 'feel' like getting up at 6:30 a.m. but my act of will, fused with the commitment to my spiritual path, is stimulated by this act.

"Once in the service I enjoy the sense that for so many hundreds of years my people have said these words in this way. Plus in all our prayer services there is a glorious flow—from acknowledging G-d, then praising. Then having the *Amidah*, which is a private conversation/communion with G-d. This can be a time of venting my distress and it can also be the time/place where I palpably experience something that feels like entering into a closer relationship with the Bigness of the Universe and beyond. It is pretty 'wow.'"

When religion or a committed spirituality plays anything like a significant part in shaping our identity the effects of this will be felt in every aspect of our lives, including the crucial dimension of what we expect to give *to* life, and not just what we will receive from it.

Jane Sloane is a Quaker friend and the executive director of a nongovernmental aid organization. Jane gives an example of how necessary it is for her to have a genuine congruence between her private beliefs and her public life.

"Some years ago I was working for a company that did a lot of work for a government agency [that works for peace and justice, especially within our region]. The company's chief operating officer took his executive team on a leadership half-day and during the course of that time took us to a shooting gallery to 'teach us to shoot on target and eliminate our opposition.' I was so shocked when we arrived at this place that I was literally lost for words. Finally I said I couldn't participate because I was a Quaker [and committed to nonviolence]. The experience raised for me wider ethical questions about where I was working and to what end. And also what this degree of compromise was doing for my spiritual life and whether or how it was eroding my sense of self. It very much brought to the fore the question of 'right livelihood'—a key Quaker demand on our conscience as well as consciousness. I left the company soon afterward."

It is a privilege to have choices about where we will work, what kind of work we will do and whether we can feel comfortably aligned with the ethics of our workplace. But when we do have those choices, the real privilege is to take them seriously.

I will never forget arriving for the first time in India and being taken by my Brahma Kumaris friend Charlie Hogg to Gandhi's ashram in Ahmedabad in the state of Gujarat. On a wall in that bare, unpretentious place was a huge enlargement of Gandhi's handwriting saying, "My life is my message."

Taking charge of what our own "message" will be is the supreme choice that life will offer us. This will depend, in turn, on the "messages" and stories that constantly pulse through us and even more so on what we choose to "make of them."

*What values do those stories nurture? What self-image do they harbor? What connections with other people do they allow—or disallow?* And, as Jane Sloane was pushed to consider, *What are they doing for our spiritual lives or very sense of self?*

Gandhi's declaration challenges us to choose our messages and our own life "message" bravely. He knew—and we do too—that our choices will sustain us only when we make them freely and with dignity: when they are made with and reflect our most generous understanding of love.

TO ENTER A FRAME OF MIND where love is our primary identity and value, we must leave behind our fears of ridicule and insufficiency. We must loosen our ties to the literal and linear. We must embrace a spiritual logic. And we certainly must discover what it means to surrender.

Meditation can be a tremendous resource in this willing process of opening to an enhanced awareness of life's depths and meaning. The "pause" it requires and also the slight distance it gives between "us" and our thoughts lets us experience how our usual hesitancies, defenses and qualifiers can lose their grip. Perhaps more than either of those advantages, meditation also lets us see from the inside out that there is an "inside!" And that "mind" as an experience is much greater than the sum total of our cognitive abilities.

Excellent guidance comes from Venerable Bhikkhu Bodhi, a Buddhist monk born in the United States who lived in multi-faith Sri Lanka for more than twenty years. The founder of Buddhist Global Relief, he offers an exceptionally clear teaching in a recent article on "Love and Compassion" where he states that there are qualities "essential to our stature as true human beings" that "manifest our inherent divinity."

To discover our "inherent divinity" is already to transform our view.

But questions remain: How should we live those qualities? How can those qualities become our inspiration and our message? How should we make our "inherent divinity" real in the sometimes harsh and cynical alternative reality of twenty-first-century life?

Making this a little easier for us, Bodhi makes a distinction between loving-kindness (*metta*) and compassion (*karuna*) that makes the actualization of love more subtle and achievable. He then offers a way to bring them even more fully alive through carefully structured meditation practices.

Through such practices we can learn to generate those transformative qualities toward a whole range of people, starting with those easy for us to care about and gradually working our way toward those whom we are more likely to regard with indifference, anger, fear or contempt.

This wise monk is obviously a realist. At the beginning, he writes, we are unlikely to generate genuine loving-kindness. However, through training the mind to cultivate kind thoughts and send good wishes increasingly widely and unconditionally, *we will positively affect our own emotions and inner experiences*. We will also affect how we perceive and influence situations and other people. And, I would add from my own perspective, we will without doubt positively transform our inner sense of self and identity.

This lets us think more actively and honestly about compassion—so often more a high ideal than a reality. "Specifically," Bhikkhu Bodhi writes, "compassion means the feeling of empathy with those afflicted by suffering. Therefore to develop compassion as an exercise in meditation, one has to focus on those undergoing suffering."

I have found a similar practice strengthening in my own life. Like many people, I would often feel lost in helplessness as one news bulletin or newspaper after another brought tragic news into my living room—much of it caused by humanity's capacity for inhumanity. Then a friend would call with their personal confusion or heartache. Or there would be agonies in my own family, as in every person's family. *In life there is suffering.* What could I do?

What I felt I had to do was to remain open to those human experiences *and* resist the temptations of ignorance, helplessness or pessimism. I had long before learned to give practical help wherever I could. Money, service, information and engagement: these all count. But if I was to remain open and empathic I needed also to learn to pray fiercely and meditate compassionately.

Who could say that anyone will change a situation for the better by focusing on the twin powers of compassion and loving-kindness through a simple, repetitive prayer: "May they be well and happy. May their hearts be filled with peace. May they know their highest good . . . ?"

What I can report on is the change in my own thinking when it was softened by such practices and especially when I shifted my response from "worry" to "good wishes."

This doesn't mean that I ceased worrying. If only! But I have certainly tamed that rather feral capacity and am confident that when I promise people that I will pray for them or for their situation I am promising something that is genuinely connecting and encouraging.

Perhaps it is also healing. When others promise to pray for me, my heart always lifts. It feels like a gift.

Sending prayers and good wishes to all—the good, the bad, the loved, the unloved—may seem trivial. I believe it is not. It does not replace action and outward-directed service. It deepens and augments it. Nor does it mean that we cease to see that some people are victims of violence and others are perpetrators of it. That distinction remains relevant. But it does acknowledge that if those who cause damage and sorrow are to have any change of heart—to cease their violence and their self-pitying or arrogant justifications for violence—*they also need prayer.*

With its unconditional emphasis on including all members of the human and divine family, this spiritual practice shifts the way we see ourselves. And it changes forever the way in which we think about and relate to others.

Thinking, though, is never enough. Good intentions and prayers are also never enough. In transforming our attitudes, we must *live* more inclusively and caringly. This is where the strengths of the monotheistic religions really come to the fore. Yes, they are all capable of generating bigotry and violence. It is undeniable, though, that all also urge practical compassion (*caritas*) that in many instances is literally life-saving.

In his article, Bhikkhu Bodhi offers a useful perspective on this, too. "While all great world religions praise love and compassion, Buddhism stands out in offering precise, step-by-step techniques for awakening and cultivating these sublime virtues ... At the same time, however, I believe that traditional Buddhism has a critical weak spot. This is an insufficient emphasis on expressing love and compassion in concrete action aimed at promoting a more just and equitable social order ... I feel that Buddhism has much to learn from Christianity about love in action."

~~~

At the age of twenty, those simple spiritual truths were far ahead in my future. Leaving Israel behind, I went to Europe and lived there, mainly in London, for most of the next sixteen years. Quite early in that time, I moved in a freezing midwinter to what was then West Berlin for the best part of a (fractured) year. That was even more challenging than living in Israel and would play an equally significant part in my spiritual formation.

It was in Berlin that I learned how helpless I felt without any mastery of the language. (I couldn't afford German language classes, and had learned French and Latin but no German at school.) I also experienced my invisibility and vulnerability, my total lack of meaningful outer identity, while working in menial service jobs. Both of those experiences gave me raw, necessary insights into the agonies experienced by people as they are forced (which I was not) to move around the world in search of the work that others don't want to do and the pitiful income that rewards it. Without language and much sense of direction, I learned what it means to feel like "no one."

Living in a still-occupied Berlin, I also experienced at first hand the power of political institutions and ideologies, and how inevitably militarism shapes and influences every life it touches. More than twenty-five years after the war had ended, the city of Berlin continued to be vigorously and ostentatiously occupied by four "powers": in the East—part of the DDR—by the Soviet Union, and within West

Berlin by the British, French and American militaries, each with their own zone. The might of the Soviet Bloc was inescapable. So was the West's Cold War response to it.

By the time I was twenty-two, I had already been in the workforce for six years. I had lived in four countries. I had been married and divorced, and had (afterward) fallen in love with a German man who lived not in Berlin but far away in West Germany. I had chosen to expose myself to a variety of intense "faith" or political systems, none of which was my own.

My own children are now in their mid-twenties, but it was not until each of them turned twenty-two that I fully realized how dangerous or foolhardy so many of my adventures had been, how absurd it had been to attempt to create an independent life from the age of sixteen, how foolish it had been to travel so far and so long alone.

Impulsively and quite suddenly I left Berlin and returned to London. I moved into a large shared apartment near the banks of the Thames in Chelsea (starting with the smallest bedroom and working my way up) and quickly made my way into the world of book publishing.

Publishing was, for me, a homecoming. It was more than a professional homecoming; it was also spiritual. At last I could begin to create meaning in my life, inside and out. At last I could contribute. At last I could discover sense and purpose as well as latent talents. And because I had worked so unhappily for so long, first as a law clerk and then in a string of disaffecting jobs, there was no limit to my ambition.

For at least a decade, publishing and especially feminist politics dominated any conscious pursuit that I might have given to the sacred or to spirituality. Yet spirituality did not entirely desert me. At The Women's Press, a feminist publishing house I founded in the late 1970s—with the essential backing and enthusiasm of Naim Attallah, a dashing, innovative Palestinian-born, London-based entrepreneur—I was able to publish some exciting and pioneering books. Here and there among them were some that pointed a way toward at least some depth of spiritual understanding.

It was also during those years that I trained in psychosynthesis, a spiritual and psychological analysis of human experience that still stands me in remarkably good stead. For many years I also "believed" in the help possible through psychoanalysis and especially the British school of object relations. I spent perhaps twenty years deeply fascinated and influenced by analytic therapy of varying kinds. I underwent years of therapy. I explored its insights in my writing. I practiced it.

Now I see it as immensely helpful in deepening our understanding of the immense complexities that come with being human. In good hands, I see it as an effective therapy. But as an "awakening" of our full potential, I believe it's limited. It could not assuage my spiritual longings, offer a language for them or even acknowledge them. It could not adequately address my chronic and often debilitating self criticism and self-doubt that sometimes showed itself as depression, sometimes as manic activity and chronic overwork. It did not point to or uncover the wisdom I could mine from my own experiences. It gave me no signposts to suggest where at an inner or external level I uniquely and unconditionally belong.

But of course those deficits were exactly what I needed to take my searching and inquiring in more appropriate directions.

Without any conscious realization of what I was seeking, I used the increasing proliferation of talks, teachings and workshops that characterized "alternative" London in the late 1970s and early 1980s to begin to explore around the edges of Eastern spiritual practices.

By the mid-1980s I would come back to a new perspective on the gifts and wisdom of Christianity in the company of the Religious Society of Friends (Quakers). Prompted by a series of dreams, I would even discover a joyful, all-accepting divine "brother" as well as teacher in Christ. I would come to a place where I could sense (not just "believe"—always more limited for me) the unfailingly faithful presence of the Holy Spirit. But that all lay ahead, facilitated in part by my physical move to Australia and even more by the psychological and spiritual transformations of becoming a mother.

Meanwhile in London, and while still an ardent feminist and social activist, I discovered the psychological as well as philosophical and spiritual depths of Buddhism in its different forms. I read some Sufi books. For the first time, I read the poetry of Rilke. I pored over a rather dull translation of the sublime Bhagavad Gita. In the company of Buddhists, I learned to meditate and mainly forgot to meditate. I shifted, a little, from the unquestioning worship I had once given to the power of the intellect. Like someone sensing a change in the seasons even before the temperature rises or the leaves fall, I began to sense the ineffable power of spirit.

As I moved toward my mid-thirties, and from England to Australia, from the world of publishing to the worlds of writing and psychotherapy, from being single to being a partner and a mother, the murmurings of my soul were growing more convincing. I read more poetry than I had for years. I wrote down and listened more attentively to my dreams. I wrote fiction (*Running Backwards Over*

*Sand*), then *Intimacy and Solitude*. I read Jung rather than Freud or the post-Freudians. I remembered the spiritual passion of my school years. I closely watched as well as watched over my beloved, beautiful children.

I glimpsed, as from a great distance, what a direct experience of the Mystery might be. And I experienced an increasing thirst. But for what?

Was there something deeper than even the most exciting intellectual, political or relational engagement could offer? This was seeking of a very particular kind.

IT IS ONLY THE MOST OBVIOUS parts of our stories that are easily revealed. Some of what is most formative will be unconscious. Some of it will be forgotten or discounted by our conscious minds or fallible memories. Some of it will feel too awkward, too hesitant or unready to be shared.

Looking back at my own early story of spiritual seeking I see that several themes emerge. The first is a tenacious belief that there is "more" to life than achievement, as entrancing as achievement can be. That matters to me because for many years my professional ambitions and drive for excellence as a publisher and then as a writer certainly did give me a crucial sense both of belonging and of meaning. Achieving success in those very public spheres was far less a matter for me of applause or financial security, although both those things mattered, than it was a testament to the value of my life.

This is such a common story that you might read those lines wondering why I am even mentioning it. That must have been my view also because, as I have already said, it took me so many years to discover that the value of my life does not rest on my work. My life—like yours—is *intrinsically* precious. Has intrinsic meaning. Is *already* a gift and always has been.

This makes it more and not less important how I "spend" it. But the measures I now have for "wise spending" may not always be what the world "counts" or regards most highly. (Isn't it interesting how many financial terms we use to describe our well-being?)

What also emerges for me is a lifelong commitment to ethics as the highest expression of spirituality, recognizing that while it is feasible to be scrupulously ethical but neither religious nor spiritual it is *impossible* to be credibly religious or spiritual without also taking seriously one's own behavior and the effects of that on other people.

~~~~~~

In the last section of this book, I will write more about the later years of my spiritual journey, and what a significant difference the experiences and identity of "mother" made for me. As decisive was becoming increasingly openly immersed in spirituality and religion(s): joining with others, learning alongside others. And through each of those sometimes separate, sometimes interconnected worlds, I could see how unquestionably significant community is to our growth as spiritual beings.

Simultaneously I could see that the converse is also true.

Our communities, from family to local to global, depend for their health on our growth as spiritual beings. They depend on our abilities to see our difficulties—and the easing of those difficulties—as spiritual challenges that will never be solved through violence or opposition but only through cooperation.

Recognizing who we *are* in common, and what we *have* in common, is the primary expression of the inter-being to which I consistently refer in this book. (The air I breathe out is the air you breathe in. The air you breathe out is the air I breathe in.)

Learning from one another expresses this. This has been true in my work as a psychotherapist also, which sat alongside my writing for a good many years. And perhaps it is even more evident in ministry, where larger numbers of people from many kinds of backgrounds and with diverse needs must, in any given moment, move between difference and sameness with consideration and grace—and find themselves capable of doing so.

Perhaps unsurprisingly, I also see reading and writing as highly "communal" and sometimes unequivocally spiritual activities, our contemporary equivalent of campfire times, sharing meaning around the "flames" of inspiration, sharing experiences too and hard-won wisdom: listening to ourselves; listening to one another. All sacred.

⁓ↄℇↄℇↄↄ⁓

Those subtle processes of reflection are integral to all the most essential aspects of daily living. They are essential to identity. They are essential to seeking.

Such processes become more refined, and we become more skilled at using them, when we do so consciously and appreciatively. Realizing this may save you from "spending" your life unwisely or recklessly. It may save you also from doubting the value of your existence—here and now.

Such depth of reflection is not a question of time. Courage and openness are what's needed, and a good dash of curiosity about what's working more—or less—well. This brings you an inward security and confidence that will let you quite naturally think compassionately and encouragingly about yourself. And it will let you look outward in ways that are genuinely empathic, ethical and supportive.

～❧～

With the force of nature, our inner stories and convictions shape our attitudes and actions. Our values express our beliefs. Our choices and behaviors express our values. Spiritual seeking is a social and historical journey almost as much as it is a personal one. Time, place and culture all indelibly shape us. They affect how we will ask our questions, how we will tell our stories, how we will seek to define a sense of self and bring meaning to our existence. But there is still room for tremendous variations in understanding, attitude and actions that we can only attribute to the individual soul or psyche.

The primary teachings on love in all the world's faiths and scriptural traditions could not be more explicit. A subtle shift in perspective can bring about real change. This doesn't mean that we become a different person. But we are likely to value our lives differently and live with greater kindness, optimism, generosity and acceptance.

We may still sometimes behave in ways that are petty, self-pitying or mean-spirited. We will have the courage, though, to see that and make amends. For is it not the case that whatever our status, education or culture, we are free to affect the world around us for the better? We can do that for love, too, and not because we fear punishment or seek reward in this life or the possible next. And is that not the purpose of a spiritually focused life: to understand what relieves suffering and increases happiness—and to leave the world a little better off for our time here?

Our outer circumstances will affect us deeply. But they will not determine whether we choose to cultivate a generosity or even a magnificence of spirit. It is not by chance that the deeper into our hearts we travel, the easier we will find it to identify with our highest values and vision and draw strength from that. As we do so, the less conditional our expressions of love and appreciation will become. *Growing into life, we participate in the transformation that we are seeking.*

Gandhi again inspires me: "I believe in the essential unity of all people," he wrote, "and, for that matter, of all that lives. Therefore I believe that if one person gains spiritually, the whole world gains, and if one person falls, the whole world falls to that extent."

# LOVE

*Some day, after mastering the winds,*
*the waves, the tides and gravity,*
*we shall harness for God*
*the energies of love, and then,*
*for a second time in the history of the world,*
*humankind will have discovered fire.*

Pierre Teilhard de Chardin (1881–1955)

HERE'S WHAT WE KNOW: HUMAN BEINGS thrive in
the presence of love. We grow more loving where love is present.
Inspiration itself stirs and excites our capacities to love—while an
experience of love is itself inspiring. Love is also health-giving,
restorative, curative. It is the essential element of our interdependency.
We receive love more confidently when we feel able to give it.
We feel more alive when breathing in love and breathing out love
become, simply, breathing.

No wonder then that the sacred and even some of our most
cherished ideas about God are linked so intimately with our yearnings
for love. And no wonder then that the primary spiritual challenge
is not just to love but to allow love to be the foundation of our
lives: the ground of our being, the place of forgiveness and gratitude,
delight and awe, and ceaseless source of hope. When a religious
teaching leaves out love, it ceases to be religious. Where a spiritual
teaching sentimentalizes love, it ceases to be spiritual.

Is there a more beautiful teaching than this one? "Beloved: let
us love one another, for love is of God, and everyone who loves is

born of God and knows God. Anyone who does not love has not recognized God. *For God is love*" (1 John 4:7–8).

For many, and I am certainly among them, the sacred is an opening to love and a meeting with love. A time of quiet reflection or prayer, offering a kindness or forgiveness, participation in a ritual, reading poetry or scripture, holding someone as they grieve, laughing with a child, listening with care to a colleague or a friend, allowing oneself to be awestruck in nature: these moments connect us deeply within and without. Perhaps we feel and experience the balm of such moments particularly strongly when they come unexpectedly or at times of confusion, pain, grief or sorrow. Sometimes those moments are not just loving and restorative but also palpably sacred. Life's holiness is restored.

One of the most vivid examples of this comes in the writings of Oscar Wilde, the brilliant nineteenth-century Irish writer who was shamed, pilloried and jailed for his sexuality. In his extraordinary book *De Profundis* (*Out of the Depths*), Wilde describes being taken from his prison cell to the Court of Bankruptcy, walking between two policemen. As he made his way toward a new round of humiliation he saw a friend whom he doesn't name. This is how he describes the event and what it meant to him: "—— waited in the long dreary corridor that ... he might gravely raise his hat to me, as, handcuffed and with bowed head, I passed him by. Men have gone to heaven for smaller things than that. It was in this spirit, and with this mode of love, that the saints knelt down to wash the feet of the poor, or stooped to kiss the leper on the cheek ... When wisdom has been profitless to me, philosophy barren, and the proverbs and phrases of those who have sought to give me consolation as dust and ashes in my mouth, the memory of that little, lovely, silent act of love has unsealed for me all the wells of pity; brought me out of the bitterness of lonely exile into harmony with the wounded, broken, and great heart of the world."

In our own lives, "little, lovely, silent acts of love," whether we are giving or receiving them, are life-giving and even transformative. Transcending the categories of kindness, compassion and even beauty, these acts of love offer us glimpses of the sacred that are highly stabilizing. Whatever our outer circumstances they allow us to remember: "I am part of something wondrous. My life has value."

So vitalizing are these insights into our need for love and into the nature of love that they also transcend the categories of religion. It is only in transcending those categories, in fact, that love can truly be honored and appreciated. Mystics throughout the centuries and from all cultures have been explicit about this. No one "owns" love. No one "owns" God, either—although many would scramble, fight and kill to make that claim. A mystical view would tell us that we don't even "own" this life: all the more reason to treasure and love it. In one of Rumi's most famous poems he sings of the unbounded, unbiased, infinitely spacious nature of love:

> *Define me, shrink me: you starve your self of Self.*
> *Keep me nailed in a box of unyielding words,*
> *That box becomes your coffin.*
> *I do not know who I am.*
> *I live in brilliant astonishment.*
> *I am not a Christian. I am not a Jew. I am not a Zoroastrian.*
> *Even a Muslim, I am not.*
> *I don't belong to land, or to known or unknown seas.*

*I am not to be claimed by nature or by heaven.*

*Not by India, China or Bulgaria.*

*No place is my birthplace . . .*

*You say that you can see my mouth, ears, eyes and nose?*

*They are not mine.*

*I am the life of life.*

*I am that cat and this stone.*

*I am no one.*

*I have discarded duality like a worn cloth.*

*I see and know all times and universes*

*As one, one, eternally one.*

*What must I do to get you to know who is speaking?*

*Know this—and change everything!*

*This! Your voice resounding on the walls of God.*

~~~

As we have seen earlier, theologian Marcus Borg uses the terms "God," or the sacred, or Spirit interchangeably. Out of his own faith tradition of Christianity he asks a question that could apply to all traditions—and to those for whom seeking is itself the path: "Is the Christian life centrally about believing, or is it about relationship?" And also: "Is it about believing in a God 'out there' or about a relationship with a God who is right here . . . ?"

Borg's emphasis on the immediacy of relationship and experience, rather than belief (and speculation), will resonate for many contemporary seekers. We could argue about or go to war over ideas *about* God or the sacred. What will make far more difference to the quality of all our lives is to risk living lovingly: to gamble everything for love.

~୬୭୲୭ୢ~

The directness of our relationship to love, and perhaps also to the sacred and to God, is one of the most exhilarating and liberating characteristics of twenty-first-century spiritual life. We don't all need a middleman (as the poet Rilke disparagingly called priests) to flatten the path to God for us. We don't all need dogma. We certainly don't all need to be puffed up by claims of being somehow better than others in the eyes of God.

What seekers do need and often yearn for is what writer Andrew Harvey describes in *The Direct Path* as a "direct and unmediated contact with the Divine, free of the divisiveness, body hatred, and bias toward transcendence that disfigures all the inherited patriarchal religions." This is already electrifying. It's what makes sense of rare visionary poetry like Rilke's, Hafiz's or Rumi's. It makes new sense of the ancient "receptive" sacred practices like chanting, meditation and contemplation, and it accounts in large part for their contemporary renaissance.

It also makes sense of the emphasis in these pages on ethical living founded on inspiration, interconnectedness and love: seeing all beings through the eyes of the Beloved, finding the Beloved everywhere—and allowing our behavior to reflect that transformational insight. As Harvey explains, this gives us a chance "... at last to inhabit time, the body, and the earth with ecstatic consciousness and a passionate and radical sense of responsibility toward all living things."

Ecstasy and responsibility *is* the new spirituality: one changing our understanding of the other almost entirely. One quality pointing us toward heaven; the other connecting us more securely to this earth.

～⁀∽⁀∽～

You met Daya in the previous section. A mathematician who has lived in India, Britain and Australia, she explains in a most touching way the transformative power of seeing her own life as well as life itself "through the eyes of love."

"There was an epiphany moment in my spiritual life which just changed everything, and I'm still empowered, carried and driven by the experience and insights. It was about three and a half years into my spiritual journey when I had the opportunity to spend a couple of hours in silence as part of a weekend meditation retreat. During those hours of silence, I went for a walk in the gardens and just sat and contemplated how I would view myself, others and the world if I were just a tiny living being of pure beautiful energy—situated in this physical body.

"As I went deeper singularly into this consciousness, suddenly I felt I just 'understood' the journey of the 'soul' away from its 'truth' and every single soul's effort in getting back to its 'truth'—and an overwhelming feeling of mercy, love and compassion for myself, others and the world emerged. At the same time, in the silence, I felt so incredibly full of love, peace, inner power, happiness . . . and yet more and more love . . . I felt as if my face had expanded so much! Since then, for me everything changed in terms of how I see others, myself, the world (and even God). And how I navigate my life. In the silence, I felt I 'saw' what words, for me, had never come close to touching . . . and the depth of silence draws me still."

It is marvelous and truly liberating to align our conscious intentions with the soul and its strengths rather than with the limited ego and all its familiar fragility. This is something far more reliable, stabilizing and powerful than self-confidence or self-esteem. A softly spoken, unassuming woman with a formidable intellect, what Daya understands by her soul strengths is clearly evident in the way she listens, pays attention, supports and encourages other people—and remains poised and calm within herself. It also comes through in the choices she makes about how she will use her time, where she will give her attention and from what she will draw her sense of herself as well as her strength.

This should not suggest any kind of piety or withdrawal from life. In fact it allows for a depth of engagement and robust attention that a more cynical or self-protective view could never achieve. Daya's way of understanding this is that her soul journeyed back to its truth—and that its truth is love. She feels at home with a loving perspective. Her life shows that.

"You are precious in my eyes, and honored, and I love you," were the words that the ancient Hebrew prophet Isaiah believed he received from God. And in the next verse: "Do not be afraid *for I am with you*" (Isaiah 43:4,5).

These are the words of a mother. Receiving them is to be blessed.

Yet a sense that our inner world is a place of love and a resource for all the highest qualities can be extremely difficult to grasp with the intellect alone. Surrender of some of our usual ways of thinking is needed to make way for these kinds of experiences.

Daya makes her experience of love so simple and that simplicity is itself contagious. We would literally bring the kingdom of heaven to earth if we were able to "navigate our lives" with the confidence in love that Daya describes. Or if we were able to shed our fears of insufficiency to experience ourselves as precious, as Isaiah did. Or to trust as Isaiah also did in the faithful presence of the sacred.

TO RECEIVE AND EMBODY WHAT LOVE can give we must be *present*. It's what the Buddhists call "waking up." And so much can get in the way of that. Yet in receiving love—as well as giving it—we also give ourselves our best chance to come into the presence of the sacred, of God, of the "world we carry within us" as Rilke called it. "What happens in your innermost being is worthy of your whole love," he wrote in his famous *Letters to a Young Poet*. "You must somehow keep working at it and not lose too much time and too much courage in explaining your position to others . . ."

Certainly that is what my life tells me, both that we are easily distracted or uncertain about the inner world we carry with us (or that carries us), and also that we are never *not* in the presence of the sacred.

It's *we* who are often absent or perhaps forgetful.

But whether you share my view or doubt it, you will know from your own experience that it is sometimes easier to be closed to love rather than open to it. Habits of fear, disappointment, bitterness, an absence of forgiveness of God, life or another human being, cynicism, despair: these can all get in the way.

That's why I am so touched by this simple story from Graham Long, minister at Sydney's Wayside Chapel where he serves some of the least respected members of our society. He explains, "As I was attempting to leave [the Chapel premises] last night a woman threw her arms around me and hung on for ages. She said, 'Pray for me, Father. I'm at rock bottom.' I could feel this lady shaking in my arms and I sensed that the realization she was at 'rock bottom' was the pertinent ingredient of this moment. I held her and whispered a prayer in her ear and held her face in my hands. It was an uncommon moment of love between two people who had never met."

~~~

To open to what love can pour into us and how love can heal us there must be at least some willingness on our side, some degree of conscious yearning as we sense that all our usual distractions are not enough. It's love and the meaning that comes with love that we have to have. During our darkest nights of the soul, the consolations of love can seem far away. That distance is itself the theme of much of our suffering. Yet, like so many of us, I know that it is also when my need has been most desperate, confused and anguished that I am most open to receiving those priceless hints of softening, opening and reconciling with the life within me and beyond me.

It's often a shift in bodily posture that makes the heart and mind ready. This might include sitting still and quiet on our meditation chair or cushion even when "nothing" apparently happens yet the mind also settles. It might include a willingness to express our needs aloud, as when that brave woman said to Graham, "Pray for me, Father. I'm at rock bottom." Or when the Psalmist David cries, in Psalm 25, "Show me thy ways, Lord. Teach me thy path." Or when Christ himself called from the cross in his dying moments: "Abba (Father). Into your hands I surrender my spirit" (Luke 23:46).

It might include a simple willingness to bow our heads, turning inward, or to kneel in prayer. Kneeling rather than sitting is a gesture of humility and openness that has become quite lost to many non-Islamic Westerners in recent decades. And that is a great shame because the benefits of shutting out the usual daily clamor and kneeling, whether in prayer or simple contemplation, can be intense. It may even be full prostrations—laying our whole body face down on the floor. This was typical in ordination and profession ceremonies in the Catholic world for centuries, and symbolized dying to the world and living only for God. Prostrating would be unthinkable to most people these days other than Buddhists and particularly Western Tibetan Buddhists who do this eagerly and report its benefits with great enthusiasm.

But it need not be exclusively a sacred gesture or spiritual practice that readies us for love. What may matter even more are the attitudes we are habitually cultivating in our lives and souls. Where are those attitudes taking us? What are our liveliest expectations? Do we dare open to love *in the presence of our fears and terrors*?

◖◗

It lifts my heart always to hear people say how much more secure they feel as well as more hopeful, poised and more loving when they begin to live a more spiritually focused and supported life.

This doesn't mean pious, removed from life or judgmental. On the contrary, what it often seems to mean is they don't any longer feel limited to the faculties of the familiar "self" the world sees and judges on the basis of highly conditioned views of race, social class, culture, religion, gender, sexuality or status. And they don't either see their experiences or understanding of "love" as solely dependent on a single individual or a group of close friends or family.

Some would describe their opening to love and their willingness to receive (and give) love as essential to their spiritual identity. For many, that *is* their spiritual identity. They may even echo Daya's portrayal of herself as "a tiny living being of pure beautiful energy—situated in this physical body," or as a soul, spirit or divine spark. The descriptions are variable (and necessarily imprecise), but what they add up to is the famous aphorism attributed to Catholic priest Pierre Teilhard de Chardin: "We are not human beings having spiritual experiences. We are spiritual beings living a human life."

This doesn't mean detaching from our everyday selves or discounting those individual and familiar drives, behaviors, reactions and responses that are the stuff of everyday living. But it often does mean that tolerance for our own everyday selves—and for everyone else's human shortcomings—becomes far more generous when we recognize that what we can see, touch, measure and describe is not all of who we are.

In Nancy Malone's memoir, *Walking a Literary Labyrinth*, she draws on the rich perspective of age to reflect on the girls living near her current home on City Island in New York City. Writing about these girls, she touches on many of our lives also. Certainly what she says comes right home to me as I also look down the tunnel of time.

"Every time I pass the teenage girls on City Island Avenue," Nancy writes, "with their magenta lipstick and tight jeans, dancing around boys, I regret that I can't tell them, as I would like to have been told, that there is a self within them, worthy of their own esteem, precious to God, and quite independent of the opinion of the little buggers whose attention they are so desperately trying to attract."

You may not wish to attribute any metaphysical characteristics to your innermost sense of self—or to love. That may be my desire and not yours. Even so, to sense love's power as a force for transformation you have only to bring to mind what it's like to be moved by an experience of kindness and acceptance, whether this is an experience you have been able to offer or receive. You have only to remember moments when love has seemed inevitable—untainted by anxiety or possession. Or when a shift occurred from aloneness and loneliness to solitude and contentment. Or how good it feels to be appreciated or understood. Or the relief when a bleak way of interpreting an event gives way to a more spacious point of view.

WE ALSO KNOW THIS: THAT LOVE is not love when it is demanding, manipulative, self-focused or judgmental. Love must take us beyond the constraints of egocentricity. Sexual love is sometimes our way out of egocentricity (and loneliness), but equally it can be an extension of it. Perhaps we adore the way someone else makes us feel, and call that love. A more reliable and authentic understanding of love asks that we discover how possible it is even when our passions are not aroused and our needs are not being met.

At its best, love is anarchic and untamable, strengthening as well as softening. We can make changes for the sake of love that might seem impossible under any other conditions. Love can literally heal our hearts and restore meaning.

Scriptures from all the traditions speak of love as the essential saving grace of our human nature. These days, it may need to become the saving grace of *all* nature. The logic of love expresses itself in care-taking, selflessness and a keen recognition of common interests. If we don't love the earth and its creatures perceptively and urgently we risk losing everything that we depend upon. And if we don't come to terms with the meaning that love brings to life—with altruism as its expression—we risk our happiness and emotional well-being.

We know to our sorrow that in a so-called rational world people must "belong" to us or be significantly like us to matter. Or they must "win" or deserve our love and we must win or deserve theirs. In that same world, we all play favorites and create outcasts.

The sacred offers another dimension.

His Holiness the Dalai Lama has spoken extremely frankly about how dependent we are upon living wisely and kindly. "There is an inextricable link," he says, "between one's personal happiness and kindness, compassion and caring for others." In other words, *caring about other people's well-being is the best possible way to take care of our own.*

We live in a world where we praise yet plunder nature. And we praise yet plunder and exploit our own human natures. In *Spiritual Politics* Corinne McLaughlin and Gordon Davidson write with grief, following a massive oil spill: "If our obsession with consumption and materialistic pursuits continues unchecked, we too will be coated in heavy, black muck, unable to free ourselves to the flow of the Spirit."

Our safety, physical health, relationships, our freedom to walk down the streets of our neighborhoods without fear, our most fertile and fragile landscapes, the nonhuman species that become fewer each day, everything that we value survives only because of the mutuality of trust and care *for which each one of us is responsible.* With our own eyes we can see our interdependence and everything that depends on it.

Many of our worst fears circle around the loss of love. And many of our worst behaviors reflect an agonizing incapacity to take love seriously, to take it in—or give it. Poet and Vietnamese Zen monk Thich Nhat Hanh is just one of many writers who points out that if we practice love both through reflection, prayer and meditation, and through the conduct we choose in the many moments of our everyday lives, we can heal what he calls the "illnesses" of the painful, conflicting emotions like anger, insecurity, loneliness, hatred, resentment and sadness. These are the emotions that drive our most common addictions, as well as much of the violence, betrayal and insecurity that torment our hearts and minds. He also says, in his book *Anger*, "Your capacity for loving another person depends entirely on your capacity for loving yourself, for taking care of yourself."

A sense of connectedness and confidence are the immense gifts of raising our expectations of love—and practice of it—to their highest levels. Those gifts can also bring us back to love. Sometimes this involves regarding love as a teacher, the inner discipline of love replacing old habits with new. A very special example comes from the nineteenth-century Russian spiritual classic *The Way of a Pilgrim*, where we learn that the Pilgrim, the seeker, wants to learn to "pray without ceasing" as suggested in Paul's epistle to the Thessalonians.

The Pilgrim comes across a suggestion to say what we would call a mantra "very frequently." The mantra is: "Lord Jesus Christ, have mercy on me." For the first three weeks, he finds this tedious. He is then told to say the mantra three thousand times the first day, six thousand times for two days, then twelve thousand times, then without a limit, counting these numbers on a rosary.

The Pilgrim follows these instructions and, despite his earlier boredom, this time he finds only the first two days taxing. After that, the prayer wakes him in the morning and accompanies him through the day. He reports, "I felt there was no happier person on earth than I ... The whole outside world also seemed to me full of charm and delight. Everything drew me to love and thank God: people, trees, plants and animals. I saw them all as my kinfolk; I found in all of them the magic of the name of Jesus."

~~~

Our need for love is instinctive and primal. When this need is satisfied we experience life quite differently from when love seems lost to us. The sense of connection and affirmation that love brings is indispensable to our psychological and spiritual well-being. This is the obvious reason why some people who have "everything" are nevertheless bereft and grasping, and why others who have "next to nothing" seem to live a life of radiance and quiet satisfaction.

SEEKING AN INCLUSIVE, PROFOUND VISION OF love is synonymous for many people with seeking the sacred. Inspiration and relationship play their essential part here but they come to life as we learn, moment by moment, what "living lovingly" actually means.

If love becomes an instrument of manipulation it is not love; it is self-interest. Good intentions are not enough, either. Action is essential. "Dear children, let us not love with words or tongue but with actions and in truth" (1 John 3:18).

Love must be lived and tested and shaken up and called upon in the ambiguities and shadows of everyday life to become the force for transformation that it is. It must guide our actions and become our actions, otherwise it is nothing but a charming idea.

Understanding what love is, we need to be clear what love is asking of us. We should also be clear what we are asking of love.

*Love doesn't mean treating everyone exactly the same.*

It doesn't mean struggling to like everyone equally. Some people are far more uplifting than others; some are more precious. Those are facts of life that need not imply *dehumanizing or discounting those you like or understand least.*

It doesn't mean putting up with hurtful or unjust behavior, or "tolerating" what's cruel or unjust. It doesn't mean losing sight of what is right and what is wrong.

It doesn't mean that things will not sometimes go wrong and have to be put right.

Several years ago Catherine Greer, the writer and young mother who worked so generously with me on *Choosing Happiness*, sent me a particularly wise note about how she sees love and self-love. She names self-love as "the gateway to acceptance and happiness." More usefully still, she says, "To love yourself, you have to believe there *is* a self. And to become a self, you have to set boundaries. *This* is me and *this* is not me. Some of us have been taught not to set boundaries, that it's selfish or mean or not within our authority.

"Think about the boundary of skin, for example, and the horror of childhood abuse. I could name a hundred other examples of a lack of boundaries stopping self-love, all relating to personal space, and Virginia Woolf's old-fashioned but ever relevant 'room of one's own.'"

Love has so many expressions: respect, kindness, thoughtfulness; speaking up, not speaking; learning and teaching; supporting; praying for and with; the creation of beauty; tolerance of grief; fidelity; freedom; loyalty; devotion; service; laughing, singing or comforting; forgiving; joy, peace and bliss. Its repertoire is infinite. Often restraint is also love because it so powerfully reminds you of the vulnerability, sensitivities and truth of the "other," and of your capacity to heal rather than harm. But as Catherine so powerfully and effectively points out, love is not love when it does not keep you safe.

Understanding how the sublime ideal of love can be expressed through our choices and behaviors will bring it closer: into our bodies and into the relational "bodies" of our encounters as we literally embody it. That may mean showing tolerance to the people who irritate us; restraining our impulses to demean, shame, control or try to change the people around us; offering and accepting forgiveness; moving on from past hurts; generating good rather than bad humor; doing something about the injustices we see; doing something about our compulsions or addictions; spending recklessly the divine currencies of gratitude and appreciation; taking action on behalf of the wordless—and the planet; sending prayers and good wishes broadly; giving others the benefit of the doubt; keeping our word; listening without correcting; cultivating enthusiasm and creativity; extending ourselves beyond our own immediate interests; praying the prayers of traditions that are not familiar to us; understanding what inspires people quite unlike ourselves.

All that is the stuff of spiritual realization.

~ல௵௸௸~

A touching reflection comes from Sydney writer Walter Mason. A warm childhood and a lifetime commitment to his Vietnamese-born partner Thang have given him insight into a broad and generous view of existence. For Walter this is grounded in the infinitely precious moments of daily existence that mirror precisely his view of the sacred. He explains, "I see myself as a Universalist though I know this is probably quite unfashionable these days when people are so keen to emphasize the particular. But I do believe that there is a core in every person and in every religious and philosophical system that is shared.

"I used to struggle with this, but now I am happy to call it God. I'm not afraid to say 'God' and have it mean exactly what I want it to—not bound by the definitions of others. I am also less and less inclined to identify myself with any one school of thought or spirituality. Last time I was in Vietnam [where he travels frequently] I spent a lot of time at the neighborhood Cao Dai temple, and often went to prayers. Frequently the priest and I were the only people there and afterward he would give me tea and little biscuits. He would speak to me passionately about the oneness of God and the shared experience of all humanity: the shared knowing that there is something beyond the physical. The priest said to me, 'People try to make God so small, so as to belong to only them or their religion. But God is vast.' This really affected me—I was filled at that moment with the vastness of it all."

Conscious of that vastness and fully alive to it, it is easy for Walter to say, "I no longer need or want to define myself as some particular spiritual 'thing.' For years I identified as a Buddhist and was adamant that a firm spiritual identity and a careful adherence to rules were both necessary to advancement [on the spiritual 'path']. I would lose patience with people who said they didn't like to put a label on their spiritual ideas—they would exasperate me. Now I am one of them!"

A "mature spirituality" for Walter means more than refusing a particular religious or spiritual label, and the identity that comes with it. "Accepting that others may have quite a different path, a path that serves them well [matters to me]. Thang and I live in Cabramatta [an area of Sydney where many residents are of Vietnamese origin] and we spend a lot of time at the local Buddhist temples. They are filled with elderly people, most of whom at some stage in their lives have lost almost everything they ever owned. But now they are happy. They have no great grasp of Buddhist theory, no sophisticated insights to speak of—just a happiness to be alive and a careful regard for others."

Kindness, happiness, trust and "a careful regard for others" are not simply ideals to be learned on our way through life: they are also the rewards of an inclusive way of living and being. They defy lazy pessimism and dangerous nihilism. *They are exemplifications of the sacred* regardless of external circumstances.

Walter makes this clear when he explains, "I look for 'the sacred' in others. I find that people are constantly kind to me, especially when I travel. And my partner [Thang] makes the most immense sacrifices for me, with no possible hope for reward or compensation, simply because he loves me. That moves me immensely and *causes* me to have faith.

"My grandmother and her sister, my great-aunt Audrey, were also my most influential teachers. They were warm, loving and entirely accepting of everyone they encountered. They were big women, great huggers and kissers, and loved by everyone who ever met them. They were also singers and dancers, laughers and smilers, forgivers of others' trespasses. They were filled with joy, and infected others with that same sense of joy. Love in action. They taught me to smile at everyone and to treat everyone I encounter with respect."

THERE ARE PROFOUND BENEFITS IN relying on love as a spiritual resource and inner teacher. These are richly described by Therese, a psychotherapist in her forties who has been through several tough years with health issues, including cancer. During this demanding time, Therese has been remarkably willing to draw on her knowledge and practice of love. When I asked her about her spiritual experiences it was easy for her to remember a quite beautiful experience that occurred when she was meditating on retreat. She explains, "I opened my eyes and saw the people in the rows facing me and the wall behind them as shimmering, vibrating molecules, enabling me to see through to the trees and garden beyond. This spoke to me of the impermanent nature of being; that it is in constant flux and not as solid and fixed as we normally experience it."

To deepen her understanding of love and her capacity to receive and express it, Therese visualizes manifestations (images) of the Buddha and bodhisattvas (enlightened beings). She explains, "Sometimes I am creating them in my imagination and sometimes they just arise in my mind's eye. However, on one occasion the Buddha arrived as a luminous, alive, potent presence from beyond my psyche. It's hard to describe this experience as it is at a level beyond words and ordinary experience. For me it was a kind of initiation. I already felt called, but this visit from the Buddha confirmed that deeply for me and has sustained me for many years. Variations on this experience followed, but this was the defining one."

From these experiences Therese has defined several key ways to keep herself steadily tuned to the benefits of a loving spiritual practice. As she explained them to me, these practices are all designed to be *inwardly supportive* through caring about and noticing the effects of her *outer actions*. This kind of consistency is powerful enough to "mend" those painful, wordless gaps we may feel between our inner and outer lives. They also keep our lives consistent and less inwardly chaotic or cluttered.

Therese's current practices include persevering when times are tough, regardless of whether she "feels like it." They also include taking responsibility for the effect of her words and actions, and not giving in to baser impulses to retaliate if she's hurt or angry. The qualities of kindness, compassion and patience with oneself and others are central to her spiritual commitment. Therese interprets this by attempting to act ethically in all situations, regardless of whether anyone will ever know. In addition to actions, Therese emphasizes cultivating an inner generosity of heart and spirit. Last, but not least, she is committed to creating the conditions that will support her spiritual nourishment.

This last point is so easily overlooked, yet it relates strongly to the sense of being "present to love" that I wrote of earlier. In a song I used to play often I especially treasured the words, "I want to be ready, an opening for God." To be "ready" to be an opening for the sacred or for love—and for God—we may need to spend time where love and the sacred are wholeheartedly honored, articulated, affirmed and even glorified. That's what makes spiritual companions and often a spiritual community so heartening on our journey forward. Alongside others and learning from them, giving and receiving can become sacramental as well as robustly life-giving.

In Buddhism the "threefold way" of meditation, ethics and wisdom mirrors the "three jewels" of the Buddha, the Dharma (teachings) and the Sangha (community). These combine as "teachers of love" and give practitioners like Therese priceless support even in tough times. She explains, "[These practices] give me something to hold on to when I feel confused, downhearted, hurt, upset or angry, helping to steady me in those moments and find a better path through them."

The spiritual truths that highlight the power of conscious choosing are captured in this verse, attributed to the Buddha himself:

*To study the way of the Buddha is to study oneself.*
*To study oneself is to forget oneself.*
*To forget oneself is to be enlightened by everything in the world.*
*To be enlightened by everything is to surrender one's own body*
  *and mind.*

~୧୨୧୨~

There is so much to appreciate in Therese's account, but what strikes me most is how much inward steadiness and confidence she gains through identifying with the explicit values of her Buddhist practices as well as from her ever-deepening identification with both the historical Buddha and the enlightened beings, achieved through those gifts of visual imagery and meditation. This takes us straight back to the theme of the previous chapter, noticing how much difference it makes to our peace of mind and well-being when we bring our inner identity into alignment with our most nourishing values. I love the sense of abundance and possibility this offers, virtually regardless of our starting point. (*This moment* is a starting point: always.)

So often we turn to some version of self-improvement, whether it is psychotherapy, counseling, self-awareness courses, groups or books, out of feelings of insufficiency, fear or inadequacy. A galloping case of "not-enough," or "not-good-enough," can dominate someone's thinking so completely that it literally taints all their experiences and decisions.

More dangerous still, a perception that "I don't have enough" or "I am not good enough" can become not just a compelling inner story but an entire identity.

When that kind of thinking dominates, it will always dramatically affect what the person feels entitled to do or enjoy, how much pleasure they will get from life—or offer others—and where their attention most routinely strays and stays.

An insufficiency "consciousness" is highly contemporary and massively widespread. And it's always unloving. It makes us greedy as well as fearful and the cultures of status, envy and competition depend on it. Entire industries, in fact, rest on this illusion that we will never have enough or be enough, no matter how hard we try. Given the struggle that many of us have to establish a strong sense of self—with or without a spiritual basis—people will always find plenty of reasons to justify this kind of thinking.

From Munich in Germany I receive a welcome letter from Kerstin Kamm, a mother, Buddhist and science teacher, telling me of her excitement in discovering that spiritual devotion does not mean giving up a part of herself. That it is easy for her to perceive "strong forces out there, a highly sensitive web that connects all life forms." This sense of "web" aligns with Kerstin's deep love of nature, which she regards as her main source of inspiration, and the powerful atmosphere of places she regards as sacred. It also increasingly aligns with the way she sees herself, particularly when she recalls being present at a retreat I gave some years ago at Mana Retreat Centre in New Zealand when, totally spontaneously but compelled in and from a deep place, I walked around the group of standing, silent participants and increasingly slowly said to each of them, "You are enough."

Kerstin remembers that moment: "You said, 'Kerstin, you are *enough* . . .' It was so powerful, so moving."

Such a simple thing, but what made it almost painfully poignant for everyone there that day was that in the precious moments of hearing "You are enough," each of us had also to recognize and heal those limitless moments of living with the idea that we are not enough.

⁓ᥱᥣᥲ⁓

Many of us are skilled at focusing on and creating difficulties so that even if we eventually have what "everyone" wants—beauty, wealth, talent, acclaim, security, partner and children—we remain anxious. Perhaps we are afraid of losing what we have. Or of others taking what we have or spoiling it by envying us. Perhaps we tell ourselves that we do not really deserve it. Or that it's ours only by sleight of hand. Or we fear that even the abundance we have is not enough. Focusing relentlessly on our shortcomings or losses, we may believe that nothing is enough. The anxieties aroused by a fragile ego can be remorseless.

The trajectory of such thinking must always be challenged. It will never be another course, another guru, lover or therapist, more hours on the meditation cushion or in the pew that will "save" you or transform your view. It won't be another degree or promotion, as welcome as they may be. It is *waking up to who and what you already are.*

By contrast, to allow the mind to rest in a moment of sufficiency or simple gratitude is deeply peaceful. It is also a choice.

THE CALL TO THE SACRED URGES us to regard our lives with gratitude and hope *whatever our external circumstances*. It shows how naturally love can become our primary expectation and guide. Stepping over our fears of failure or ridicule, or our anxiety that our understanding and experience of love may be hollow or sentimental, we can find new meanings for love. These require clear thinking. And they not only mend bridges between "heart" and "head," they make such bridges unnecessary. True love requires strength of mind and purpose. True love is liberating. So is learning to think about our *obstacles to love* with greater tolerance, good humor and compassion.

Meister Eckhart, the fourteenth-century German Christian mystic and seer, states plainly who we are and what we should do with this knowledge when he writes: "The seed of God is in us. Given an intelligent farmer and a diligent field hand, it will thrive and grow up to God whose seed it is and, accordingly, its fruit will be God-nature. Pear seeds grow into pear trees; nut seeds into nut trees; and God-seeds into God . . . Go to the depths of the soul, the secret place of the Most High, to the roots, to the heights; for all that God can do is focused there."

Twentieth-century Catholic priest and writer Thomas Merton adds something marvelous. In *New Seeds of Contemplation* he writes, "To say that I am made in the image of God is to say that love is the reason for my existence, for God is love. Love is my true identity. Selflessness is my true self. Love is my true character. Love is my name."

*Love is my true identity . . . my true character. Love is my name.*

What would enable us to live as though we believed that? And how different would our lives be?

∼ᢗᢁᢚᢙᢗᢋᢁᢙᢇ

In twenty-first-century life so many people who are warm, well fed and safe have real difficulty offering themselves inner shelter, comfort and a reliable sense of being at home in their own lives. Many of us remain stuck, like the teenage girls Nancy Malone observed on City Island Avenue, dependent on the opinions of others to reassure us that our lives matter and that we are lovable. In those circumstances, status, youth, worldly riches, sexual appeal and beauty come to matter disproportionately. They may even enslave us.

Love may seem like a mirage or torment when others seem to "have it" but we do not. Perhaps our childhood has been affectionate and supportive. Perhaps we have a fine education and an admirable career. Yet still we *gnaw* at ourselves, psychologically speaking. Still we pick at the one percent of whatever it is that does not go well, ignoring the ninety-nine percent where we are doing fine. Still we blame and rail at others when they can't make up to us the deficits in our own self-regard.

How *un*surprising it is then that our concern and support for others is often so unstable or arbitrary. Or that we are confused about what kindness to others could actually mean.

*Meeting our defenses with compassion is essential.* And that rests on learning also to see life itself with greater appreciation and gratitude. If your first impulse is always to dwell on what's wrong, *notice that*—and shift your attention. ("What's needed here? What would support me through this? How can I be more creative or strategic in my thinking rather than scared or helpless? What are my *soul strengths* that I am ignoring?")

Condemning those obstacles, or blaming yourself for having them, will never help. Far better to see that the reasons you are not loving to yourself or others developed from a time when you did not know how to take better care of yourself. Those patterns are also influenced by a culture that's largely superficial in its judgments and disdaining of the values and attributes that are most sustaining.

But those habits and patterns can change. *You can change them.*

Blame is never helpful; nor is self-pity. Patience, tenacity, good humor: these are the qualities we can *afford* to embrace.

⁓ↄʋ\ʋↄ⁓

Perhaps it is an understandable fear of falling into narcissism or of becoming overly self-involved or selfish that explains why loving our own lives—our own self—is for so many people the toughest call of all. I understand this struggle. It is something that I have had to face in the most hidden, shadowy aspects of my existence. Yet what I have learned is this: what seems to begin in me or to be about me will not end in me; and what seems to begin in you, or to be about you, will not end in you. We live in a constant flux of experience, influencing as well as being influenced, taking in and giving out, and rarely knowing exactly which moments will be most significant in defining what is coming.

> *The kingdom of heaven is like a mustard seed*
> *That someone took and sowed in their field.*
> *It is the smallest of all seeds, but when it is grown*
> *It is the greatest of shrubs and becomes a tree*
> *So that the birds of the air can come*
> *And can make their nests in its branches.* (Matthew 13:31–32)

*Envisaging yourself positively* is essential to self-love. Putting yourself down, belittling or humiliating yourself is harm of a most corrosive kind. So is assuming that you are too weak to face up to your own failings or wrongdoings—or to move forward from them, chastened certainly but also wiser.

Inward steadiness comes from trusting that you can indeed bear the inevitable ambiguities of human existence: that you can call on your values in tough times and express your joy unequivocally in the better times.

It also comes from "bearing"—or better, genuinely accepting—the ambiguities in other people's lives and conduct. Their inconsistencies will undoubtedly be alarmingly like your own. That may make you feel more irritated and less compassionate. It may also make you feel justified as well as tempted to take over when you can see clearly what needs to be done. But love is *never* expressed through constant harping, nagging, whining, bickering or controlling. Love is never expressed—or honored—by attacking someone or humiliating them. And especially not when this is purportedly done for the sake of the other person ("This is for your own good."). Or when the claim is made that the other person "caused" our angry response ("You make me so mad."). Releasing our anger or frustrations by attacking or demeaning others is unambiguously *un*loving. Nothing justifies it. Taking responsibility never to act in these ways is the only liberation possible. It is this that restores the feelings of gratitude, connection and especially acceptance that are the hallmarks of love.

Encouragement and appreciation are as essential for building trust as they are for intimacy. And they are crucial in building a picture of ourselves as people capable of giving love generously, as well as receiving it.

*Envisaging yourself positively*, you also align yourself with the sacred, however subjectively you interpret that.

Here is a very practical example of love working for me in my own life. I find it extremely calming to see myself as part of the bigger universe and, even more helpful, to see whatever is currently worrying or troubling me also as part of the biggest possible picture. *This too will pass. This event will take its place in life's big picture.* Saving myself from feeling overwhelmed, I can so much more easily think about whatever it is with clarity and focus.

Holding a strong, respectful image of yourself can be a regular part of your meditation practice. It can be part of what soothes you in difficult moments or times when your mind would otherwise be flooded with apprehension. It is what can take you to sleep at night and wake with you in the morning.

Whatever our history has been, it is possible gradually to learn to appreciate ourselves as loving and loved persons, a source of love for others and for ourselves: *May I be well and happy . . . May all beings be well and happy.* Seeing ourselves in this way is itself an act of love and an authentic honoring of our gift of existence.

This doesn't mean imagining that you are better or more special than the next person. Far more humbly than that, it means holding in your mind confidence that you are worthy of your own good will and affection; that your precious, unique life is worth treasuring; that your capacity for love can also include your own self and will quite naturally express itself to other people and in how you value and connect with the physical world.

This may be the most profound and effective self-therapy we will ever achieve. Certainly it makes our seeking of the sacred intensely personal as well as profound. And it powerfully and immediately benefits everyone else.

I know from my own life that it is my experiences of the sacred that have allowed me to accept my imperfections, to learn from and forgive myself for my many failures and mistakes, to reset my priorities, to rejoice in the connections and pleasures that life so abundantly gives and to be far more accepting and appreciative of others.

"As long as you remain blind to your own truth, you keep putting yourself down and referring to everyone else as better, holier, and more loved than you are," writes Catholic priest Henri Nouwen in *The Inner Voice of Love.* In this intensely personal journal, Nouwen is addressing himself as "you," but is inviting us to identify with ways in which he is also speaking of our condition.

"You look up to everyone in whom you see goodness, beauty and love because you do not see these qualities in yourself. As a result, you begin leaning on others without realizing that you have everything you need to stand on your own feet."

When someone tells me how impossible self-love is, or how persuasive their feelings of insufficiency are, I often urge them to consider this change of mind for the sake of everyone else. (I also suggest that they start by simply being more encouraging and less critical; finding modest chances to express appreciation and gratitude; taking a closer interest in other people and particularly behaving toward themselves as they would to any good friend.)

A poor view of ourselves places a huge demand on our relationships. It leaks out as self-pity and self-absorption as often as it does through bitterness, frustration or envy, or the kind of pettiness I wrote of earlier. In some people a lack of self-acceptance will show in the criticisms they make of those nearest to them, especially when they project onto others their lack of inner trust, or exploit the epithets to harass or hurt others that they themselves most fear ("lazy," "aimless," "insensitive," even "worthless"). We gain insight as well as humility when we review with some detachment what we are prepared to "call" others.

Any version of this makes us less than ideal company—even for ourselves. And it often means that we will consciously or unconsciously require others to compensate for our own unloving attitudes, yet will rarely be satisfied when they attempt to do that.

"I think you are a terrific person. And I love you."

"You don't really mean it. You are only saying it . . ."

SEEKING the SACRED

A lack of self-acceptance and self-love keeps our attention too firmly focused on ourselves and especially on our anxieties and shortcomings. *This also prevents us from being a wholehearted source of love for others.*

Feeling better about ourselves and less self-involved, we can engage with others more generously. And we can take in and accept the praise, kindness and appreciation that they want to offer.

"I think you are a terrific person. And I love you."

"Thanks! You've made my day . . ."

On this the famed psychiatrist and writer M. Scott Peck goes so far as to say, "We are incapable of loving another unless we love ourselves, just as we are incapable of teaching our children self-discipline unless we ourselves are self-disciplined. It is actually impossible to forsake our own spiritual development in favor of someone else's."

As long as the dynamic of insufficiency dominates our horizon, our spiritual strengths will lie fallow.

❧

The social paradigm of "not enough" sits in sharp contrast to the spiritual paradigm of "you are enough." This is very much part of the identity story that I covered earlier in this book but here, too, in the presence of love, we can see that achievements, credentials, effort-making, worldly glory—if you so choose—can as easily emerge from being "enough" rather than as compensation for "not being enough."

That you are at this very moment *inwardly rich and treasured* is the authentic meaning of the spiritual quality of abundance. It has nothing to do with acquiring material wealth or fame; on the contrary. Regarding your own life with a sense of plenty, it becomes easy and natural to water that "God-seed" within you, to leave self-consciousness at least somewhat behind, to worry far less about how others might be judging you and to throw yourself with enthusiasm into whatever interests, relationships, dreams, passions and causes engage you.

What a delight to find that you are not the center of an anxious universe, with other people waiting to judge and condemn you, but that instead you are part of an intricately connected, sacred universe, filled with people whom *you* can positively influence, support and encourage—and who will sometimes similarly support you.

In the most "ordinary" of existences there are opportunities for us to reach out toward others and allow others to reach toward us. At a recent dinner I attended a busy, newly single mother and businesswoman told a detailed story about moving to a new home and trying to buy a mower that both she and her ten-year-old son could use. While she was dealing with that, a hundred other things, her own indecision and the hard reality of finding herself, as she put it, "responsible for everything," her neighbor—himself a busy executive—quietly mowed her lawn.

Taking those opportunities and creating new ones is nothing less than life-enhancing. But beyond reaching out in those immediate and necessary ways—and noticing the many ways in which *our own lives are supported*—the sacred teachings about our interdependence have a quite different reason for gaining urgency. It is gradually dawning upon us that our inevitable interdependence is not a matter of ethics only. It is also a matter of physical and spiritual survival. This was clearly stated by theoretical physicist Albert Einstein in the following sublime quotation.

"A human being is a part of the whole, called by us the 'Universe,' a part limited in time and space. He experiences himself, his thoughts and feelings, as something separate from the rest—a kind of optical delusion of his consciousness. This delusion is a kind of prison for us, restricting us to our personal desires and to affection for a few persons nearest to us. Our task must be to free ourselves from this prison by widening our circle of compassion to embrace all living creatures and the whole of nature in its beauty. Nobody is able to achieve this completely, but the striving for such achievement is in itself a part of the liberation and a foundation for inner security."

And why would you even contemplate attempting to "strive" in this way?

In part, and yet again, for the most practical reason possible: we protect ourselves as well as the people we know and love best when we live with awareness of our unique part in a greater "whole." We protect ourselves—and the earth on which we entirely depend—when we dare to find out what it means to live *from* that awareness, allowing it to guide and temper our priorities, decisions and choices. We protect ourselves when we start to recognize that this shift in consciousness and conduct must always start with our own behavior—and never finishes there.

Living peacefully and cooperatively, *we create peace and cooperation.* Living justly, *we create justice.* Living lovingly, *we generate love.* Caring about beauty, *we generate and protect beauty.*

Those awe-inspiring qualities come to life only when they are "embodied" by us, when they become the drivers of our personal and collective behavior.

The most universal and uplifting prayers and teachings describe love as the power that connects us to one another and also to the Source of Love that we might call God. Such writings exhort us to know love as the power that "wakes us up" and moves us on from small-self feelings of isolation, hopelessness, despair. In fact, those teachings don't just praise love. They evoke it as the only possible salvation, not salvation for the unfathomable "next life" but for this familiar one: for each one of us moving through a human existence that will uniformly be marked by fear, sorrow, stupidity, ignorance, cruelty, loss and death, as well as insight, hope, grace, forgiveness and bliss.

"Be still," we hear in the supreme Psalm 46, verse 10, "Be still, and know that I am God." In stillness and mindfulness of Love, we are restored to ourselves.

NOTHING IS MORE TRANSFORMATIVE than discovering how possible it is to see our choices, strengths and weaknesses, longings, desires and ambitions—our very self—through the eyes of love. Love is the pulse as well as the heart of spirituality. As love becomes integral to our identity, many of our choices will change. How we think about time, as well as how we spend it, may change. What's most important to us will change, as will our priorities. We will reassess our values and what we most value about ourselves. Some of what we fretted about most will slip off our radar. Nothing but a more loving view could achieve this level of benefit to every aspect of our lives simultaneously.

A glimpse of what Sydney man Rodney Cole has both experienced and achieved is helpful here. Now in his forties, and leading a crucial suicide-prevention program, his work and life have pushed him to reflect particularly deeply. When I asked Rodney if there were times when self-love had seemed elusive, or when his spiritual life was empty or flat, he told me, "If I think in terms of living from a place of our most essential spiritual nature, my childhood and adolescence were some of the blackest and darkest times of my life, and in some ways I am still recovering from them. The isolation, desperation and struggle in trying to deal as a child with something as complex as a gender identity crisis left me feeling spiritually void. God was nowhere to be seen and in my eyes I was not 'worthy' for feeling so different.

"After attempting to live a fulfilling life as a gay man in my twenties, as I approached my thirties I could sense the isolation and loneliness I had felt as a child returning. I felt like I didn't fit in the gay community and in some respects didn't want to fit in or participate in such limiting and at times destructive behaviors and practices that dominate [Sydney gay] community life.

"Ten years on my struggle with fitting in still continues, and renewal for me is still ongoing. I now have a strong sense of what feeds me spiritually and I am no longer fearful of my faith—which I was, terribly. While I can appreciate how private someone's faith is to them, I have found sharing it respectfully with others very empowering and it has helped enormously in being able to unpack it, ask questions, seek guidance at times."

Rodney is confident that as his spirituality has matured his sense of identity has changed for the better.

His story continues. "I will never forget the moments that led to me claiming and owning my spirituality. For many years I had played with the notion of labeling myself spiritual, yet I did very little to nurture or develop it. Looking back now I can see my spirituality was more like a fashion accessory. While it wasn't false, and occasionally was very bright and made me look good, it didn't feel real.

"I felt that my spirituality lacked depth and authenticity. I hadn't worked out what my faith looked like, what it felt like, what it meant to me. I had a lot of questions to ask it: how is my spirituality supposed to support me, why do I feel challenged and sometimes embarrassed by it, what are the limitations it places on me?

"Curious about the answers to the questions, I decided to go on a silent retreat [in a Christian abbey] and gave myself permission to really explore my spirituality in the hope of becoming clearer about its place and role in my life.

"At the retreat, I noticed quite early on that I had become fascinated with a large fig tree near my cabin. It had a massive solid trunk which supported the myriad of twisted and intertwined branches that flowed from it. It looked both unbalanced and in perfect harmony at the same time.

"Throughout the retreat I kept focusing on the tree, as if it held the key to some secret I was trying to uncover. Finally, on the last day, I looked at the tree and heard this voice say from deep within, 'I am no longer one of the branches of the tree subject to the mercy of the wind and other elements. I am the solidness of the trunk, from which everything grows and is supported.'

"I left the retreat knowing that my spirituality was no longer a tiny part of me, that I wanted it to be the core of me. I wanted it to be my foundation from which everything flowed.

"In the years following the retreat what I have noticed in my day to day life is a greater feeling of compassion and kindness—for myself and others—to know that even when I feel most alone that I am not as alone as I feel. This has been a great comfort and a tremendous stabilizer for me. I have noticed that I desire less and, in general, need fewer things to function in the world. And, paradoxically, I feel I have more than I need.

"I remember a workshop that you [Stephanie] gave on forgiveness when you suggested we approach forgiveness with a thinking heart and a feeling mind. This has been almost a mantra that I use to remind myself to foster better understanding between myself and others.

"In my current work in suicide prevention, I'm not sure I could sit with people in their despair, to hear and acknowledge the ambivalence they feel, without my spirituality actively supporting me."

Like Rodney, each time we deal with a situation with greater confidence and stability, we grow more trusting also of our inner world and its capacities. Recognizing new strengths and choices, we will loosen our need for behaviors that have restricted us. What will also change is our trust in and knowledge of love.

❧

This is how Subhana Barzaghi describes one of her most significant experiences of learning what love is. Subhana is both a Zen Buddhist Roshi (ordained teacher) and a skilled Vipassana teacher of many years' standing. She has been a midwife in the past and is now a psychotherapist. In her role as spiritual teacher she leads many retreats. But the story she tells here comes from a time of great vulnerability and it speaks so strongly to me.

Subhana says, "When I first met Robert Aitken Roshi [Subhana's primary teacher and a famed Zen writer], I was twenty-five years of age and in considerable anguish and distress. After hearing his teachings, I felt an overwhelming sense of trust, that here was a wise teacher who could help me. I attended my first seven-day Zen sesshin [retreat] at the Convent of the Sacred Heart at Burradoo, south of Sydney.

"Aitken Roshi is a man of few words, but those words were poignant and potent. After the first few days, I realized that I found it difficult to look Roshi in the eye. His gaze was penetrating, and I felt that he could see right through me, so I avoided his gaze.

"I began to wonder why I could not look at him and realized that I felt ashamed of myself, for there were a number of things that I had done, how I had hurt others, that I felt remorseful about. I realized that I did not love and accept myself. I was capable of giving out a lot, loving others, but it had never occurred to me to love myself, fully and completely. So I sat with the intention to love and forgive myself unconditionally.

"This softening of the heart toward myself shifted my response to Roshi. I could then look him in the eye without shame or embarrassment. This experience of self-acceptance and self-love initiated a much deeper and more profound awakening experience. I sat [in meditation] long hours, well into the night. I had very little need of sleep. My mind was steady, calm and still. I arrived at a place where everything that I felt and thought about myself, everything that I knew, started to fall away. I had no idea who I was, where I was or what I was anymore. All known reference points of my failures, successes, achievements, knowledge, roles and identity simply fell away. It was like I had fallen into an abyss or a great void of 'not knowing,' yet I was incredibly alert and focused.

"Roshi asked me to focus on the koan *Mu* (which means 'nothing'). Koans are primary questions used to awaken the heart-mind. There was nothing left to cling on to. I thought I was going crazy, losing my mind. At that moment a great fear arose and I thought I was going to die. The 'I' that I had known and had believed to be myself at that moment did, in fact, die. The words 'though I walk through the valley of the shadow of death, I will fear no evil' came to me and comforted me.

"I embraced the fear and just kept walking. What followed is hard to explain. I realized the exquisite emptiness of *Mu*, which was beyond being and nonbeing; freedom, peace and the joy of liberation pervaded my mind. This experience of *kensho*—realization of the unborn unconditioned—transformed my life. It was like the world turned inside out and upside down. I was no longer inside the world but the world was inside me. The 'I'/'me' story and drama just seemed like a soap opera, an empty illusion. The division and duality between my self and 'other' had also dropped away and what remained was love, a timeless, boundless immeasurable ocean and presence.

"One of my favorite verses, that I think is so beautiful and encapsulates the whole teachings in two lines, is from a Vedanta teacher in India, [Sri] Nisargadatta Maharaj, who said, 'Wisdom teaches me I am nothing. Love teaches me I am everything. Between these two poles my life flows.'"

Growing into the great potential that love promises is best achieved, in my somewhat chastened experience, *in the spirit of what one is seeking.* As Subhana's story so gracefully reveals, we can choose to claim love as our reference point, however awkward or unpracticed we may feel. This means dealing with our difficulties intelligently rather than harshly. It certainly means learning how to be generous and forgiving toward ourselves while also taking seriously the invaluable lessons of our own experiences.

Subhana is one of the most naturally generous people I know and I'm confident that she would agree that we do not and cannot become more loving by chiding or berating ourselves or others, by obsessing about our own or other people's failures and failings, or by living in terror about what we or the rest of the human race might be tempted to do next.

I know that none of us grows happier or more resilient dwelling on our shortcomings. If we are religious, we do not grow more loving either by obsessing about sin, or by seeing ourselves or anyone else as sinful or "unworthy" of God's or our own love. The Jewish mystic Ba'al Shem Tov makes this last thought particularly clear. "Brooding on one's sinfulness is merely a trick to keep [humankind] far from God. The service of God requires the deepest joy and such joy cannot be experienced in a divided self. Repent of evil, know that God in His love accepts your penitence, and return to serve him with joy and wholeness ..."

∽༄⁊༅∾

Again, our lives would transform in an instant if we could comprehend the power of love within us and beyond us. *Love is the language of the sacred.* It is a language of attitude, gesture, symbol, dreaming, desiring, creativity and especially silence as much as it is vocabulary. Words can take us only so far in understanding love; living it is essential. Motivation matters too. And expectations: both what we expect of ourselves and of any situation.

Why are we being more loving? For whose benefit: to prove or improve what?

Twentieth-century Hindu master Meher Baba expresses this with memorable simplicity: "There is no path greater than love. There is no law higher than love. And there is no goal beyond love. God and love are One."

Claiming our spiritual birthright, we would know that all of life is suffused with love: love for nature, people, creatures; for what we can do, imagine and create; for the ambiguity and fragile mortality of it all; for the astonishing variety of it; for life's shadows; for the reluctance with which we leave the body when the time comes for our dying; for the grief and sorrow and suffering that only love can begin to heal.

Love is path, purpose and practice. As we learn love, we become more empathic, sensitive and appreciative—with increasingly fewer conditions. As we learn love, we literally *look forward* with greater confidence, enthusiasm and hope. We find meaning wherever we are because love does not bring meaning; love *is* meaning.

Appreciation and gratitude come to the forefront in our lives. Grasping and possessing make less sense. So does insisting on our own point of view, or condemning others when their way of living or seeing the world is different from our own.

In the Atharva Veda from the Hindu tradition we hear this testimony to love:

*Love is the firstborn, loftier than the gods, the High Ones, and*
*    humankind.*
*You, O Love, are the most ancient of all . . .*
*. . . In all forms of goodness, O Love, you show your face.*

Is love our way of tuning in to and reflecting the nature of God—or does it "just" reflect the highest capacities of our human nature? Any answer to that will be highly subjective. What is tangible is how love is revealed through "all forms of goodness," including creativity, passion, consolation, compassion and connection.

IT IS ALSO LOVE THAT CONNECTS the worlds, that makes remotely comprehensible the notion of "life" in its essential spiritual aspects weaving its way through the seen and unseen: the worlds of matter and of spirit.

Susan MacFarlane is a meditation teacher as well as a therapist. Like many people whose deep stories I have heard it has been death as well as life that has taught her much about love's infinite dimensions. Susan describes this.

"One of the most crucial and formative spiritual experiences I have had was when my sister Lizzie, fifteen years younger than me, was dying. The more her body faded the more the light of her spirit filled the room. Light and presence were palpable and yet her physical life force was dissolving. I realized that her beauty was her soul. This was the first time that my spiritual beliefs about the continuity of life were so acutely tested. Lizzie's great gift to me was to allow me to witness the emergence of her beautiful spirit. How could I grieve the loss of something which wasn't gone and that never died? Those hours after her death, as we bathed her body and sat in reverence and awe at the miracle of her radiant presence with us, will never leave me."

This experience has influenced the way that Susan can think about her own inevitable death, but this "knowing"—beyond words—is also profoundly influenced by her committed spiritual practices.

Again she explains. "What I believe will help me most when I leave this world is what I have learned and continue to learn through contemplation, silence and focused meditation. I have had the direct experience of there only being one world and that it is my mind that creates the separation. Knowing the Presence of Love to be everywhere and all-pervading, in the visible and unseen world, I know that after my body dies my consciousness will continue to dissolve its sense of individuality into the 'Great Ocean of Divinity'—or 'GOD.'

"I don't feel a need to know the details of the afterlife experience. I have a profound trust that my spirit knows where it came from and therefore knows where it is going. All I need to do is to open my heart and allow the light and love of my essential being to guide me. I'm inspired by Jelaluddin Rumi's words: 'My death is my wedding with Eternity.'"

꧁ ꧂

Love connects us powerfully *and* it takes us way beyond our usual understandings of connection. "Connection" already implies separation. Love transcends separation—even, as Susan shows, the separation of life and death.

A Cherokee teaching on peace gives us some sense of what our losses are when we forget the roots that we share and the origins of our diverse expression of a single yearning: "All of us can trace our roots to that one Great Tree of Peace, life itself. Whatever our tribe, our language, our race, our culture, there is one truth, one reality, that unites us all as people."

Looking around, we will see that we cannot hurt someone else without harming ourselves. We cannot do good without also benefiting. This is the theme of all of the universal spiritual teachings: that we swim in a single ocean (called life); that we have continuously unfolding choices to do good rather than harm. And that the direction we take determines our happiness as well as who and what we are becoming.

I suspect that every one of us knows this, not intellectually only but in our bones. Yet how it translates and gains meaning is when each one of us individually discovers how to live lovingly with increasingly fewer conditions and with increasingly fewer reasons why we would *not* love.

This requires us to think hard about the limits of our loving: whom we are willing to love and especially whom we are willing to regard and treat as "our neighbor."

~~~∽⌒∾⌒∾~~~

"Love your neighbor as yourself" is the Golden Rule that illuminates and attempts to make sense of the central teachings of unity and reciprocity in all the known world religions. It is the ethical meeting point of the world's most significant philosophies. It is the rule that makes sense of even the most primitive understanding of our interdependence. It "awakens" and puts into play all the qualities that we now associate with moral and emotional intelligence, including imagination, empathy, self-awareness and self-control. Crucially, it pushes us to take other people's needs and wants seriously, even and especially when they don't match our own.

The Golden Rule offers an essential wisdom that if taken half seriously could literally transform the view we have of others and ourselves. It marries our internal awareness with our outer actions, bringing us to a crucial level of wholeness within and without. It is without parallel in its simplicity and clarity. And throughout the ages it would seem that people of faith find it every bit as difficult to live as people without faith.

A few years ago I wrote a book called *The Universal Heart*. Without overtly emphasizing the Golden Rule, that book was nevertheless inspired by and based on it. What I was particularly interested in exploring was this paradox: most of us feel a great deal better when we are behaving at least relatively thoughtfully—*so why don't we do that more of the time?*

What stops us from using the Golden Rule as the constant and unifying ethical foundation of our private and public lives? Why is it that so many religiously minded people can get themselves in a shocking tangle about rules, regulations, observances, laws and dogma, while leaving the most "Golden" and pivotal rule of all way out of the picture? How can a priest, imam or rabbi confidently and arrogantly condemn their fellow human beings—or claim certainty that God is condemning them—when *the first rule of their faiths is to love divinely, inclusively and unconditionally?*

This truly makes no sense, for if we are indeed in any way tuned to the mystery we call God, or wishing to seek or live the sacred, we cannot avoid taking the Golden Rule completely seriously. If we wish to flourish psychologically and grow spiritually in any way worth a teaspoon of salt, we cannot avoid basing our lives on it.

~♥~

From the Torah, in the Book of Leviticus (19:18), this is how we hear the Golden Rule described: "You shall not take vengeance or bear a grudge. Love others as you would yourself." Moments later in Leviticus (19:34) comes the same message: "The stranger who dwells with you shall be like one of you, and you will love him as you do yourself." Here it is not just the neighbor we should include in our concern; no "stranger" is to be left out.

In one of the most famous accounts in the Christian gospels (Matthew 22: 36–39), Jesus is asked which is the greatest of the commandments. His answer is clear. "Love the Lord who is your God with all the power of your heart, your soul and your thoughts. That is the great and first commandment. But the second is like it. Love others as you love yourself. In these two commandments is contained the whole Law and the books of the prophets."

In the Gospel of Luke (6:31), as well as earlier in Matthew (7:12), the Golden Rule arises again: "Do to others as you would have them do to you."

Emphasizing the spiritual as well as the social truth of our interdependence, the Prophet Mohammed said, "None of you truly believe until you wish for others what you wish for yourself"(An-Nawawi's 40 Hadith 13). And this also: "Do you love your Creator? Love your fellow beings first."

(Oh how much easier to love your Creator than the "fellow being" who gets in your way, takes the last parking space, fails to appreciate you, cheats you, lies to you, insults you, abandons you with little children, takes your land or livelihood, holds a grudge into eternity, harms or abuses you ... How wise the Prophet was on that score.)

From two and a half thousand years ago we hear the historical Buddha urging us to come awake to this same depth of perception. "Consider others as yourself." And also: "He who experiences the unity of life sees his own Self in all beings."

More ancient still are these key verses in the Isa Upanishad (6–7) from the Hindu tradition: "Those who see all creatures in themselves, and themselves in all creatures, have nothing to fear. Those who see all creatures in themselves, and themselves in all creatures, know no grief. How can the multiplicity of life delude the one who sees its unity?"

"How can the multiplicity of life delude the one who sees its unity?"

The primary problem here is surely one of "seeing": of seeing the "multiplicity" with deep appreciation *and* the unity, and seeing this interconnected truth through and beyond the conditioned mind.

"Open your eyes and the whole world is full of God," said the German poet Goethe.

And from Sufi universalist Hazrat Inayat Khan: "Behind us all is one spirit and one life. How then can we be happy if our neighbour is unhappy? ... The same bridge which connects two souls in the world, when stretched, becomes the path of God."

*Listen*, they seem to be saying. *Listen, see, touch, pause*: let your sense and senses be your teacher.

As I sit here writing late into the evening, relishing the peace of my own home, in one of the safest suburbs in one of the safest urban centers in the developed world, significant numbers of people in our human family are waking to their day, ready to kill, abuse, denigrate and cause indescribable harm in the name of religion. Reading the mind of God—as they claim—they may even judge their actions to be pleasing to God. Many more millions are willing to crush the spirit or break the hearts of those who don't believe as they do.

Wherever our world is troubled or violent, unforgiving or unjust, we will see evidence that "loving our neighbor"—and the safety and well-being that flow from it—is surely the greatest of all hurdles in a spiritually focused life, and the most necessary call to heed. No religious sacrifice, however arduous, is as meaningful or as confronting as living up to the Golden Rule.

༄༄

"We don't love ourselves enough to believe God loves us," I heard Father Michael Whelan, a gifted, compassionate Catholic priest and writer, say recently to a packed church in my home city of Sydney. That should be a usefully shocking statement: shocking us out of our usual presumptions. And we could go further. We often don't love ourselves enough to make sense of the Golden Rule. And to live it.

Problems accelerate when we doubt ourselves as the instruments of love and doubt God as the infinite source of love. (Far better to disbelieve in God entirely than to doubt that.) Many convinced "believers" self-evidently believe in a monstrous God. It's unsurprising then that they would fear God more fiercely than they love "Him." Fearing God, and believing in the kind of justice that sees sheep sorted from goats, and sinners condemned to the fires of hell for all eternity, it becomes inevitable that followers of that wrathful deity would treat other human beings harshly and arrogantly, elevating some and regarding others as barely human. Fearing God, they live in terror. Fearing their capacities for sin, they surely doubt their abilities to forgive, tolerate and love.

✦❧✦

How we behave will always give the most truthful account of what we believe. When teaching on the Golden Rule, Jesus said, "This is my commandment, that you should love one another. Love one another as I have loved you. And through this, *people will see that you are my followers*" (John 13:34).

We need not doubt that countless selfless, compassionate Christians have lived that message, and continue to do so. But do we dare wonder how different the last two thousand years would have been if the vast majority had taken love as their rock, light and guide: And through this, *people will see that you are my followers*.

So as shocking as Michael Whelan's remark may seem, it is possibly not shocking enough. Wherever God is viewed as less than Love itself, wherever fear and condemnation dominate, it is tragically difficult for followers to live freely and joyfully, to love one another wholeheartedly, and to accept and love themselves.

How far those familiar limitations take us from the following verse, as ancient as the rest, in Deuteronomy (30:19):

> *I call upon heaven and earth this day to bear witness*
> *that I have set before you life and death, blessings and curses.*
> Choose life.

*Choose life so that you and your descendants may live.*
*Choose life!*

⤙⤙⤙

It seems fair to say that no matter what the religious tradition, nor how powerful or ancient its claims, the litmus test for ordinary decency, spirituality and certainly for organized religion is quite straightforward. Are the rules we are trying to live by supporting us to "choose life"—or not? Are they emphasizing our connections to other people—or dividing us? Are they healing harm—or causing it? Are they opening us to humility—or arrogance? Do they condemn those who believe or live differently from us? Do they condemn *anyone*?

Are they inspiring us to become exuberantly life-loving—or not?

⤙⤙⤙

There is no ideal higher than love. And no experience that is more healing. Love is our first lesson on the spiritual journey and the last. Spiritual realization (*realizing* our spiritual nature and living accordingly) will only be achieved through conduct that mirrors love and is inspired by it. There is a familiar story about the monk who explodes when he is interrupted during his meditation. "Can't you see you are disturbing my *peace*?" It's a story that should make us laugh, and think again, because it is not the monk only who can be misguided in how he sorts his priorities; it is all of us.

Contemporary British religious writer Karen Armstrong makes a similar point in her memoir, *The Spiral Staircase.* "I have discovered that the religious quest is not about discovering 'the truth' or 'the meaning of life,' but about living as intensely as possible in the here and now. The idea is not to latch on to some superhuman personality or to get to heaven but to discover how to be fully human ... Men and women have a potential for the divine, and are not complete unless they realize it within themselves."

A former nun and now a leading English-language scholar in the field of religion, Armstrong also says, "In the past my own practice of religion had diminished me, whereas true faith, I now believe, should make you more human than before."

⤳~ↄᴗↄ~⤲

Some of us will feel certain that we are best guided and supported by a religious faith. Some of us will follow more universal ethical and spiritual principles. But whatever the foundation of our lives, we need to know what beliefs and assumptions are motivating our most significant choices—and where they are taking us. We need to feel in tune with our own seeking. Perhaps the most touching aspect of love is that we must choose it. Or at least choose to live it meaningfully. Doing that, we will discover quite naturally how love is also choosing us.

It is Teilhard de Chardin who again gives us some wonderful words. "Joy," he wrote, "is the most infallible sign of the presence of God." Joy, and connection, wholeness and tenderness too, are infallible signs also of the presence of the sacred, of love.

The Australian Aboriginal lawman and Ngarinyin elder David Mowaljarlai expresses the joy of the sacred even more passionately. "You know ... when daylight starts, it wakes me up ... It wakes the whole body. So I turn round to have a look ... Morning gives you the flow of a new day—ah! With this beautiful color inside, the sun is coming up, with that glow that comes straightaway in the morning. The color comes toward me and the day is waiting. You have a feeling in your heart that you're going to feed your body this day, get more knowledge. You go out now, see animals moving, see trees, a river. You are looking at nature and giving it your full attention, seeing all its beauty. Your vision has opened and you start learning now.

"When you touch them, all things talk to you, give you their story. It makes you really surprised. You feel you want to get deeper, so you start moving around and stamp your feet—to come closer and recognize what you are seeing. You understand that your mind has been opened to all those things because you are seeing them, because your presence and their presence meet together and you recognize each other. These things recognize you. They give you wisdom and their understanding to you when you come close to them.

"In the distance you feel, 'Ah—I am going to go there and have a closer look!' You know it is pulling you. When you recognize it, it gives strength—a new flow. You have life now."

# "DO NO HARM"

*I refuse to accept the view that mankind is so tragically bound to the starless midnight of racism and war that the bright daybreak of peace and brotherhood can never become a reality . . . I believe that unarmed truth and unconditional love will have the final word.*

*Non-violence means avoiding not only external physical violence but also internal violence of spirit. You not only refuse to shoot a man. You refuse to hate him.*

Dr. Martin Luther King, Jr. (1929–1968)

REFUSING TO CAUSE OR PROLONG HARM would already create the spiritual revolution that our world needs. Wars could not be waged. Children could not be deserted, starved or abused. Women and children could not be trafficked and enslaved. Nation-states could not torture and murder. Women and men could not "solve" their problems through violence and corruption. Terror could not reign if that simple truth were to be engraved across our hearts and taken seriously.

Choosing a more abundant and generous way of life, choosing empathy, kindness and forgiveness, we would begin to know what it means to honor life. We would begin to know what unconditionality amounts to. We would surely know what the sacred is. And only then would we live its meaning.

There is no valid seeking of the sacred without thinking freshly and vigorously about what love asks of us as well as what it gives.

There is no valid withdrawing from harm, or recognizing the devastations that "harm" causes, without first remembering and desiring love.

Certainly love gives us our best chance to live like the spiritual beings we are while in the human body. In Australian Aboriginal spirituality the belief is strong that the whole of life is a spiritual experience and that human beings are more spirit than matter, not at a time to come, but right now.

From India, twentieth-century teacher Sri Aurobindo put it like this: "The Spirit shall look out through Matter's gaze, and Matter shall reveal the Spirit's face ... and all the earth shall become a single life."

"All the earth" already *is* a single life. That's the miracle of inter-being. We cannot harm someone else without harming ourselves. We cannot relieve others' suffering without also benefiting.

What Sri Aurobindo in his wisdom was pointing to is a question of perception. Ego gets in the way repeatedly. So do habits of insufficiency. How we use the mind to direct the mind is critical here, as it is everywhere. What are we allowing ourselves to see? What version of the world are we creating through our perceptions? What are we *leaving out* as well as identifying with? On what is our life centered?

～✺～

One of my favorite of all teachings on the power of perception comes from Quaker writer Thomas R. Kelly in his exceptionally fine book, *A Testament of Devotion*. Kelly writes: "We Western peoples are apt to think our great problems are external, environmental. We are not skilled in the inner life where the real roots of our problems lie ... We are trying to be several selves at once, without all our selves being organised by a single, mastering Life within us ...

"Life is meant to be lived from a Centre, a divine Centre. Each one of us can live such a life of amazing power and peace and serenity, of integration and confidence and simplified multiplicity, on one condition—that is, *if we really want to*. There is a divine Abyss within us all, a holy Infinite Centre, a Heart, a Life who speaks in us and through us to the world."

And what would prevent us from living such a life? You will have your own answers. You will know your own hesitancies and reluctance all too well. Kelly sums it up like this: "We have not counted this Holy Thing within us to be the most precious thing in the world. We have not surrendered all else, to attend to it alone. Let me repeat. Most of us, I fear, have not surrendered all else, in order to attend to the Holy Within."

Without surrendering to this sacred reality, the challenge of living lovingly, of living *unconditionally* lovingly—just as the Golden Rule asks of us—may make little sense. It may feel too naked. It may arouse fears of vulnerability. It may be confused with weakness. It may seem ridiculous or just feel too hard. How consoling then to discover that the Golden Rule offers another and perhaps more accessible way to live with greater social and spiritual awareness.

And to do so in a way that is certainly not "second best."

In my discussion of identity, I have already quoted the most famous version of the Golden Rule's teaching on "do no harm." This is where Rabbi Hillel sums up the Torah by saying, "What is hateful to you, do not do to your neighbor. That is the whole of the Torah. The rest is commentary. Go and learn it."

In the Udana-Varga (5:18) from the Hindu tradition we hear something remarkably similar: "Treat not others in ways that you yourself would find hurtful." And in the Mahabharata (Anusasana Parva 113:8), "One should not behave towards others in a way which is disagreeable to oneself. This is the essence of morality. All other activities are due to selfish desires." And also (in 5:1517), "This is the sum of duty: do not do to others what would cause pain if done to you."

In the Jain Kritanga Sutra the teaching goes beyond people: "Treat all creatures in the world as you want to be treated."

In the Analects (12:2), we hear Confucius saying, "Do not do to others what you would not like yourself."

In the Taoist Thâi Shang it is written: "The good person will regard others' gains like their own and others' losses in the same way."

In the ancient religion of Zoroastrianism we hear it again: "Do not do to others whatever is injurious to your own self" (Shayast-na-Shayast).

Are we capable of this? Are we capable of hearing and heeding? A commentary from Confucian teacher Meng Tzu, who died in 289 BC, would suggest this is so. "Each person has a heart that pities others ... If a person sees a child about to fall into a well, he will be moved by mercy. Not because he wishes to make friends with the child's parents or to win praise but because the child's cries pierce him. This shows that no one is without a merciful, tender heart. No one is without a heart for shame and hatred. No one is without a heart to give way and surrender. No one is without a heart for right and wrong."

It is in allowing our hearts to be *pierced* and opened that we become fully human.

⁓⊶⊷⁓

This is the "other face" of the Golden Rule. It is less familiar. It is just as serious. In fact, I wonder whether "not harming" or not hurting other people—near and far—feels more reasonably within reach than *loving* them?

As you think about it now, and perhaps also about some complex or challenging situations in your own life, does it seem more realistic to affirm that you could refrain from harming, rather than "loving" others?

Perhaps it is more realistic, although it is obvious from the prevalence of harm and hurt in our world that this, too, takes considerable self-awareness and restraint.

Few of us wake up in the morning and decide that today we will ruin someone else's happiness or peace of mind. Nonetheless, just through an ordinary lack of self-awareness and depth of concern we also miss many opportunities to *avoid* causing harm. Perhaps what's most obviously missing on those occasions is any degree of consciousness that in all our encounters *we have a choice to leave the person better or worse off for their time in our company.* The difference may be very slight, but no encounter is neutral. It is influencing that other person; it is creating who we ourselves are becoming.

For some people, "causing harm" can seem like a fine way to exert power. This can start very young when a child who feels wretched within him- or herself becomes a bully. The attention of being feared can seem preferable to getting no attention. And this can become addictive. We have only to read the day's newspaper, switch on the news or look around to see that there are significant numbers of people in our most civilized communities who take pleasure in causing others distress. The effects of this may be worst in our intimate relationships, but in workplaces and schools, in community activities and in religious and political groups, variations on the "bullying" or undermining tactics of skilled bullies often prevail and, worse, are sometimes mistaken for efficiency and are rewarded.

Even without wishing to cause pain, we are often careless about the effects of our choices on others. We may be skilled at self-justifying. We may let ourselves be ruled by what *we feel like doing* rather than what we could or should do. We may blame the other person for *making* us behave like a shrew, an ogre or a frustrated three-year-old.

As long as our choices depend on how we are currently feeling, or how those choices make us look in others' eyes, we remain enslaved.

Civil rights leader Dr. Martin Luther King, Jr., was one of the most outstanding crusaders for nonviolence and justice in the twentieth century. He was also clear on where harm should stop. "One of the most persistent ambiguities that we face is that everybody talks about peace as a goal. However, it does not take sharpest-eyed sophistication to discern that while everybody talks about peace, peace has become practically nobody's business among the power-wielders. Many men cry Peace! Peace! but they refuse to do the things that make for peace."

As perceptively, Dr. King said, "The time is always right to do the right thing." People may like to split hairs and argue about what "the right thing" is (while Rome burns). "Do no harm" clarifies this—or should. We free ourselves the moment we recognize that our choices are our own to make. This is true of all our choices. It is especially true of *our choice to cause no harm.*

The Rabbi Hillel story is surely apocryphal yet its survival as a teaching story is significant. Whether he was standing on one leg or two, the rabbi and those who have preserved this story for us would have been quite familiar with the teaching in Leviticus to love others as we love ourselves. Yet when asked to *sum up* the Torah, this humane teacher came forward not with a repetition of the Leviticus teaching, nor even a reminder about loving God, but instead summarized this plea to do no harm. It is tempting to assume he thought this more manageable—and more likely to be achieved.

Not only that, he makes it clear that "not harming" involves using our human gifts of imagination, empathy and restraint. "Imagine," he seems to be saying, "what you would most hate or fear. See it in your mind's eye. Taste its bitterness in your own mouth. Feel the disgust it evokes. Feel your own heart pounding. Feel your shame and fury as well as fear. And now—think about your neighbor. Is there any reason to assume your neighbor would feel any differently about this than you do? So let that knowledge of what you share be your teacher. Let it stay your hand. Let it open your heart. This is peacemaking of the most serious kind. *What you would hate, do not do to anyone else."*

⤳⟲⟳⤶

The longer I have sat with Rabbi Hillel's teaching the more I have come to see the kindness as well as the wisdom of his entreaty to "do no harm."

I sit now at my desk, one of our devoted gray cats on my knee, and wonder: What would it take for us to become *embodiments of hope?*

A REFUSAL TO HARM ANOTHER (even when we believe we are entitled to do so) honors our primary spiritual connections *regardless of how like or unlike we are at the levels of belief, personality, race, culture*. It asserts our spiritual identity over all others. It allows us to live from the security of the "divine Centre," as Thomas Kelly urged.

"I am a spiritual being before I am a Christian," Jack said to me recently, thoughtful in his mid-twenties. "I am a spiritual being even before I am a husband, son and teacher—although that's how I am expressing myself."

And this too from Caroline Ward, an Australian longtime meditator who now lives in Chile. "My primary spiritual identity is that I am a being of light: an immortal, conscious and self-aware spark of pure life-force energy, living in this body. When I 'feel' myself as this, not just know it as an intellectual construct, everything changes. I know myself to be inherently good, beautiful, stable, secure and strong. I feel that I am love; that love and peace are my true nature. Born from this state is deep compassion and understanding for myself and for others."

For many years Caroline has been successfully teaching and training other people in a variety of management disciplines. That makes it particularly touching when she highlights the difference between spiritual knowledge and cognitive or intellectual learning. "I must know the reality of my identity as an experience, not solely as a teaching. And for me, when I touch this experience, I know it to be truth. Eternity becomes my home. I rest in the security of a unified oneness, not where I disappear into nothingness, rather, where the need fades to put myself at the center of all things. I am gently yet utterly present and connected with all life. Knowing who I most essentially am—and knowing this as a deep experience—also helps me recognize when I am *not* being who I truly am. [At those times] *I don't feel good.* A simple way to say it, but that's how it is. My energy is skewed. I get tired easily. I notice doubts emerging within me. I compare and compete. I blame or look for something or someone to blame ... I live in a duality of good and bad, right and wrong ... full of judgment and lacking in understanding and kindness. And I don't feel good at all! So when I recognize I have "left myself," then I can reorient my vision inward, reconnect and remember and all the disorder dissipates and a harmonious alignment returns."

Caroline is gifted with a rare degree of natural warmth and is very much a "people person." As she explains, her self-identity and attunement directly affect the way she perceives others and feels free to behave with them. "In this soul-aware state, I understand so much more. I am not bound by the limits of my own narcissistic story where I am the center of all things. I am centered in truth and connected energetically and intuitively. I can sense and sometimes know the details of another's pain. More often, I can understand how easy it is to behave without dignity or grace when disconnected from my true identity and disconnected from the Source. It is like being a refugee, lost to the home of one's own self and security, becoming a survivor and behaving under survival conditions. I know this to be true for myself and I understand it to be true for others. I can be more compassionate, more understanding and kinder. My perceiving is amplified and my feeling is gentle and nonviolent.

"As my spirituality has matured, I have become less important. I have less *need* to be at all important. I find myself happy to retire into a quiet existence of kindness. This is not how it is playing out, however I truly feel content to be simple and part of the oneness, the unity of all."

❧❧❧

Holding firm to the reality of our connections to all of life is the primary commitment of a spiritually focused life. Writing this, I am aware of my silence as millions of uprooted people are moving around the world in search of a home—and being treated like criminals. I am aware that in sophisticated France, a country I have always loved, one becomes a criminal oneself for attempting to help them.

As a species, we remain deeply tribal. This is more obvious in some parts of the world than in others, yet even in our most advanced, progressive societies we clearly form alliances along strong lines of similarity and familiarity. Instinct and emotions run deep. As a mother, I am well aware that I have always been ready to defend my own children far more ferociously than I would stand up for other people—all children once.

Is this something we assume is inevitable? Or dare we investigate it?

Religious institutions themselves play upon and also breed tribal differences and conflict. We don't have to go further than modern Europe to see that. The recent sorrows of Northern Ireland and Serbia and Croatia are just the most prominent examples. Across the Middle and Near East and much of Asia, some Hindus, Muslims, Christians and Jews are far indeed from turning their swords into ploughshares. The authentically alluring sense of belonging that a religious group can offer its members is frequently predicated upon seeing other people as outsiders. Sometimes those "others" profess a different faith; sometimes they are splinter groups within a single small denomination.

Surely we can do more? Surely we can care more?

~∽⌒∽~

For many years I have been thinking, writing and praying about forgiveness. Gradually I have become convinced that the most significant step on the forgiveness trail is also dependent on "doing no harm." This liberating moment is achieved when you resolve that you will not wish or cause harm to another, *even and especially those who have harmed you.* This may not always amount to forgiveness. Certainly it does not mean that what was harmful has ceased to matter. What it does achieve is a highly significant inner assertion that however enraged or wounded we are, we cannot benefit from making someone else suffer, no matter how tempting this can seem.

"I want her to suffer even more than I have."

"I long for him to know what chaos and pain he's caused."

"I pray each day they will live in torment—as we do."

"For them no punishment is 'good enough.'"

These are understandable desires *and* they keep us deeply and intimately connected to those who have already caused us sorrow. As long as those are the thoughts we are constantly repeating, "justice" will mean punishment and revenge. And thoughts of that person—alive or dead—will fill our inner horizon. The past will dominate the present. The future will remain something to be feared. More crucially still, these thoughts keep us locked into a logic that normalizes the cycles of harm and retaliation—rather than liberating us from them.

> *We are what we think,* teaches the Buddhist Dhammapada,
> *All that we are arises with our thoughts.*
> *With our thoughts we make the world,*
> *Speak or act with a troubled mind*
> *And trouble will follow you*
> *like the wheel follows the ox that pulls the cart.*
> *Speak or act with a peaceful mind*
> *And happiness will follow you like your shadow, unshakeable.*

Ceasing to wish harm to another person is only part of the complex forgiveness process. Restitution, repentance and a resolve never to repeat the behavior or action: these are also complex acts that can take the process a whole lot further.

If we are the one who has caused harm the least we can do is think extremely seriously about how we will initiate the repentance and change in behavior the situation demands.

If we are the person who has been hurt we will know that the actions of reconciliation and the awareness that drives them are not always available to us. Sometimes the person who has hurt us is incapable of repenting. Sometimes they are dead or absent. And sometimes it is not another person but life itself against which we rage. Or it is the injustices endemic within our political or corporate systems that have hurt us. Or it is God we can neither understand nor forgive.

In all those situations our feelings of powerlessness as well as hurt can be acute.

A DESIRE FOR REVENGE IS RIPE in our human nature. We have an instinct for it that has been honed over thousands of years, fueled by generations of self-righteous power-seeking in the name of survival.

"Vengeance is mine, saith the Lord!" which could—in the best possible light—simply mean, "Leave it to me and to my ideas about divine justice! Don't stoop to taking revenge yourselves." Perhaps this oblique teaching also warns that a desire for revenge makes perfect sense to our emotional minds. It makes no sense at all, however, within a spiritual framework.

*We cannot relieve our own pain by causing or wishing pain to another.*

Such thinking denies our spiritual reality. As Caroline Ward so accurately expressed it in the quote I shared earlier, "Knowing who I most essentially am . . . also helps me recognize when I am *not* being who I truly am. [At those times] *I don't feel good . . .*"

A spiritual reality pushes us to recognize that someone causes harm or pain through ignorance of his or her power to make different and better choices. This is not to make an excuse for their wrongdoing or what we might be tempted to call evil. On the contrary, when we call someone "evil" it supports the notion that this person is somehow essentially different from you or me. By contrast, what a spiritual perspective insists upon is that as disgusting, as abhorrent as that other person's actions may be, the person is and remains a member of our single human and divine family.

─◦୨୧◦─

Unshackling your thoughts from a desire for revenge and punishment already lightens your heart. It also wakes up your inner power. You are "choosing wisely." And your choices reflect your own highest ideals and insights rather than being *dictated to or choreographed by the actions of the other person.* This is immensely significant. Withdrawing your desire to cause harm or to be implicated in prolonging harm, you support your own soul's strengths and particularly self-knowledge, self-mastery and self-respect.

This does not mean pretending that something that once mattered no longer matters. It may not even mean giving your cloak as well as your coat, walking a second mile, or turning the other cheek to be struck, as Christ urged us to do. What it does mean is refusing to dwell on this injury or to let it become your reason for living, rather than *holding steady to your own highest identity.*

Let me share an example of what I mean.

Mariella is someone who has been coming to my retreats and talks for years—when she is well enough. She would say that in relation to all the reading she has done and her years of meditation and classes, what has been most transformative is the value and validity of her own insights: those private moments of epiphany that have gradually led her to put her spiritual identity above all else. But it's not always easy for her to stay in touch with that.

During a recent time together, I asked her explicitly about what her life (and insights about her life) has taught her about the sacred. Her response surprised me.

"You know, I feel as if I have been talking to you through a mask. When I think about the moments of great beauty or tenderness in my life, or the moments of naked sorrow and raging grief, or when I remember times when I felt at one with the infinite universe even for a few seconds, or have been able to exceed my usual self, then I know for sure that the sacred has broken through my usual defenses. *And I know that I know!*"

Mariella had a severe breakdown in her last year at university, and years later is still vulnerable to occasional periods of anxiety and panic. She is raising two boys without their father, her much-loved partner, who died suddenly when their sons were preschoolers. She has valid reasons to be angry or self-pitying, but is neither.

"People ask me sometimes whether I am angry with God about Damien's passing. First of all, I don't believe in God's personal hand in my life in that way. I don't believe in a God 'up there' somewhere who's saying, 'Damien's time is up and Mariella and their boys can deal with it.' Or a God who is deciding, 'I will save her and her kids from this but not that.' That means I can't either go with the kind of thinking that says, 'This is meant to be,' or, 'There's always a purpose.' When it comes to human affairs I think things are far more complex than that.

"What I do believe, though, is pretty blessed and sustaining. And that is that my God is with me, however vague my beliefs are about exactly who or what God is, however unorthodox my ways of praying and so on are. *God is with me.* That's my truth."

Like Mariella, I too know how possible it is to have a relationship with "God" that is highly sustaining and deeply intimate without needing to compartmentalize God or reduce the mystery of the divine down to terms easily grasped by the human mind. Also like Mariella, it is the intensity and constancy of this relationship that gives me my strongest trust in my own spiritual identity even and often especially when things are rough.

Mariella continues: "This is what I learned from having that breakdown when I was twenty-two. *No one can know me better than I can know myself.* No one can live my everyday life for me. And I can't live others' lives for them—as tempting as it may sometimes be to try to! I am not prepared to take my identity from Damien's death nor even from being my boys' mum. My identity has to be independent of those roles even though I'm affected by them every minute of each day. Part of this discovery is about staying open at the soul level to your [Stephanie's] teachings and insights, or other teachers', and getting the benefits of support and encouragement from people I meet in all kinds of situations, from prayer, etc. I am open to the events that have happened, for sure. Missing Damien is sometimes agonizing and I can rage about everything that we have all missed because of his death. But that's only part of it. I know that I will only go as far on this sacred journey as I dare to go alone. Others will cheer me along. But it is my trek."

Taking our identity from *who we are* rather than from *what has happened to us* is the true meaning of self-mastery. It is implied in the phrase of ultimate surrender: "Not my will but thine be done." It is also captured in the first lines of the serenity prayer used daily by millions in recovery from the agonies of addiction: "God grant me the serenity to accept the things I cannot change, courage to change the things I can, and wisdom to know the difference."

Along with the awareness and restraint that express our self-mastery, this prevents us from being enslaved by any thinking that prolongs or exacerbates suffering—however justified or inevitable such thinking may seem.

In other words, when thoughts of revenge or condemnation arise, with all their attendant emotions, the healthiest and most healing response is persistently to turn your mind to the bigger picture of your life; to what is unfolding into the future; to your inner strengths and the people who can support you; to ways in which you can support others who have suffered similarly; to the prayers or spiritual practices that bring peace; to the small domestic moments of each day that remain grounding and rewarding; to the psychological benefits of intense physical engagement like sports, walking, gardening, or enjoying the sensual details of the natural world and allowing them to reveal themselves freshly to you.

In following up the desire to "do no harm" to ourselves or, indeed, anyone else, and to protect ourselves and others, we can benefit greatly by following the Buddhist guidance in the "Eightfold Path" that liberates us from at least some of our suffering.

Each of us will need to take particular notice of this in different combinations, but it involves paying attention to attitude, intention, speech, action, livelihood (which is more than how we earn money; it is also how we engage with community), effort, mindfulness and concentration.

Such self-control is not easy. Such mindfulness is not easy. Far better than "easy," this kind of refocusing is life-saving and life-enhancing *even when it is only partially achieved.*

WHEN IT COMES TO HARM, I find myself wondering if war is the most extreme travesty of our human and sacred potential. Or is war only its most arrogant and deluded expression?

"War is a lot of things," writes Sebastian Junger in *War*, a book based on his experiences with American fighting forces in Afghanistan, "and it's useless to pretend that exciting isn't one of them. It's insanely exciting. The machinery of war and the sound it makes and urgency of its use and the consequences of almost everything about it are the most exciting things anyone ever engaged in war will ever know. Soldiers discuss that fact with each other and eventually with their chaplains and their shrinks and maybe even their spouses, but the public will never hear about it. It's just not something that anyone wants to hear acknowledged."

~~~~~

"... Caesar's spirit, ranging for revenge," writes William Shakespeare in *Julius Caesar*,

*With Atë by his side come hot from hell,*
*Shall in these confines with a monarch's voice*
*Cry "Havoc!" and let slip the dogs of war.* (Act III, Scene I)

Atë is the ancient Greek goddess who, mythology tells us, was exiled from heaven by her father, Zeus, the greatest of the gods. Possessed by rage and desolation Atë wanders the world causing whatever havoc she can, in part by treading on "the heads of mortals" rather than on the earth itself. (Her agonies are never "grounded." They roar and flame in the "air" of her thinking and imagination.) In contemporary parlance we would say Atë's head has been "done in" by her father's betrayal. In retaliation she literalizes this harm by "treading on the heads of mortals" and doing their heads in also (confusing them, blinding them to their sacred reality and potential, urging them to actions that mirror closely her own anguish).

Atë, of course, lives on. And continues to be worshipped. Whether or not we know her name, she exists as a profound archetype in the minds of millions of human beings, justifying the hell she causes by the hell she has experienced in ways that will be wearyingly familiar to any contemporary observer.

꧁ఎసిఞ꧂

James Hillman is a Jungian analyst whose many books include *A Terrible Love of War*. Written some years before Junger's book, Hillman's thesis in some ways anticipates what Junger writes. Humankind, Hillman asserts, loves war, is devoted to it, seeks it out, yearns for it and with immense fidelity and success brings it into existence.

"During the five thousand six hundred years of written history," writes Hillman, "fourteen thousand six hundred wars have been recorded. Two or three wars each year of human history." What's more, "... the turning points of Western civilization occur in battles and their 'killing sprees' ... the ultimate determination of historical fate depends on battle whose outcome ... depends on an invisible genius, a leader, a hero, who, at a critical moment, or in prior indefatigable preparation, 'saves the day.' In him a transcendent spirit is manifested. The battle and its personified epitome, this victor, this genius, become salvational representations in our secular history."

Here we have "harm" running amok, ruling the consciousness of almost everyone it touches. Hillman also argues: "When war clouds gather, religious belief electrifies the air." Such "belief" may pertain to and be driven by religious faith in the conventional sense. It can also be and often is the "religion" of nationalism. Then it is a flag that becomes the sacred focus both of myth and adoration; then sacred ritual becomes the lavish display of military power with machines as music and uniforms as honoured vestments.

Thinking of war, and the hysteria that allows war and perpetuates it, it becomes obvious that religion and religious identity can evoke loyalties as divisive and ferocious as any other version of nationalistic or totalitarian thinking.

Hillman again: "The single focus on One True God requires that belief be cohesive, organised ... [But] because a monotheistic psychology must be dedicated to unity, its psychopathology is intolerance of difference."

"Intolerance of difference" is deep in the human psyche. Religion is simply a great place and good reason to express this. We fear difference. We despise it. When we can, we crush it. When nations go to war to crush it, we use the phrase "war has broken out." Yet what has really broken out is our own eagerness for war. And our willingness to justify it.

With the weariness and stubbornness of a lifelong pacifist, I would argue with all my heart as well as mind that there is no such thing as a "just war," however eloquently Martin Luther King, Jr., or countless thinkers before or since have argued for it. There may be "just" reasons for conflict, but war is never anything but a wholly unintelligent and morally indefensible response to the differences in perspective or action that bring conflict about.

Unless one "believes" in the religion of war, *war makes no sense.* And the harm that war causes, generates and prolongs is unrelievedly tragic.

It would be fascinating to take to task the ubiquitous "religion" of war, rather as Christopher Hitchens, Richard Dawkins, Sam Harris and others have taken religious faith to task in recent years. Meanwhile, we live in a world where far more people believe in the inevitability of war and violence (as Hillman himself does) than believe in religion—or the healing power of love. Entire economies continue literally to be oiled by war "efforts."

Worldwide spending on war and war readiness is greater than the sum needed for every human being on earth to have food, clean water and shelter, and the chance to live in their homeland. Dr. Thoraya Obaid, who is executive director of the United Nations Population Fund, has said, "It would cost the world less than *two-and-a-half-days' worth of military spending* to save the lives of six million mothers, newborns and children every year." Yet so ubiquitous and apparently persuasive is this religion of war that governments, academia and industry invest virtually nothing in investigating life-giving rather than life-destroying means of resolving the inevitable conflicts there will always be between people.

In the world you and I inhabit war is "normal." No, it is way bigger than "normal" suggests: it is thrilling, entrancing, collectivizing and mythic. In battle, death itself becomes larger than life. It becomes a legend.

Weeks after I had written the paragraph above I read this from Junger: "War is supposed to feel bad because undeniably bad things happen in it, but for a 19-year-old at the working end of a .50 cal during a firefight that everyone comes out of OK, war is life multiplied by some number no one has ever heard of. In some ways 20 minutes of combat is more life than you could scrape together in a lifetime of doing something else ... Don't underestimate the power of that revelation. Don't underestimate the things young men will wager in order to play that game one more time."

$\sim\!\!\sim\!\!\sim$

I was born after the end of the Second World War. Virtually every family I knew as I was growing up, including my own, had sacrificed young men to that war and lost peace and happiness because of those who returned but could not recover from it. During my childhood in safe, isolated New Zealand, farmers had a burst of wealth as they sold their wool to be made into uniforms for men fighting in the Korean War. As I became an adult, people in my own and older generations were protesting the Vietnam War. As

I have discussed in the section on identity, at the age of twenty I lived for some months in Israel, a nation that has rarely not been at some version of war, and a year or two later I lived in a divided Berlin while the Cold War raged and the Vietnam War was "lost." During my twenties and early thirties, I lived in Britain during the many years of the "Troubles" in Northern Ireland (that spilled over also into Ireland more generally and sometimes, direly, into England, including London).

In my lifetime of peace there has been no peace for our global family. One of the personal memories that stands out most strongly for me came from my talented late writer friend Sally Belfrage, an American citizen and London resident who went to Northern Ireland many times in the 1980s in order to write a book about the tribal troubles there (*The Crack*). She was able to confirm widely published reports that the area of the United Kingdom that had the lowest levels of depression and anxiety (but not domestic violence) was Belfast.

⚬⚬⚬

The seductive power of large-scale violence is immense. It focuses the mind. It makes the pulse race. It gives people something other than themselves in which to believe. It brings them together around a common cause. It simplifies life. It makes rage, prejudice and hatred reasonable. It excuses and makes possible many small, individual acts of violence. It clarifies whose side God is on. It puts evil at a distance and offers the illusion that it is easy to tell right from wrong. It postpones boredom and trivia. It makes some individuals and corporations insanely rich.

One last quote from Sebastian Junger: "There's so much human energy involved [in war]—so much courage, so much honor, so much blood—you could easily go a year here without questioning whether any of this needs to be happening in the first place."

~✵~

Here is a sobering teaching from Sufi master Hazrat Inayat Khan about why we fall into wars and call it inevitable. "Whenever wars have occurred, whenever there has been bloodshed in the world, whenever there have been revolutions and upheavals in life, all the various disasters that have taken place are due to these same causes: on the one side man's selfishness, and on the other his lack of understanding of the law of nature and the law of happiness.

"Our limited self is like a wall separating us from the Self of God. God is as far away from us as that wall is thick. The wisdom and justice of God are within us, and yet they are far away under the covering of the veil of the limited self.

"Whoever has arrived at that realization of the nature of God's justice is able to see all things in a different way from others. His whole outlook on life becomes different ... *[Humankind] has now become cold, ignorant, and blind to the law that life depends on the happiness of those with whom we live. The whole of life is one. In all these different names and manifestations life is one.* The true thought is, 'If my [spouse] is not happy, if my children, my neighbours ... are not happy, how can I ever be happy?' How simple it is. Yet how difficult for man to understand! It is simple to him who observes life keenly. It is difficult to him who is absorbed in himself."

War is the extreme face of acceptable violence. And there is no doubt that it is highly and widely acceptable. Hazrat Inayat Khan's teaching would fall on deaf ears in most quarters. In a battle between the kind of happiness that he describes and the kind of excitement that Hillman and Junger capture, excitement's "victory" would be all too easy.

In 2002, long after Hazrat Inayat Khan was writing the words I quote just above, the Assisi Decalogue for Peace was held in Italy. It was the largest meeting of world religious leaders in history, more than two hundred in total. It included dozens of ministers representing various Protestant denominations and the World Council of Churches, dozens of monks, gurus and others representing Hindus, Buddhists, Sikhs and Zoroastrians, leaders of native African religions, the then Pope, John Paul II, a number of cardinals, Bartholomew I, spiritual leader of Orthodox Christians, a dozen Jewish rabbis, including a few from Israel, and at least thirty Muslim imams from Iran, Iraq, Saudi Arabia, Egypt and Pakistan. These religious leaders prayed together as well as talked, and while they did not condemn war unconditionally, alas, they did condemn "every recourse to violence and war in the name of God or religion." And they did commit themselves to "educating people to mutual respect and esteem, in order to help bring about a peaceful and fraternal coexistence between people of different ethnic groups, cultures and religions."

Yet in many countries in the world the Decalogue was barely reported and certainly did not make headlines. It was the cause or catalyst of neither shock nor awe.

War, like peace, begins in the human mind. It is sustained by the human imagination and depends on individual acts of cooperation, compliance and will.

"Be patterns, be examples in all countries, places, islands, nations, wherever you come; that your carriage and life may preach among all sorts of people, and to them," wrote George Fox, one of the earliest and most influential Quakers. "Then you will come to walk cheerfully over the world answering that of God in everyone."

It is up to each of us, though, to take that wisdom seriously. To imagine it and live it. To "walk cheerfully over the world answering that of God in everyone." Unconditionally. To refuse the inner seductions of Atë and of Thanatos, god of war. To make peace within ourselves possible. To make peace between ourselves real.

PERHAPS WE WILL NEVER WAVE SOLDIERS off to war or actively support a war effort. We may, nonetheless, sometimes or frequently be at war within ourselves. Equally, we may be at war with people we know—or once knew. We may regard life itself, or illness, as a "struggle" or "battle." And, as our "struggles" with forgiveness make clear, we may be sorely tempted sometimes to ease our pain by causing pain to others.

In the complex world of human relations it is quite possible that the "others" whom we may feel almost compelled to hurt may *not* have hurt us—at least, not directly. (That's also true of larger acts of war.) Perhaps they don't even know us or don't know how much they irritate or frustrate us, or how they arouse our self-pity, shame or guilt, or our agonies of indecision or inadequacy. Perhaps they arouse our prejudices and we hate them for that. Perhaps they simply have what we most want—and we resent that. Perhaps it's their loving partner, delightful children or good job that makes us feel like lashing out. Or perhaps they have a sense of meaning or purpose or a religious faith that gives them a degree of confidence and stability that we resent and want to spoil.

The "spoils" of war are usually seen as what can be carried off: including acts of rape as well as pillage. Spoiling can also mean over-indulging or favoring. But spoiling has another and far more intimate meaning and purpose also that is always harmful. Spoil can mean to ruin, damage or lower the value not just of something but also someone. The more intimate our relationship, the more vital it is that we monitor with fierce vigilance whatever bad temper, envy, malice and pettiness allows us to *spoil* someone's trust, peace of mind or happiness. "Spoiling" is harm that is easily trivialized. The effects of such harm on the human spirit, however, are corrosive, toxic and eventually destructive.

꒰꒱

It is also possible, and maybe even increasingly so, that the person we most want to harm is our own self. Perhaps we are literalizing this harm: cutting, starving, bingeing on alcohol or food; taking sexual risks; engaging in debasing, degrading behaviors; thrill-seeking in ways that endanger our life and perhaps others' lives also; or through our choices and decisions inviting others to treat us badly. Perhaps we are refusing to do something about the addiction that is running our life and causing others grief. Perhaps we are lost in self-pity, apathy or helplessness.

Humankind is richly creative. We have invented infinite ways to cause or perpetuate harm. So it is liberating as well as spiritually empowering to discover that we can *take charge of where harm stops. Unconditionally.*

Harming others—or ourselves—makes no sense within a context of spirituality that is primarily relational. African American writer Howard Thurman, raised in a savagely segregated America, gives us a marvelous clue when he writes, "In the presence of God there is neither male nor female, white nor black, Gentile nor Jew, Protestant nor Catholic, Hindu, Buddhist, nor Muslim, but a human spirit stripped to the literal substance of itself before God."

Such a vision connects us *through care* to all forms of life—including ourselves. It does not deny the ways in which we are male [and] female, white [and] black, Gentile [and] Jew, Protestant, Catholic, Hindu, Buddhist [and] Muslim. We are those things, and many other categories besides. And I for one treasure that diversity, and the diversity within every one of those categories. But there are also moments when all labels can be set aside and we can meet on common ground. Or meet our own selves in the spirit of acceptance and reconciliation.

This is memorably expressed in the classic Buddhist instruction, the Metta Sutra.

*This is what should be done,*
*by one who is skilled in goodness . . .*
*Wishing: in gladness and in safety.*
*May all beings be at ease . . .*
*Whether they are weak or strong . . .*
*Seen and unseen . . .*
*Living near or far away,*
*Born or yet to be born,*
*May all beings be at ease!*

A way of life that wishes that *all beings may be at ease* is not built on unattainable perfection. It grows like a lotus from the "mud" of ordinariness. It grows from what we learn each time we fall down as well as what we learn as we rise up. It grows from listening deeply. It grows from observing mindfully. What's more, it is something to claim rather than "deserve."

"Deserving" belongs to a quite different paradigm from "claiming." But it needs to be thought about intelligently wherever the temptation comes to debase or disregard ourselves. "You are a child of the universe no less than the trees and the stars," we hear in one of the most memorable lines in Max Ehrmann's famous prose poem, "The Desiderata." And later in the same poem: "Therefore be at peace with God, whatever you conceive Him to be ... in the noisy confusion of life, keep peace in your soul."

These words are better than beautiful. They guide us to consider what we are capable of being. They also push us toward considering the effects of that on our self-perception as well as our way of being with other people. Each time we treat another person harshly we diminish that potential—and ourselves. Each time we allow ourselves to be an embodiment of courtesy, interest, good humor, respect and kindness we positively affect others—and we significantly affect ourselves.

It is in growing in self-confidence and self-respect from the perspective of the soul or spirit rather than from the perspective of the ego that makes the crucial difference.

Frances Wickes, a Jungian analyst, writes that "true creativity is not concerned with the ego but with the Self." From this perspective and with this attitude, our drive to live well—to honor the gift of life that we have—will not be satisfied with meaninglessness or purposelessness. It will not be satisfied either by material prizes only. We will feel the harm we are doing to ourselves when we have "better" choices and turn away from them; or when we treat ourselves like a machine rather than a human being; or when we let other people know that they are merely toys in our toy box or cogs in our machines.

From that same perspective we can see our own lives more completely. And we can see that we are only part of a greater whole.

*We are not the center of the universe.* Perhaps we are the center of our loved ones' universe, as they may be of ours. But stepping back just a little, the view changes.

Everything that happens around us is not "about" us. Other people's apparent responses to us should be taken entirely seriously, but may sometimes have more to do with whether they got up today in a good mood or a bad one than with who we are, what we are doing and how we are doing it. Who we are and many other factors matter. *And* those factors and influences are not everything.

How liberating it is to know that we have constant choices. Even if it is "only" around attitude and perspective—and our own responses.

How liberating it is to know that we are not the center of the universe. *And* that we are part of a greater whole (a unique part of an astonishing universe).

Each and every time I allow myself to be conscious of this, I am soothed.

~~~

Harm begins in the mind. Sometimes it "arrives" from outside us. But our thoughts and imagination sustain it. Imagination is critical in this story of harm. We have instincts that can also drive and justify harm. But it is imagination that carries them forward.

Imagination can also soothe us. So can "relaxing more deeply into participation."

This evocative phrase came to me from Bill Idol, formerly a consultant and businessman and now active in Third Age education from his two homes in the United States and New Zealand. He relates this idea to another. Bill explains, "For some time I've thought of myself as a four-dimensional being at least: physical, intellectual, emotional and spiritual (the 3-D concept of body, mind and soul or spirit lacks the emotional which has been the most powerful for me over time). My best glimpse of our primary paradoxes are *both* Spirit *and* Flesh, and *both* Feeling *and* Thinking. That a single one should be super-ordinate violates the notion of what I believe to be our majestically mysterious paradoxical nature. Earlier in life I thought my 'thinking self' would eventually figure out in much greater detail the nature of my connection to Spirit. Now I doubt that's the case. If I'm going to experience greater depths of this connection, I believe my avenues now lie in this very notion of 'relaxing into participation' more fully on the other three dimensions."

Imagination, participation: what better to remind us of what we are and what we already feel and know?

This can underscore our links to other people as well as to the "parts" that make us "whole." This can arouse the saving graces of empathy. This can connect us to our very finest ideals. This can heal and save lives.

IT WAS IMPOSSIBLE FOR ME TO complete this book without thinking deeply about the harm done in the name of religion and sometimes in the name of God. Shame, contempt, fear: how shocking it is that this piling of one tragic attitude upon another is for many the dominant religious story. In *American Fascists*, his scalding account of Christian fundamentalism in America, Chris Hedges writes of a "Janus-like God"—a God with two faces: a memorable but tragic image—"one terrifying and one loving, in dizzying confusion."

In *The Soul of Christianity*, religious philosopher Huston Smith draws our attention to how crucially love is determined by what we see and then how we interpret what we see. That brings us back to reconsider the extent to which we are "conditioned" in our attitudes and behavior, and the extent to which we are "choosing." Correctly, Smith points out how "deeply Jewish" Jesus was, yet how strenuously he objected to the prevailing rules of "holiness" being used to divide people, elevating and reassuring some at the harrowing expense of others.

We see the effects of holiness codes running riot in Islamic countries and communities where male religious leaders deny women their most basic human rights, including the right to be seen as a human being rather than as a potential object of lust that must be hidden and veiled. This is religion at its most explicitly enslaving. But many of us will know far milder versions at first hand.

I grew up with versions of holiness codes myself, at a time when for a Roman Catholic child to eat meat on Friday was a far greater sin—risking hell for eternity—than cheating in class or hurting another child, and when it was not permitted to pray in a Christian church of another denomination or for a Catholic and "non-Catholic" to be married in front of a Catholic altar. Modesty, too, was an obsession, with fears that through showing part of a knee or shoulder we could become "an occasion of sin" for any passing man. It seems incredible now but then, as now, using contraception was as great a sin as murder and the only people fit to be ordained and to say Mass were, and still are, men.

Smith says of the Jewish holiness code, well known to Jesus, that it began by "categorizing acts and things as clean or unclean ... [then] went on to categorize people according to whether they respected those distinctions. The result was a social structure riven with barriers: between people who were clean and unclean, pure and defiled, sacred and profane, Jew and Gentile, righteous and sinner."

That still sounds chillingly familiar.

It was the social divisions and the devastating pain and injustice that the holiness codes caused that Jesus could not accept. Huston Smith continues: "... [Jesus'] own encounter with God led him to conclude that, as practiced in his time, the purity system had created social divisions that compromised God's impartial, all-encompassing love for everyone."

To exemplify his protest as a "social prophet," according to Smith, "Jesus parleyed with tax collectors, dined with outcasts and sinners, socialized with prostitutes, and healed on the Sabbath when compassion prompted his doing so."

A vision of all-encompassing love is our most powerful antidote to harm. Perhaps in its uncompromising vastness, it is our *only* antidote to harm. It begins with our own selves. It flourishes out of a profoundly connected concern for other people. It emphasizes freedom and self-respect as crucial aspects of the sacred.

༄

Sometimes the harm done by religions stimulates us in our seeking of the sacred. It may drive us to *choose* more consciously and actively, to find new forms, companions, teachings and meanings. Sometimes, though, the harm done by religions drives us away from the sacred for many years.

Yet however frequently we witness religion's shadows and devastations, they remain only a part of the complex religious story.

Many people's *chosen* experiences are or can become something quite different. For some with a continuing religious faith—as well as those who would see themselves as "committed but unaligned seekers," as one young couple described it to me—this is a post-dogmatic, perhaps post-religious but not a post-spiritual age. And that's exhilarating.

In ways that are emerging with increasing clarity, the way is open to develop *a spiritual vision that emerges from a love for life and the sacred.* This work is part of that.

~~~

An exceptionally moving story is recounted by Reverend Dr. Martin Luther King, Jr., in his book *Strength to Love*. The title of his book is already striking. Violence is cheap. It cheapens life. It is also close to hand. It takes self-possession and strength of quite a different order to love and to heal, to practice restraint rather than dehumanize or resort to violence.

In this personal recollection, Dr. King describes himself as being in a state of profound exhaustion, with his courage almost gone. In that highly vulnerable frame of mind, with people still looking to him for leadership and example, he had nowhere to turn but inward.

He takes up his own story. "I determined to take my problem to God. My head in my hands, I bowed over the kitchen table and prayed aloud. The words I spoke to God that midnight are still vivid in my memory. 'I am here taking a stand for what I believe is right. But now I am afraid . . . I am at the end of my powers, I have nothing left . . .'

"At that moment I experienced the presence of the Divine as I had never before experienced him. It seemed as though I could hear the quiet assurance of an inner voice saying, 'Stand up for righteousness, stand up for truth. God will be at your side forever.' . . .

"Three nights later, our house was bombed. Strangely enough, I accepted the word of the bombing calmly. My experience with

God had given me a new strength and trust. I knew now that God is able to give us the interior resources to face the storms and problems of life.

"Let this affirmation be our ringing cry. It will give us courage to face the uncertainties of the future ... When our days become dreary with low-hovering clouds and our nights become darker than a thousand midnights, let us remember that there is a great benign Power in the universe whose name is God, and he is able to make a way out of no way, and transform dark yesterdays into bright tomorrows. This is our hope for becoming better people. This is our mandate for seeking to make a better world."

Perhaps that's all spiritual practice is: finding the courage to ask for what we need and the courage to receive those "interior resources to face the storms and problems of life."

"Let us remember" may be all we need to remember!

"Let us remember" who we are and, above all, *what* we are.

Surely that is the wonder of spirituality, that love, trust and sometimes presence survives all that we humans can do? That spirit and Spirit pour forth unceasingly despite all that we humans can do? And that our seeking lets us experience that?

Religions continue to be deeply and sometimes gravely flawed. Spiritual seeking is sometimes confused and confusing. But for all that, countless people continue to find something within religion or spiritual practice that is authentically and convincingly uniting rather than divisive, uplifting rather than terrifying, healing rather than harming.

Diana Eck, an esteemed American academic and religious writer, and director of Harvard's Pluralism Project, is just one voice of many pointing out (in *Encountering God*) that the greatest tensions between the religions "are not found between the Western and Eastern traditions, between the prophetic and the mystical traditions, or indeed between any one religion and another; they are the tensions that stretch between those at opposite ends of the spectrum in each and every religious tradition. Exclusivists and pluralists, fundamentalists and liberals, wall-builders and bridge-builders—are there in a variety of forms in every religious tradition . . . Very often the religious conflicts that flare up [within religions as well as between them] have less to do with *what* one believes than with *how* one believes what one believes."

༺༻

Even where harm also lives, there is an astonishing tenacity in the ways that people will seek the peace, comfort and forgiveness that are characteristic of genuine spiritual sustenance. And will also find ways to offer those qualities or support others with them. For them, the word *religion* may well be restored to its original meaning: to tie or fasten not to dogma or interpretations or even to the "word of God"—as shaky as that can sometimes be—but to the source and spirit of life itself.

MAGGIE IS A KEEN PARTICIPANT IN spiritual life who regularly sends me brief uplifting notes of encouragement from her home in Melbourne. She describes the possibilities of a more expansive and inclusive "view" particularly well.

"I have long thought that one of my life's great blessings lies in a diminished perception or sense of the so-called other. For this reason I believe that religious and racial bigotry is by no means inevitable but rather a learned response to others of different cultures and antecedents. While I have an Anglo-Celtic background I was born in Karachi, Pakistan, soon after the partition of India [in 1947]. Pakistan was thus created and became an independent nation-state.

"During my first five years I experienced much love from my parents but also from various other individuals of differing faiths (and skin color), my elder brother speaking Hindustani along with English. An enduring but critical part of my now long-deceased parents' legacy was this inclusive view of humanity: 'One Race, the Human Race.' Perhaps of special significance was my father's

274

lifelong sadness and genuine feelings of grief related to the immense suffering caused by the actual process of partition. This poorly planned and hastily executed mass migration of millions of people of various faiths resulted in dislocation, lost children and huge loss of life. Though my father only spoke of these events on a handful of occasions, it taught me much of the concept of Universal Love and compassion."

Maggie was raised as a Roman Catholic and before her retirement was a nurse for more than twenty years. It is unsurprising that she identifies her favorite Christian parable as that of the Good Samaritan. If taken seriously, this familiar story challenges all our conditioned notions of who—and what—really matters. As the story is told in Luke's Gospel, a lawyer asks Jesus what he must do to achieve eternal life. Jesus—with humor—turns the question around like a good Socratic debater: "Well, what do you know that is written in the law?"

The lawyer responds with the classic Jewish teaching: to love the Lord your God with heart, soul, strength and mind, and to love your neighbor as you love yourself.

But Jesus' quick reassurance that this is the correct answer is not enough for the lawyer. He is a lawyer, after all, and wants to know exactly *who his neighbor is*. Isn't this also where we get tripped up?

The question "Who am I?" may be our primary existential inquiry. "Who are you?" has to be as essential as we make sense of our spiritual outlook and world. It was in response to such formative existential and ethical questions that Jesus told this story:

Once a man was going down from Jerusalem to Jericho and he fell into the hands of robbers. They robbed him of his clothes, beat him half dead and, leaving him lying there helpless, they ran off.

It so happened that a priest was going down that same way, but when he saw the man he walked on past him. A Levite who was on that road also walked past the man as he lay there.

But then a Samaritan came by. When he saw the man, he had compassion for him, went up to him, bandaged his wounds, pouring on oil and wine, set him on his own beast, took him to an inn and looked after him. And the next day the Samaritan took out two denarii, gave them to the landlord of the inn and said to him, "Take care of him, and if you need to spend more, when I come again, I will repay you."

Which of these three, do you think, proved himself to be a neighbor to the man who was attacked by thieves?

The lawyer said, "The one who showed compassion to him."

Then Jesus said to the lawyer, "Go, and do likewise."

As with all the great teaching stories, there is a timelessness to this one that pushes us to see that two thousand years on from the time of its telling we could be any one of those characters. We could be the Samaritan who goes out of his way to help a fellow human being with money, time and care—despite the fact that the Samaritan himself would have been viewed by those around him as despised, disgusting, "low class," "unclean." We could be the priest or Levite who tells himself that his fellow human's suffering is none of his business. Or that it ought to be someone else's business. Or perhaps does not *see* the injured man at all, so caught up is he with the concerns swirling inside his own mind.

We could also be the person severely injured on the "road" of life, beset by circumstances outside our control, "robbed" of safety, security or health.

Perhaps we are even and unpalatably sometimes the "robber," holding back praise or encouragement that it would cost us nothing to give; spoiling someone's pleasure with our envy or possessiveness; starving our life of everything but our addiction; telling ourselves we have no time to spend with friends or family because "getting ahead" is everything; telling ourselves "it's not worth trying" because we are possessed by apathy or a fear of failure; telling ourselves that we are entitled to hurt or shame others because we believe we ourselves have been robbed of inner security, love and peace of mind.

⚬⚬⚬

Some people within each of the faiths surely live as lovingly as they can; some do not. Some people of no formal faith live as lovingly as they can, seeing it as the basis for decent living regardless of religious belief. Studying one another at increasingly close quarters, as contemporary life pushes us to do, it really does seem that no simple conclusions can be drawn about the efficacy of the different faiths in teaching or indeed following the moral ideals that they largely share. What seems to count most in forging and sustaining an inclusive, tolerant, compassionate view is the philosophical as well as the spiritual basis on which people value—or devalue—life.

Maggie's comments are again relevant. "Through the parable of the Good Samaritan, Christ interprets who our 'neighbor' is and so identifies a universal and inclusive love. How could one 'cross the road,' so to speak, and ignore the dire suffering of another human being? To do so would be to deny that great potential that humanity affords us."

Yet even in the light of Maggie's clarity, the "how to" question remains pressing. For love to release us from egocentricity to at least some version of selflessness, it must surely be honed through a conscious acknowledgment of *the value of all beings*, whoever they are and however differently they live.

⁓∽∾⁓

When I wanted to share an inspirational example of the benefits of a more inclusive way of thinking and living I thought of Thang, an Australian of Vietnamese origin whose life has been deeply shaped by two faiths and two cultures. He explains: "I grew up in a Protestant Asian family. The concept of original sin was preached literally every Sunday, while at home it was the unspoken idea of karma that was practiced. I have a naturally optimistic personality, which helps me deal with life's challenges. Part of that optimism is knowing that my actions will, one way or another, influence my life and those around me. I can relate to karma and became more repelled by the idea that there can only be one true [way to] God.

"I identify closest with Buddhism in my spiritual outlook. As I mature, it was only natural that my spiritual outlook moved more toward Buddhism. I can see that everybody is an enlightened being [but] we choose to be or not. It helps me to see everyone as someone special and it helps me to love myself more—faults and all!

"Knowing we're all potential enlightened beings helps me love the people closest to me—warts and all—because it's easy to see beauty in them. I'm forty-four years old and have worked for more than two decades, lived on three continents and had seven jobs. I've mixed, and still do, with an incredible range of people. I can say I don't wish ill toward anyone because, regardless of how they treat me, I can see their beauty. I know we are all special beings whether we choose to recognize this or not.

"The greatest spiritual challenge [to more people living like this] is still the silos that are intentionally and subconsciously built between different faiths—the belief that theirs is 'the only true way.' And I don't mean just Islam or fundamentalist Christian religions, even more progressive faiths. I find people still carry this 'I am more progressive than thou' attitude, which of course is another way of saying 'mine is the only true way.'

"I've been blessed in that I've been able to deal with most challenges that come my way. And you build up confidence if you see time and time again you've been able to overcome big and small problems life throws at you. I believe that I and everyone around me are beings on a continuous course of self-discovery. That has really helped me to understand my place, how I relate to other beings. We're similar beings traveling on our path. It also helps me to accept the cycle of birth and rebirth and deal with my mother's sudden passing away. It helps me to accept growing old as another place in my journey.

"I see God in my life through the consequences of our actions. Even in cruel events, I see that karma is being released in readiness for loving acts. In death, I see the opportunity for rebirth and more learning."

At nine years old, Thang came to Australia with his parents from a country devastated and divided by the effects of colonialism and war. When I asked Buddhist-leaning Thang what was the most validating gift around spirituality or religion that he had from his childhood, his answer surprised me.

"It's the idea of a Jesus who dies for the sins of the world. While I don't subscribe to [the Christian doctrine of] original sin, the concept of selfless sacrifice is so beautiful.

"Acts like this on a smaller scale I've experienced all my life—like my parents, leaving everything behind in Vietnam so that I could have a better future. It's indescribable the idea of leaving behind your family, friends, job, coming to a new country where you can't speak the language or have any meaningful connections like you'd have at home. All this sacrifice for a child of nine years of age!

"The confidence I have, the sense of an 'order' [to life], has been amazing in dealing with difficult situations. It has given me a sense of stability—I guess it's what you refer to as 'home.' I know that I can always reach inside and find comfort. That's been amazingly peaceful and has given me a great sense of confidence."

I am inspired by the examples that Thang quotes. Only love can persuade us to step beyond the claustrophobia of self-interest. Such love connects us to others. And it reunites us with our own selves.

EACH TIME WE REFUSE HARM'S INVITATION, we grow stronger. And love's invitation grows stronger within us. "Doing no harm" and living more generously and lovingly will inevitably be easier in some circumstances than others. (Easy to be considerate to other people when life's going our way. Easy to be kind to those we want to impress or those we hope will be impressed by us. Easy to be self-accepting and encouraging when we are "on top" of things rather than buried by them.) But how we behave cannot depend on what's beyond our immediate control. That dependency robs us of our spiritual as well as psychological power: the power to choose. It also robs us of one of our most essential freedoms.

In the ancient Chinese wisdom teaching Tao Te Ching (49), that thought is expressed with exquisite ease. "Those who are good I treat as good. Those who are not good, I treat as good. In so doing, I discover goodness. Those who are of good faith I have faith in. Those who are lacking in good faith, I have faith in. In so doing I gain in good faith."

Again we find a brilliant correspondence to this teaching in another scripture that originated far away, and in a different tradition, but is pointing us in the same direction. In the Bhagavad Gita (2:47–8, 57) we can read, "You have a right to your actions, but not to the rewards of your actions. Do what needs to be done for its own sake. Do your work with the peace of Yoga [a stable mind] and, free from selfish desires, be impressed neither by success nor failure. Yoga is stability of mind, a peace that is constant. The wise person lets go of results, good or bad, and is focused on the value of the action alone."

That person is, of course, stable inwardly and genuinely free.

◦◦◦◦◦◦

The greatest teachings on love and on "do no harm" transcend both origin and "religion." Or they *are* religion, in its truest sense. The mystic's heart is open to the whole world; the "whole world" is welcomed in the mystic's heart. Again we must ask: What is this teaching me, what am I learning from it, where is it allowing me to go, and what kind of person is it teaching me to be?

This brief account from Freda Morgan expresses that in a way you might also recognize: "I suppose my spiritual awareness began because of the love of nature in a very smoky industrial mining village [in England]. Then of course the words of the Bible, poetry to my ears, and the sermons and the Alleluias from the congregation of the Baptist chapel. The 'thou shalt not' got to me though and I began to question what I did believe. I then married a man who became a priest and my first understanding of the spirit beyond becoming part of me came in the miracle of life, giving birth to my first son. After that the search continued, stymied by Anglican rigor mortis. After divorce, the Quakers proved a silent healing ground and now I'm back with the Anglicans but picking and choosing and with the [Auckland, NZ, interfaith] meditation group, who do no harm, provide a peaceful retreat from the world and bring a healing light to our bruised souls.

"Aren't we lucky to be human?"

It is easy to find powerful calls to inclusiveness in all religious texts. In *Spiritual Unity of East and West*, German writer Ursula Groll conveys this beautifully: "The way back to the spiritual homeland should be the true goal of every person. It is a lifelong process of spiritual development arising through an act of free will … humankind was created as a vessel to receive the Divine, that spiritual light which pervades the whole universe."

It is difficult to take those calls seriously, however, or to heed them in a spirit of generosity, if we are not also able to include ourselves in the infinite breadth and depth of that spiritual vision. *We need to regard our own existence as sacred.* But, equally, if it is only our own life or the lives of those we know intimately that we can truly value, the holiness of life will elude us.

Hindu master Sri Nisargadatta Maharaj makes this clear: "*Use your body and mind wisely in the service of the self … Be true to your own self absolutely.* Do not pretend that you love others as yourself. Unless you have realized them as one with yourself, you cannot love them … *When you know beyond all doubting that the same life flows through all that is and you are that life, you will love all naturally and spontaneously. When you realize the depth and fullness of your love of yourself, you know that every living being and the entire universe are included in your affection."*

Trusting that *the entire universe could be included in our affection* is no small matter. This alone is what can keep us from harm, and keep us regretting the harm that we cause. When we cause harm, we need to be willing to face up to this, own up to it, learn from it, make up for it when we can—and move on. *Love allows this.*

For love to be sacred enough to defy and heal harm, it must transcend all labels, including the labels of religion. This does not mean that the labels don't matter. Or that each label is the same as the next one. At the profoundly significant levels of symbol, meaning and identity, none of those assumptions is true. Labels matter acutely. Labels differ extremely. Nonetheless, facing and welcoming the truth of our infinite diversity (within and beyond our "labels"), we must go beyond labels to consider love. And not just what love is, but how to live it.

Living love, we discover and continuously rediscover its power to heal, inspire, soften and connect. We discover that love cannot be given or withdrawn like a currency. It can't be produced to get our own way or to impress. It can't be the carrot, either, with "harm" as the stick.

It also means limiting harm and healing the harm done.

Seeking the sacred, from whichever direction we are called, our minds can move freely between the transcendent and the familiar, between the familiar and the emergent. Living in global community and domestic intimacy, we discover it is surely our fellow humans who are the source of our greatest agonies and frustrations—and our greatest satisfaction and contentment. We learn love from others and in their presence. And they learn love from us, and in our presence.

We cannot undo harm without caring about others; without caring about our own selves; without caring about what most intrinsically binds us.

We cannot undo harm without touching and embodying love.

# TRANSFORMATION

*I offer you peace.*
*I offer you love.*
*I offer you friendship.*
*I see your beauty.*
*I hear your need.*
*I feel your feelings.*
*My wisdom flows from the Highest Source.*
*I greet that Source in you.*
*Let us work together for unity and love.*

Mahatma Gandhi (1869–1948)

THROUGHOUT RECORDED HISTORY women and men have gone beyond their everyday preoccupations to seek the dimension of existence that we call the sacred—and to be *transformed by this seeking experience.* Seeking, yearning and "tasting" the sacred becomes the very heart and soul of existence. Beliefs, dogma, theologies—all the costumes of religion—vary dramatically through time and place. But the call to know love as the ground of our being, and to honor our gift of life through the way that we live it: this does not vary.

Seeking, yearning, tasting and transforming are certainly heart, soul and meaning of my own existence. And always in the midst of what we call "everything."

My children have transformed me more than any spiritual teacher. So did the death and absence of my mother, as well as her short life. My years of writing have been essential to this moment. So has conversation, praying, reflecting and coming up hard against my own shortcomings. Relationships that have ended have transformed me at least as markedly as those that remain buoyant and continue. Grief, joy, creativity, openness, disappointment, despair, courage and rebellion: my entire vocabulary of experience is present in my transforming. Religious experience. Not-religious experience. All one. Some things become easier. Other things become irrelevant or impossible. Life makes a different sense.

More, I am responsible for only some of it. I am also *being transformed*.

⌒✷◟✷⌒

Heeding the call to love and heeding the call *of* Love, we are already transforming. Theories abound about the nature of that call. But like the famous finger pointing to the moon, they may give an accurate direction but they do not give the essence, the experience of "moon" and its light (in the darkness) that we may be craving.

Transformation occurs in ways for which we barely have adequate words. Despite this imprecision, its effects will be profound. The vital element is perception: who we believe we are and who we believe others to be. Perhaps also what we believe life, the Mystery, divine or Buddha nature to be—and our own nature also.

"Do you know that your heart is a temple?" we hear, not from an esoteric source but from Paul's epistle to the people of Corinth (1 Corinthians 3:16–17). "And that the Divine Spirit makes its home in you? . . . The temple of God is sacred and *that is what you are*."

Our decisive narratives about who and what we are will differ according to time, place and culture, including the cultures of religion. But this same simple truth rings out repeatedly.

Glimpsing existence as sacred, our relationship to it changes. Our relationship to all of life changes. We *see* differently. We *respond* differently. Living with concern for others makes sense to us. Living self-respectfully and with gratitude makes sense. Harming or disparaging others makes no sense. Peace of mind becomes possible. So does consolation in times of agony, loneliness or terrifying confusion.

"Sacred" doesn't mean detached or self-important. It doesn't necessitate calling on the language of mysticism or even spirituality. On the contrary, it means not much more (or less) than quietly knowing our unconditional place in the universe.

The British writer Evelyn Underhill expresses this sublimely in *The Spiritual Life*: "We realise with amazement what a human creature really is—a finite centre of consciousness which is able to apprehend and long for Infinity."

Early in this book I used the phrase from the famous hymn "Amazing Grace": "Once . . . was blind . . . but now I see." *Seeing* our part in things, *seeing* what we can do for other people and how we can most fruitfully develop ourselves, creates the ultimate path of learning: of learning as we go.

What kind of person are we becoming?

What is usefully challenging our self-focus and self-interest?

What is softening us inwardly and expanding our horizons?

Increasing awareness is part of it. Choice, too. But as many of the stories in this book show, transformation also happens to us or within us—if we are willing to be moved by it. *Moved*, our lives deepen as well as broaden. Awe and gratitude revive. Forgiveness becomes possible. Mindfulness becomes natural.

*Transforming*, in a spiritual context, we understand instinctively how interconnected our lives are.

*Transforming*, we understand how much we have to be thankful for in the infinite ways that others support our lives and keep us safe. We understand that the externals to which we pay such close attention are often little more than labels. *All passing.* We understand the mutuality essential to cooperation and cease trying to plunder other people for what we can get from them.

*Transforming*, we observe with care what is influencing our thinking, what we are "taking in" as well as giving out. We notice what will affect and influence other people, whether we leave them better or worse off for knowing us. Such awareness is vital in our intimate and social connections. It matters also in our most casual encounters. It matters increasingly in the workplace, where the mechanization of life can be most fierce. It matters in our many overlapping communities.

*Transforming*, we understand that we are part of a wondrous universe. No effort. No "trying." We *are*.

~~~~~

Sometimes this transformation and the clarity that comes with it happen dramatically. I am struck by this account from a writer named Juliet. She is a natural "deep thinker" in her sixties who is also a trained psychotherapist. Yet the moment that transformed her "view" came unexpectedly and not through conscious work or effort. She describes it like this.

"When I was forty years old I met my Guru [a woman]. This changed everything: the way I perceived life, the reason for living, and the way I was living. It was a revelation to sit in the presence of spiritual power such as I had never known. Her radiant presence opened my heart and soul to dimensions of life of which I had only had glimpses.

"I awoke the next morning after this experience and was flooded with joy. The joy was in me; it *was* me. The meaning of life became clear: to live from this source; to live in the fullest and most expanded way possible. I had been living a life of struggle before that, always grappling with, 'What do *I* want? What can *I* do?' Now I had a vision of a way of living beyond the needs of the ego: a life that could be larger, more joyous, more courageous, more loving and giving.

"Through the guidance and grace of my Guru, and by following the spiritual practices she gives, I have learned to access more and more of that radiance and integrate it into my life."

I am wondering what your feelings are as you read about Juliet's experiences. When people talk openly and excitedly about their moments of epiphany or transformative spiritual experience I often see mixed emotions on the faces of listeners. Perhaps the listeners are wondering if those experiences are authentic. They may also be thinking, "If that person has such amazing meditations or feels so intimately 'in touch with' God or their spiritual teacher or guru, or relishes weeks in silent meditation, or simply feels so confident about what they believe and where it's taking them, why can't or why don't I?"

The short answer may need to come in two parts.

First, I am convinced that transformation is a lifelong process and that a sense of constancy or commitment to spiritual practice and inquiry is more vital and sustaining than the lightning flash of insight that few will receive or perhaps need to receive. Juliet spoke at length to me about this and described in detail her commitment to continuing study as well as meditation, chanting and spiritual service. These daily commitments nourish her and allow her increasingly to realize and *live* the life she perceived more than twenty years ago: "larger, more joyous, more courageous, more loving and giving."

A small moment of peace at a time of suffering, an insight you had not expected, a consolation given and received at a time of need, an old teaching newly understood, a sense of inner connection or community with others, a clarifying dream or moment of synchronicity are more familiar experiences. Far from being mundane, they are significant, even transformative expressions of grace.

In fact, I have heard wise spiritual teachers assuring their students who are stunned by the magnificence of their meditation or visualization experiences that "they will get over it," meaning that they need to check any self-importance that might arise from this and simply allow themselves to move more deeply and confidently into the complexity of life.

Juliet's example of this is clear, especially when she adds, "I try to carry the awareness of service with me every day, and approach the things I do with the attitude of setting my ego aside and serving selflessly. Studying the teachings of the spiritual masters is also part of my daily life. I will often contemplate a simple teaching throughout the day, holding it in my awareness like a navigation beacon. I read and listen to tapes or CDs. On my car dashboard I currently have three different cards, each containing a teaching I am working with. I've typed it out and pasted it onto a card and colored a beautiful border. I rotate the three cards from time to time depending on which one I most need to remember."

It may be also that some of us have greater appetites than others for spiritual depth and experiences. We seek them more avidly. We open up to them more brazenly. Often we can't help ourselves. At the same time it is helpful to remember that questioning as much as seeking is one of the hallmarks of twenty-first-century life. This is by no means a negative.

Rabbi Heschel, in *God in Search of Man*, writes, "A sense of wonder, awe, and mystery does not give us knowledge of God. It only leads to a plane where the question about God becomes an inescapable concern."

My strong impression from spending time with seekers from many backgrounds is that it is possible to have a deep calling to the sacred, or a transformative intimacy with God or the idea of "something" divine and eternal, while "believing" little in any formal sense. This is a quite different position from conventional agnosticism or, as one young woman expressed it, "Whatever-ism!" And it certainly does not describe any kind of indifference.

Making *The Case for God*, contemporary religious historian Karen Armstrong reminds us of the limits of knowledge and the importance of "silence, reticence and awe." This reticence does not indicate a lack of interest but, rather, awareness that when it comes to the deepest reaches of the sacred—perhaps to "God"—our usual ways of "grasping" knowledge simply won't do. Until the rise of modernity in the West, she points out, "People believed that God exceeded our thoughts and concepts and could be known only by dedicated practice."

Central to such practice is a willingness to be transformed by what you are experiencing. In some traditions this is called self-realization:

realizing who and what you truly are and, therefore, who and what all others are. This demands a particularly fruitful innocence, by which I mean the courage to set aside prejudice, presuppositions and assumptions, however convincing they might be.

Armstrong continues: "One of the conditions of enlightenment has always been a willingness to let go of what we thought we knew in order to appreciate truths we had never dreamed of."

A few years earlier, in her memoir *The Spiral Staircase*, Armstrong had reflected on T. S. Eliot's poem "Ash Wednesday," remarking upon the complex sensations evoked in that poem of making little headway but pressing on, nonetheless.

She continues: "My own life has progressed in the same way. For years it seemed a hard Lenten journey, but without the prospect of Easter. I toiled round and round in pointless circles, covering the same ground, repeating the same mistakes, quite unable to see where I was going. Yet all the time, without realizing it, I was slowly climbing out of the darkness ... For a long time, I assumed that I had finished with religion forever, yet, in the end, the strange and seemingly arbitrary revolutions of my life led me to the kind of transformation that, I now believe, was what I had been seeking all those years ago when I packed my suitcase, entered my convent and set off to find God."

Bags packed. Sights set. A sense of voyage is unmistakable.

TRANSFORMING, WE DO NOT BECOME different people. We may see things differently. We probably will. We may make quite different decisions and use different values as our guide. But rather than becoming "different" we become more freely ourselves. And we can't go back.

Ali Coomber was raised by a Samoan mother and her New Zealand father and New Zealand grandparents at different stages of her life, and is fortunate enough to have been exposed to the joyfulness and generosity of Pacific worship. As a young woman, Ali walked away from her Catholic origins but not from seeking.

She describes a time of significant transformation. "At one of the absolute lowest times of my life, in my thirties, I remember calling out to God for help and was completely blown away by the enormous feeling of love that suddenly overwhelmed me. Colors became bright. The clarity of everything around me was incredibly heightened and I felt connected with everything. I wasn't separate from anything. Everything was one and the same. As many people have said before me and will say after, words do not and cannot describe the intensity of this revelation. What happened was so unexpected. God responded to my plea for help and answered in what is still to me now the most incredible way. I have never had that feeling anywhere as fully as that again and have come to realize that if this is to be the only time it happens, I am truly grateful for being blessed with it."

Not conventionally religious but committed to the path of seeking, Ali makes it clear how that formative experience continues to resonate a decade later.

"I now cherish the moment that God showed me the depth of his love and that has never left me. No matter what happens, some part of me feels incredibly safe in God's love. I have never felt completely and utterly alone. I always know God is around. I have been through so much through the last few years and prayed through the tough times and *never*—even at my worst and darkest places—have I felt alone. *God has been there.* It is so wonderful for me now to be in a place where I can just express gratitude. The one thing I do ask for is guidance along the path and trust that I am awake to it in the moments it is sent. That's my job—to be awake to it."

ﾟ⁓ꞇꙌ◌ꙍ⁓

As Ali identifies, to be *awake* to the guidance we are seeking is profoundly empowering. To trust the "small, still voice within"—however we define this—is to know a resource and source of wisdom that is literally priceless.

Discovering this is rarely dependent on outer circumstances. Some outer circumstances are certainly conducive to inner transformation of the most liberating kinds. Yet most of us know firsthand that it can be in the most desolate circumstances that we come to see our own most holy potential in humbling and sometimes life-changing ways.

In Psalm 138 we hear: "On the day I called, you answered me. You increased my strength of soul . . . You stretch out your hand and your right hand saves me."

And in the next Psalm, 139, we hear, "Even the darkness is not dark to you. The night is as bright as day. To you, darkness is as light." Reading this line I am transported to our Christmas Eve services in the heart of Sydney where we sing each year, in the darkness of our sacred late-night gathering: "In the darkness, there is no darkness. With you, O Lord, the darkest night is clear as the day . . ."

Wishful thinking? My sense is strong that what I am describing, and what so many of the personal accounts in this book affirm, is something far more substantial than "wishing" and, in its essential mystery, also far less "substantial."

"How is it possible," I was asked recently by Eduardo, a lively seeker in his late eighties, "to be absolutely and personally *present* in the presence of a Mystery?" He laughed, expecting no response from me except my interest, and then said, "It's not a question of 'how is it possible'; it is a question of exploding the possible. I am present. And that presence is with me, as they say, through all the days of my life. My heart is full."

Experience is vital here. Abstractions aren't enough. *Consciously* choosing a more inspired way of life, we begin to allow the sacred to inhabit us. And only then meet its real meaning.

What is most holy is discovered in the ordinary *and* it is not ordinary. It is discovered only through experience *and* it exceeds experience.

"Love is life," wrote Leo Tolstoy. "All, everything I understand, I understand only because I love. Everything is, everything exists, only because I love. Everything is united by it alone. Love is God, and to die means that I, a particle of love, shall return to the general and eternal source."

～ᡉᏸᏸ⌒

What is also clear is how easily and often that call to love is ignored, hedged or qualified. Not just by other people; also by us. Yet the wonder of spirituality is that it somehow allows the deepest conceptions and practices of love to survive everything that we humans can do. It opens our minds to the fullness of existence. It lets our deepest desires soar. It encourages our hearts to heal and our minds to rest on what will stimulate as well as nourish us.

In the mystical teachings from every era and source there is profound love. There is also a profound understanding of the agonies of human suffering that we are here (I believe) to understand and relieve—not to prolong or worsen.

We circle back again to what I see as the inviolable essence of any spiritual teaching. What kinds of *behaviors* does it encourage? Who does it include (and exclude)? Does it bring people together or drive them apart? Does it engender compassion, tolerance, hope and forgiveness? What are the *attitudes* it rests on and opens out?

Does it inspire wonder, awe, forgiveness, kindness—and bliss?

Does it give us infinite reasons to kneel in love and kiss the ground?

Who is it encouraging each of us to become?

~c~⌒~∂~

Neville is a recently retired professional who describes himself as having had the good fortune to grow up (in England) in a small branch of Christianity inspired by the teaching of Emanuel Swedenborg. This is a tradition that, in Neville's words, "looks to the spiritual essence from a Divine source in all things—people, sacred scripture and every aspect of nature." It has continued to nourish him into his adult life.

Reflecting on contemporary spirituality Neville told me, "The word 'spiritual' gets bandied around a lot these days in so many differing situations and ways. But I have certainly taken on board that, along with every human being, I am gifted with an immortal soul into which Divine life flows to enable me to be the person I am. Without it, I would not exist. That is, *I cannot be purely a physical being.*"

He makes this clearer still when he says, "I process that life in the inner world of my mind with its thoughts and affections, being free to use it for purposes which either primarily serve others or mainly myself.

"This is my higher life and, like everyone, it is where I gradually work out the type of person I want to become through the choices I formulate and process.

"I see my mortal body purely as the vessel by which I can exist in this external world and put into action those purposes I have chosen at my inner-mind level. Personally, I define the higher level of life as my 'spiritual zone' and in that sense I see myself as a spiritual being. This is the same for all humans. But my spirituality will only grow when I choose to be of use to others and put that into practice in the here and now. It will stagnate and become sterile if my focus is solely on myself and my own wants."

Recognizing the "Divine source in all things" has been central for Neville. I suspect it's been transformative. He explains, "It gradually became very meaningful to me during my thirties in talking about the basic beliefs [of his tradition] to my children. The rationality that underpinned its tenets sat so well with the more external worldview I had developed independently. Everything started to fit together like a jigsaw. I realized I could now see the manifestation of the Divine/ God in my own life from a new perspective, challenging me to seek ways to express goodness and also to try to experience the goodness in others. Religion could no longer be just an intellectual exercise, a matter of faith or a Sunday activity. It needed to infiltrate every aspect of my life from the purely mundane upward.

"In my mind's eye, I see God as personal in every way even to form, and my truest friend. I cannot 'image' God in any other way. All my life, my Christian understanding has shown me that God came into the world as Jesus Christ to experience every human frailty and overcome it. For me it means that I can take any issue that I face in my life to my God in the person of Jesus Christ and talk about it knowing that I am fully understood and accepted.

"I also 'know' that my personal God will take on board what I need help with and deal with it in ways which will best serve my interests eternally. Sorting out my external life is not God's concern. In the end, that is my job and responsibility. But my own view of God in no way limits God's activity to Christianity. [My belief is that] God will look after the spiritual needs of everyone who genuinely seeks help.

"For me, my religion had become spiritual and personal: a sure foundation which could carry me through some pretty tough and very low times."

◦◦◦◦◦

To see the world through the lens of the sacred is to be transformed. Or perhaps it is to come back to ourselves: to be born again to a sense of wonder. For isn't it true that almost all tiny children reflect to us our losses of innocence, awe and even full-hearted delight? In them, we surely see our unconditioned selves, our most sacred, undefended and fully alive selves? And isn't it true that while delighting with them, we may sometimes also mourn our losses?

As I write this, my sister's little granddaughter is approaching her second birthday and my newest godson has just turned four. Both these children are abundantly loved. Both are freed by family love to see the world as unquestionably benevolent.

At this moment, each lovely child lives in a Garden of Eden. This is not to say they don't have their darker moments or frustrations; they do. But their general expectation is of a world of kindness, generosity, interest, fascination and the simple sensual pleasures of food, cuddles, noisy baths, music, dance, easy adventurous play and story; of a bee circling and a snail sliding; of the power of a kiss to "make things better." The almost-two-year-old speaks aloud her innermost thoughts. Because she is by nature reflective, and because her age makes her unguarded, it is almost trespassing to listen in. By three or four she will almost certainly not be doing this. "Within" and "without" will have become different places, perhaps not consciously but instinctively. Only two years older but at this moment twice her age, my Indian-born godson already has a clear sense of self and other, of cultural differences, of differences in skin color and religion—and of differences, too, in attitude.

'Are you vegetarian or vegan, Stephanie?' he asked recently as we ate a slow snack in a museum café, already aware that not everyone is the same and curious to know where he should place me.

~~~

There is so much we share in our journey toward (or surrender into) the sacred *and* our differences are as innumerable as the proverbial grains of sand. This surely makes our quest more and not less fascinating.

Two of the people I spoke to for this book were particularly passionate about what they are taking and have learned from nature about the sacred and the divine. I find this inspiring because unless we begin to see the sacred in the physical world or to see the physical world through the eyes of the holy—as every indigenous religion has unconditionally understood—our efforts to "save the planet" are doomed to fail. It is almost inconceivable that we would *not* see that our "salvation" and the planet's "salvation" are inextricably linked, mirroring with profound exactitude the theme I have developed so consistently through this book: that I cannot harm you without harming myself; that you cannot raise my spirits or help heal my heart without also healing yourself.

Judith Ackroyd lives on an island in the Auckland harbor and, like many people who live in close proximity to the land or ocean, her spiritual life, and her intense *sense* of spirit, is enhanced by the people she deliberately and happily gathers around her and also by her tremendous love of nature and the natural world. She describes this awareness of connection in a way that surpasses any everyday notion of communion.

"'Sacred' is a word I love. It's like holding, receiving something in the open palm and treasuring it, giving it full attention, and also knowing, as Emily Dickinson says in one of her poems, that in one moment it is there, in the palm of your hand, and then it can be gone if we turn our eyes away for a moment, and forget it. It's a poem I have remembered for more than twenty years since my first reading of it."

> *I held a Jewel in my fingers —*
> *And went to sleep —*
> *The day was warm, and winds were prosy —*
> *I said "'Twill keep" —*
> *I woke — and chid my honest fingers,*
> *The Gem was gone —*
> *And now, an Amethyst remembrance*
> *Is all I own —*

Judith continues, "Perhaps, though, the sacred is always present. It's just that we have gone to sleep on it or stopped trusting.

"'Holy' is a new word for me and I think I may begin to use it. I find that I can embrace its meaning of preciousness, its spiritual nature (which includes an element of the unknown, the notion of mysterious). And I am more willing to use this word, 'God,' to describe this inner and outer knowing and also *not knowing* but *trusting*. I am beginning to be able to attribute qualities such as holiness to it.

"Sometimes when I am in nature, on the sea or in a kayak, the sun is low in the sky, the sea is still, the *kahawhai* are shimmering close to the surface or surging through the water, the gannets are diving in front of me, then all barriers between me and the external world dissolve. I become the sea, the fish, the sky—and that is also when I know love. This is a rare moment and a gift of awe and beauty."

⌒⌒⌒

Another glowing example of inspiration from the physical world comes from Jessica Perini. I owe my friendship with Jessica to the wonders of the Internet. That's how we "met," initially through her contacting me about my books, then through her skillful photographic interpretations of some of my work, and later with her own honest writing about her struggles with anxiety, some of which she shared in one of my earlier books, *Creative Journal Writing*. Jessica and I have shared some profound moments. Yet, in a typically twenty-first-century way, we have rarely stood on the same patch of ground despite living for years in the same city.

Jessica used to be a Catholic and is now a "more generic Christian." Her view of the sacred and the world in which we all live has been transformed by nature and also by the intrinsic beauty of mathematics.

"God started in my mind as an angry man watching from the clouds with his beady little eyes, and big pointy finger. Like an angry teacher he'd rain down his curses upon me because I got a blotch of mud on my Sunday best. Every week his representative would convey God's disappointment. As soon as I was old enough I drifted from this tempestuous God. After all, he only ever made me feel bad. I didn't want to believe God was like that. In Sunday school our teachers taught us about Jesus, and his love of everyone, including those frowned upon by society. That really appealed to me [but] I just couldn't merge the vision of a kind and caring all-loving Jesus with this God of short temper and whimsical rules.

"Then I started to learn about nature, and its utter perfection. The mathematical Fibonacci spirals repeated in countless shells. The hexagonal precision of a beehive. The sun, the perfect circle of life, its circumference divided by its diameter equaling pi. The statistical improbability of life. The systems, including air, water, soil; the interconnection of it all. And I thought, no human being could ever think up such a complete and perfect picture. It has to be 'divine.' Because it is like a giant jigsaw puzzle. Because we humans, while we may be bright, we don't have the ability to step back and take it all in. That's one heck of a grand design. Abundant in every way."

~°~°~°~

The gestures of nature are everywhere. Transformation is also expressed and understood as deeply through inner and outer gesture as it is through words. Unconsciously, we turn inward in our times of greatest need. We fall silent when we enter a place that is holy. It might be a church or temple. It might be a gathering of a few people in a garden to celebrate the life of someone who has died, or to welcome a new family member following a birth. The simplest moment can stir us. The most lavish ceremony or ritual can leave us feeling abandoned, superfluous or bored.

When I speak or write about transformation, what I am referring to is a transformation of "view" primarily. This was expressed in a sublime way by the English visionary poet William Blake: "If the doors of perception were cleansed everything would appear to [humankind] as it is: infinite."

You might prefer to call this process of "viewing" consciousness or awareness. What we *notice* as we view will depend on our attitudes and values. Our attitudes and values will also dictate our *interpretations* of what we are seeing and experiencing.

Quite recently I was seated at a function with a number of people, none of whom I had met before. I turned to the man next to me, a professional in his fifties, and asked him what he had found interesting in the talk he had just heard. "Are you picking on me?" he said, to my absolute astonishment. "Everyone picks on me."

"Is that actually so?" I asked. And perhaps he was immediately regretful about that moment of stark candor that had startled him, I suspect, as much as it did me, because he then launched into a brief speech about how he really feels his life is wonderful and that he has a great deal to be grateful for. It's likely the latter is also true—yet there was something in his "slip," as Freud would have called it, that lingered in the space between us.

An exceptional thought comes to us from Hazrat Inayat Khan: "Humankind thinks and acts according to the pitch to which the soul is tuned. The highest note one could be tuned to is the divine note and it is in that pitch, once you arrive at it, that you begin to express the manner of God in everything you do, a manner which is not only beautiful, but which is beauty itself."

It's fascinating to know that Hazrat Inayat Khan was a widely admired musician before he brought Sufi teachings to the West from India in the early years of the twentieth century. His quote, drawing on the language of music, sets the scene beautifully. How are we allowing our souls to "tune" us—or perhaps our yearnings? What are we paying attention to with greatest constancy? What "choruses" are we constantly replaying? And what effect are they having on our attitudes and thinking?

What is it that we routinely fall back on when thinking about those big questions of meaning, and the everyday actions and behavior that flow from them? How do we express the "manner of God" or the "manner of the sacred" in our daily living?

Inspiration is critical here. Without it, insight is not possible and the most ethical choices and experience remain mechanical or empty.

TRANSFORMATION IS TAKING PLACE AT ALL levels of our being: conscious and unconscious. At several key moments in my life I have literally been led forward by dreams, sometimes eagerly but more often reluctantly. Dreams are not the only way that the unconscious nudges us. There are also those "involuntary outbursts," like the Freudian "slip" I recounted on page 308, or moments of dramatic synchronicity, or observing the patterns in your projections or attitudes that emerge through journal writing. Noticing the stories you routinely return to is also literally "telling." Nonetheless, there is a nice irony in the fact that it is sometimes while sleeping and surrendering our everyday defenses that we receive the most compelling of our "wake up" calls.

When I left The Women's Press and London to come to Australia to live, expecting my first child and resolving to make writing rather than publishing my principal work, this was in large part because of dreams that had become impossible to ignore. As hard as I found it to accept, publishing as a central occupation was over for me. It was time to write.

Having worked closely with many writers, I was under no illusions about the famed "life of a writer." I knew and know how relentless it is. Yet those feelings were less persuasive than my growing conviction that this move was essential.

In the mid-1980s, when I returned to the teachings of Christ in the company of Quakers, this was again prompted in part by those dreams I'd had of Christ, whom I was "seeing" in his tenderness and commitment to humanity as if for the first time.

How we view those explicitly transformative moments and interpret them for ourselves will radically determine their power to influence our lives. We can ignore them. We may be shaken up by them—or soothed and affirmed by them. Sometimes, as in my own case, they may commit us to the boldness of a new direction.

Let me give you another less dramatic but subtle and affecting example.

You met Hilary Star earlier in this book when she talked about her journey from a fundamentalist Christian childhood through years of uncertain but persistent searching to a "return to God" as, she would now say, Mystery and Beloved. She and I talk often as we share our interfaith ministries in Australia and New Zealand. Just weeks ago she sent me a note describing how she sustained herself through a difficult moment in a way that was significantly different from how she would have struggled through a similar moment years or even months earlier.

As Hilary describes it, "I woke yesterday morning to feelings so strong and totally occupying that they felt bigger than just mine. They felt 'beyond me' and I wondered, 'What is happening?' In the past when I have experienced something similar I often felt very panicked and wondered if someone I loved was in danger. This time I found myself choosing to be utterly with these feelings. Rather than trying to just get on with things or inquiring about what is going on with cognitive reasoning, I began to breathe into the feelings.

"Some of what I found in the feelings is profound grief. I have been crying deeply, still without understanding exactly what is happening. I have felt all that I can do is pray, not feeling even any certainty about who I am praying to, yet it is the best thing I can do, to express these feelings, finding myself praying for my two sons. *I am accepting all the questions, and the 'not knowing,' without judging myself.*

"I found myself choosing to be alone with myself in a way I rarely give time for in my busy life. This has enabled me to be with all that I am feeling and sensing. I am also relieved from having to try to explain what is happening because I cannot find the words to describe these feelings or why I think I am having them.

"Occasionally something has come into my awareness that provides a brief nudge of comfort. Being able to just be with it, with myself, and not thinking, 'I ought not to be feeling this,' is somewhat easing of the pain.

"I have felt at times quite paralyzed by the preoccupation with these feelings yet also knowing I do have a choice to be very gentle with myself. Rising inside me is an acceptance to be with the pain and grief, not looking for a distraction or easy answer."

Hilary concludes: "I also have the choice to trust *without explanation*—from outside or in. This is when trusting is really called for."

The very uncertainty and lack of focus of what Hilary describes goes against the grain of so much of our contemporary agenda-driven, goal-driven thinking. Her "strategy" here is subtle and inwardly accommodating. It eloquently demonstrates that we can engage with the processes of transformation. Or resist them.

Spiritual transformation can be dramatic and immediate. Isaiah's vision of God in the temple, Saul's literal "blindness" before the insight that led to him becoming Paul of the many Christian epistles, Dame Julian of Norwich's dialogues with Jesus, Hildegard of Bingen's visions that began when she was three and lasted through most of eight decades, Ramakrishna's vision of Kali, Mohammed hearing the Angel Gabriel recite the Qur'an: these are big moments by any measure. For most of us, however, I suspect that spiritual transformation began and will continue with the small. Or is it so small?

Whatever our spiritual education and training, authentic spiritual transformation arises from a moment of *personal* insight that there is something more to life than the familiar materiality of measurable and finite forms, or the received messages of our spiritual inheritance. It must arise from within. It can certainly be encouraged. I hope this book is such an encouragement. But it can't be imposed or given. It will follow a perception that along with this *finite* familiar life we also have an *infinite* life of spirit, however indeterminately we perceive that.

Rebekah is a professional woman in her forties whose outer life is lived in a highly competitive environment. Inwardly, her world is different. "When I am praying in particular, I am speaking to God who, for me, feels somehow so much greater than myself. For me, God is all around yet just right there next to me. A presence that is solid, reliable and dependable yet has no physical form. This experience of praying to God for me can be like being wrapped up in the arms of angels, safe and secure. It almost has a physical feel about it, yet there is nothing tangible to see or touch. Praying to God feels like there is someone out there who knows me like I don't even know myself. In spite of who I am with all my human frailties, I am cherished and loved for who I am."

For some people, dogma and belief will be crucial to these processes or will emerge from them. That is certainly not universally true, however. Transformation may lead to a sense that "soul" seeks expression through our personality "self." It may also lead to a life-changing consciousness that every other human being on our planet is and was and will be something more than flesh and blood: that regardless of race, gender, culture, etcetera ad infinitum, each being also has a transcendent or eternal nature and eternal life.

When we let that insight become real, it is utterly transformative. We become soul-conscious. Spirituality becomes our primary identification.

~~∽◗◖∾~~

In 2004, the year before I was ordained as an interfaith minister, I stayed on in New York after our seminary class retreat. I was then, as I am now, living in Sydney and studying by distance while also keeping my usual complex work life going, including writing. New York is one of my favorite cities in the world and I had needed no persuading to stay on to witness the ordination of the class ahead of mine. I was hugely excited about this event, knowing that I would be back the following year for my own ordination. I was also curious about what it would signify for me in the year ahead.

On the day of the ceremony a large congregation had gathered in St. John the Divine, a vast neo-Gothic cathedral on Manhattan's Upper West Side. A senior person from the seminary got up to speak. Prominent in his talk was a lengthy homage to the fantastic job "our" U.S. Army was doing in the Middle East, especially Iraq.

In the context of an interfaith, interreligious, multicultural and multinational gathering of some significance, I found it difficult to believe what I was hearing. Is it possible to be committed to an inclusive, nonviolent, spiritual perspective, while also being nationalistic and militaristic? I doubt it. But my ears were telling me otherwise.

After the ordination ceremony was over and we were socializing, I tried to speak to this man about his words, only to discover he was confused and deeply offended by my offense. In fact, he was incredulous and quickly angry. I talked to him about my many years with the Religious Society of Friends (Quakers) and their unconditional Peace Testimony. I spoke briefly about the rationale for my lifelong commitment to nonviolence. But we made no headway. I left the gathering rattled and upset.

The following year, 2005, I was back in New York for my own ordination and knew that one of the people involved in ordaining me would be this particular man. How would I deal with it?

He and I held definite but opposing views. Could I possibly see in him "that of God," an eternal soul, a Buddha nature or my own "Self?"

When my turn for ordination came, three people stood in front of me to confer this. One of them was this man. And in that moment I experienced something so unexpected that I can only describe it as an outpouring of grace. As he put his hands on my head, I experienced him as nothing but a humble instrument of the divine. And I experienced that I could hope to be nothing more.

In that long moment I also experienced my absolute sisterhood in God with him—a man with whom I would not wish to break bread or have a cup of tea. The relative *un*importance of his personality and even of his views was startlingly clear to me, along with the profound awareness that, somehow or other, I had experienced a rare and transformative moment of transcendence.

What's more, it was only because I had felt such irritation and even contempt for him as well as for his views, that I could make this uninvited discovery. Had I already felt generous toward him or had I liked him, that formative flash of insight would never have been possible.

Please don't assume by this that it doesn't matter to me what or how someone thinks. It matters. I certainly prefer to be with people who do *not* have racist, bigoted, nationalistic or patriarchal views, and I treasure my right to use whatever power I have to offer alternative views.

But in that instant, something else also became real to me: *that our perceptions of one another must be grounded in something greater than our "views" or even our conduct.*

I had long believed that. From then on I knew it.

I have written so much in this book about this transcendent perception: about the *unconditionality* of "doing no harm"; the unconditionality of regarding others as our neighbors; the uncon-ditionality of attributing to others an inner "divine," no matter how repugnant their views or how we may respond to them at the level of personality.

This startling experience of genuinely transcending "personality," views and opinions had a rare as well as raw beauty because it occurred in the midst of a ritual that had great meaning for me. Had I been asked, I might have said, "Please keep me away from this man." As it was, the experience allowed me to see and understand in a quite new way how some people in infinitely more frightening and grim situations can and will continue to treat others with unfailing respect and kindness.

~~~

The self-respect that arises from behaving wisely and well *because we can*, and because we cherish the benefits of this, is singularly appropriate to our contemporary consciousness. But the thought is not new. In the fourteenth century, mystic Meister Eckhart wrote, "I have often said that a person who wishes to begin a good life should be like the one who draws a circle. Let the center be in the right place and the circumference will be full of life. In other words, let us first learn to fix our hearts on the Sacred and then all that we do will flourish."

Fundamentalisms aside, there is no doubt that it is more empowering to live wisely and well because we are free to do so rather than because we are afraid of what other people will think of us, or fear God's wrath or judgment or the fires of hell.

An ancient prayer makes this clear. It comes from the famed female Sufi teacher Rabi'a al-Adawiyya, born in poverty in eighth-century

Basra, Iraq, and renowned for the intensity of her love for God. It is translated here by contemporary writer Hanan al-Shaykh.

> *O God, Whatever you would grant me in this life,*
> *Give it to my enemies.*
> *O God, Whatever you would give me in the life to come,*
> *Give it to my friends.*
> *You are enough for me.*
> *O God, if I worship you for fear of hell,*
> *then burn me again and again.*
> *And if I worship you*
> *for the sake of heaven only,*
> *then shut its gate in my face.*
> *But if I worship you for your own sake,*
> *Then reveal to me your eternal beauty.*

IN THE EASTERN WISDOM TRADITIONS, and perhaps also in the mystical way more generally, spiritual transformation implies stages of enlightenment: *seeing* life and our place in life and even what precedes and follows "life" in its unity, and then acting accordingly. "Saving" or salvation occurs indirectly, through compassion, inner reconciliation and example. This unfolding process can be honored, encouraged and desired for others. But it can't be achieved for them and it can't be imposed.

This makes individual yearning and insight, and the powerful changes in consciousness and behavior that follow genuine insight, more and not less important.

That note is sounded in many teachings, including these famous lines (1 Corinthians 13:10–13): "When the complete comes, the partial will come to an end. When I was a child, I spoke like a child. I thought like a child, I reasoned like a child. When I became an adult, I put away childish things. For now we see as in a glass, darkly. But soon we will see face to face. For now, I know only in part. Soon, I will know fully, even as I have been fully known.

And now faith, hope and love abide, these three. And the greatest of these is love."

~~~ಲಿ⊌ಎ~~~

Enlightenment need not be completely achieved to be of value. "Completion" would be too awesome: a vast peak few would feel able to conquer. I remain highly skeptical of anyone who claims to be enlightened. (Fortunately, few do.) There seems hubris in that. It is much more realistic to think of getting a little wiser "day by day," and of rising up after falling down.

A brief, intense prayer that I love to use comes from the ancient Hindu Upanishads. "Lead us from the unreal to the Real," it says, "from ignorance to Illumination."

What could the source of those "leadings" be other than our hearts, intuitions, insights and dreams and, especially, our souls? When something is powerful enough to shift our inner compass convincingly this will never happen through thought alone. Or even through the most careful guidance and teachings.

We need to notice what we are "taking in." We should know when the company we are keeping or the books we are reading or the television we are watching is uplifting and nourishing, or not. But in leading us "from the unreal to the Real," even the most noble ideas are not enough. They must be embodied. That includes finding out for ourselves what works—and what does not.

To support this vitalizing idea of *finding out*, here is a teaching that you might swear is Buddhist in origin. In fact, it comes from the Jewish tradition (Pirke Avot 1:10).

*No matter how famous the mouth,*
*Check the words against experience.*
*We are here to do.*
*And through learning to know;*
*And through knowing to wonder;*
*And through wonder to attain simplicity;*
*And through simplicity to give attention;*
*And through attention,*
*To see what needs to be done.*

The historical Buddha dedicated his life to self-transformation or enlightenment. His goal, too, was to discover for himself—through observation of his own experiences—what would relieve suffering and create a life of peace, tolerance, loving-kindness and compassion.

*Believe nothing,* said the Buddha, *because someone wise has said it.*
*Believe nothing because it is generally held.*
*Believe nothing because it has been written down.*
*Believe nothing because it is said to be Godly.*
*Believe nothing because someone else believes it*
*Believe only what you yourself discover to be true.*

A well-known story is told that after his own enlightenment the Buddha passed a man on the road, walking in the opposite direction. (Or perhaps the Buddha was sitting under a tree as the man passed by. That version is just as credible.) The man was struck by the Buddha's radiance and peaceful presence, and asked him, "My friend, what are you? Are you a celestial being or a god?"

"No," said the Buddha.

"Are you a magician?" asked the man.

"No," said the Buddha.

"Are you a man?" he asked.

"No," said the Buddha.

In total mystification the man asked, "Then what are you?"

The Buddha replied, "I am awake."

Awake to what matters; awake to what causes suffering and relieves it; awake to the continuities of existence as well as to what is transient; awake to the need to make some discoveries firsthand; awake to the transformative power of grace and illumination and insight: perhaps that is some of what the Buddha meant.

～ひ～

Strikingly similar lines sing out from the Christian tradition (Galatians 2, 19–20): "For through the law, I died to the law ... It is no longer I who live. It is Christ who lives in me."

It's another version of coming awake. Of being born again.

*Dying* to the limitations in the way you usually see yourself; *living* to the call and the strengths of the soul; *daring* to open to our inner beauty and strengths: that *is* spiritual transformation.

Yet I am also aware that living from the heart in a heart-fearing world, and giving up the short-term comforts of dogma or cynicism, takes great courage. The journey inward *is* risky. People know that instinctively. Maps that take us in that direction are handmade and patchy. What they may do for me today may not help me tomorrow. Staying awake demands mindfulness writ large.

Melancholy, emptiness, loneliness, cynicism or self-absorption all create long shadows on the path of inner reflection. The rewards that arise from faithful persistence are powerful but frequently hard won. And yet who among us does not know that avoiding the risks, the intensity and *poetry* of spiritual life and experience can too easily mean sticking with the *appearances* of religious belief or spiritual practice, or staying with the well trodden and well rehearsed, rather than risking the depths of self-discovery and the depths of our own yearning.

༺✦༻

Mythologist Joseph Campbell was the twentieth century's foremost interpreter of sacred traditions. Never a conventional "believer" (and never conventional), his lifelong fascination with the sacred led him to conclude that throughout human history there have been periods when the transformation [of humankind] was radical. Thrillingly, he saw our own period as "certainly one of those."

Commenting in *The Open Life*, he said of this time—of *our* time: "Horizons are smashed [and] people of different beliefs and cultures are colliding with each other. The transformation is really of the whole sense of humanity and what it means to be a cultured and world-related human being. Anything from the past—such as an idea of what [humankind] of this, that, or another culture might be, or should be—is now archaic. And so we have to leave our little provincial stories behind. They may guide us as far as structuring our lives for the moment, but we must always be ready to drop them and to grab the new experience as it comes along, and to interpret it."

Revisiting those words, I want to stand and cheer. And Campbell's call to shed our spiritual and cultural "provincialism" in favor of being "world-related" is enhanced when we consider it alongside priest and interreligious activist Raimon Panikkar's notion that religion can and should be "a lived and living experience rather than ideology." Panikkar has also said in a 1996 interview, "Peace is not simply an ideal, it's a necessity, because the alternative would be a human and planetary catastrophe. Our competitive system, in which only things which can be given a financial value are considered to have any worth, cannot go much further . . . We, by our very nature, belong both to earth and the divine."

Those twin insights point to a new era of spiritual maturity and self-responsibility as well as freedom. And to a new understanding of our urgent need for peace.

Self-responsibility here must be understood in its widest sense: as a responsibility to one's self and others, *and* the effect on others of our own choices and conduct. Those ideas, redolent with generosity, have become something of a beacon for me.

The inevitable differences in our ways of thinking and speaking about the sacred or relating to God are far less significant than how we live our seeking through our choices and behavior. Our holiest obligation is to live with awareness, to remain attentive to what we are bringing to the multiple situations that make up our lives.

We open our eyes each day in a sacred world. We close our eyes each night and enter a different dimension of a sacred world. The sacred is not found in the elsewhere. It is found in the everywhere. It is found through seeing the eternal dimensions *in* the world and through bringing an honoring of the sacred *to* the world.

Pierre Teilhard de Chardin calls this "divinizing one's activities," an immense idea he explores in his book *The Divine Milieu*, seeing this as something particularly vital in the earlier years of one's life that will be balanced—if we are fortunate—by "hallowing [making holy] one's diminishments" in the later years.

Teilhard de Chardin's words echo the call from Paul that I quoted much earlier: "Do everything in such a way that the divine can be revealed through it."

This may turn the notion of "seeking" to one of "surrendering": to discovering what is already there, what we already have, who and what we already are.

> *You wander,* says the poet Rumi, *from place to place.*
> *You hunt for a necklace of diamonds.*
> *It is already around your neck.*

IN MANY RELIGIOUS TRADITIONS the spiritual "heart" is the holiest place on earth. Some would say it is where the divine lives and finds expression. Going to that place can seem like a long journey indeed. It is a journey no one can take for you, although numerous people are taking it alongside you. Quieting our minds to leave surface clutter behind, using prayer to listen rather than speak, discovering or rediscovering the receptivity that meditation allows, assessing our reading and reverie, reflecting deeply on what motivates and inspires us, allowing ourselves to learn from nature: it all matters, not for ourselves only but also for our world. Such inner discovery and commitment is not secondary to our outer efforts, *it transforms those efforts.*

At their best, times of *being* or perhaps *sensing* enliven and stabilize us. They allow us to know that we are "someone" rather than no one. They cut across that terrible fear we humans share that we are essentially alone in the universe. They allow us to meditate without meditating and to pray without praying.

Self-awareness is an essential precursor to taking responsibility for our effect on other people. It is a spiritual discipline as much as a psychological and ethical one.

It is literally life-changing to discover how possible it is to live from the inside out rather than the outside in. To make sense of this, we need to trust that we have an inner world—and that each of us can take our sense of direction from it.

To achieve this kind of equilibrium, we need to know our inner world.

This would have been a ridiculous suggestion even fifty years ago, when anyone with the privilege of some leisure time would routinely have used it for various kinds of self-reflection. Playing music, reading, writing a journal, long thoughtful letters or poetry, taking long solitary walks, doing needlework, are just some of the many activities that can join human beings more deeply to themselves, that allow them to reflect, muse, perhaps create or simply "be."

"Time to reflect" can be a sacred pleasure. It is increasingly a rare one.

In one of our many conversations about these ideas, my dear wise friend Jane Moore pointed out that "Harmony is often far from us as an ideal and certainly as an experience. We live at a pace where it is normal to jump when someone snaps their fingers. And to feel *guilty* and ashamed if we can't. It's so normal to 'serve' a whole fleet of 'masters' that we hardly know we are doing it: the masters of the media, of commercialization, of seemingly trivial things like what we should wear or eat or how slim or fit we should be, as well as the more obvious 'masters' of work and its demands. Our inner fears, particularly of insufficiency or failure, often also have mastery over us. Again, this is keeping us from that essential inner and outer harmony on which our maximum well-being is, in point of fact, dependent. But what's scary about this is that it is so familiar and normal we have to have a pretty big shake-up to notice."

To achieve an easy familiarity with our inner world we must open up time for periods of recovery and reflection. Constant noise and interruptions, an in-tray that is never empty, hundreds of daily e-mails demanding attention, the pressure to be "across everything" instantly and to produce work at speed rather than in depth: these are all features of modern life that can be severely destructive, disallowing any feelings of completion or quiet satisfaction in something well done—or any real sense of choice or agency.

The other side of this contemporary picture is also bleak. The many people who no longer have or cannot find meaningful paid work, who no longer feel useful or able to provide adequately for their families, suffer a psychological harm of a different and often even more pernicious kind. I have written a good deal about identity and, in this situation, where the instant reference points of professional status and paid work are gone, the security of aligning ourselves with our highest sense of self, and our most sustaining values, can become newly urgent.

In the cojoined worlds of "too much" and "too little" there is an equally urgent need for inner security, a sense of being *inwardly* alive, and the peace of mind which comes with that.

We cannot control all elements of the world beyond ourselves. We cannot even control whether we will live long healthy lives or if our lives or the lives of those we most love will be cut short by accident or illness. Taking care of what we eat, drink and think about, and how we live, gives us the best possible chance to live a long and healthy life, but there are no guarantees.

Because the world outside ourselves can seem so harsh and indifferent, it makes it more and not less necessary that we take charge of whatever we can. We offer ourselves something quite exceptionally precious when we honor and affirm our inner reality. These are the experiences, insights, consolations and subtle rewards that may never make it onto your curriculum vitae but can certainly make all the difference as to whether you want to get up in the morning or how well you sleep at night.

I am moved by the following account of a bodily, emotional and spiritual transformation of a profound kind. It comes from Judith Pemell, author of the fine book *The Soul Illuminated*, but this reflection is a personal one she shared with me, arising from her confidence in the transformative recoveries made possible by Alcoholics Anonymous and similar twelve-step programs. In Judi's case, it was Smokers Anonymous. And for any of you who may think that smoking is a fairly benign addiction Judi suggests it is useful to remember that tobacco is more addictive than heroin for some. Add to that its severe health hazards and, as well, the critical nature of all addictions: "That they powerfully influence our lives and decision-making, transforming us in a negative direction."

Judi explains her struggle to be free. "After meditating for three years and experiencing a remarkable change of lifestyle I was still struggling with a smoking habit that I just couldn't shake. It was as if I was trying to run with my ankles tied together. My self-esteem was in tatters as the shame and despair of what I was doing tore at my heart.

"In the midst of this I opened the *LA Weekly* to find staring back at me a whole section on twelve-step programs. Smokers Anonymous leapt from the page like a neon sign. Within a few days I attended my first meeting, quit smoking and began the journey of my life!

"I embraced the program heart and soul, eventually finding a sponsor who would guide and mentor me through the steps. When I had been in the program for about a year, she gently prodded me that it was time to get working on the fourth step, which involves writing *a fearless and searching moral inventory of one's life.*

"We met and discussed the step work and she handed me a list of questions as a framework for my inventory. I quickly read through them, my heart skipping many a beat before I finished reading the first: *In looking back over your life, what memories still make you feel dirty, angry, guilty, ashamed?* Several more questions followed.

"It took nine months to complete my writing, nine months of sometimes agonizing reflection and inner "owning up," committing my discoveries to paper.

"Then it was time to do the fifth step—*to give my inventory to God and another human being.*

"If tackling the fourth step had been bloodcurdling and heart-stopping, the fifth, I knew, would reduce me to ashes. I was terrified. My sponsor and I met at a place of my choosing on a busy Sunday morning: Century City shopping mall [in Los Angeles]. I chose it so I could feel anonymous, invisible, a tiny speck in an ocean of people. It was a vast area filled with cafés, tables, trees and umbrellas, and most important, thousands of shoppers—in the midst of whom I imagined I might be swallowed up. Our coffees arrived and my insides turned to jelly as I picked up the thick bunch of papers before me.

"Three to four hours later I laid the last sheet of paper to rest. My relief was beyond description. I looked across the table at the slumped body of my exhausted sponsor.

"As we walked back across the café plaza I felt shattered and drained, yet light as a feather and cleaned out. They say that when you do a very deep and thorough fourth and fifth step [owning up to the pain you have caused, giving the inventory of that to God—or Higher Power—and to a sponsor] the period afterward is a very holy time. A time when you can come close to God. The helium balloon of myself floated higher and higher, lighter and lighter. I was thirty miles above Los Angeles, touching heaven, lifted into the loving arms of God."

~~~

Honoring our inner world, values and faculties is not just a question of time. Listening deeply and with care to others is also not only a question of time. Time matters. So does how we use it. But this is also a question of attitude or perception—and of what is motivating us.

A friend newly diagnosed with breast cancer wrote to me to say, "I first thought I have no time for this! And then I realized, I have no time for myself."

Judi Pemell's nine months spent preparing for those dramatic fourth and fifth steps have yielded a lifetime of benefits. And of course the irony of it being nine months' reflective gestation leading to her epiphany is not lost on her.

Perceiving time (and therefore our own selves) more spaciously may mean opening to what can feel like a dramatic or inevitable call. It may also be more subtle but no less potent: a tap on the shoulder from the universe coming in dreams, or when a book we pick up "falls open" on a particular page, answering a question not yet fully articulated.

An eloquent example is offered by Japanese-born Harumi Minagawa. Harumi is an academic and mother of two adult children who has been through many changes in her early fifties that she would not have predicted in the preceding decades. "During a period when I had left my former life of familiarity and I was walking gingerly into the unknown, I dreamed of this: somehow I fell into the abyss of a huge, deep crater and I couldn't see anything as it was pitch-dark. I felt at a loss and naturally very scared in that moment. But in no time at all I heard voices, joyous voices, which came from the rim of the crater. The voices said that there was nothing to worry about and they shone a light along the path to guide me up the crater. Walking up the crater took a great deal of physical effort, but I felt an enormous sense of security and joy in the climb. This dream set the tone of my life from that point on. Since that time, I have stopped experiencing undefined fear of the unknown.

"Coming from a culture [Japan] where conformity is considered to be a virtue, discovering or developing my authentic self and sometimes putting that first, before others, seems self-absorbed and I often feel that it is going against my spiritual progression. I just have to trust that the Universe is lovingly supporting me to experience and express my authentic self and my voice. Life becomes simpler as my trust grows."

~ひひひ~

To explore our full potential, we need to cultivate not just the strengths of our inner world but intimacy with it. Trusting and honoring our inner reality, we will use our instincts, intuitions and inspirations. And we will feel far less compelled to dump our agenda on other people or to scream or shout when their inner reality or needs don't mesh with our own.

Our moods, our social confidence and availability to others, our resilience and capacity to deal intelligently with disappointment and frustrations, our joy and appreciation in living: all of this is affected profoundly by what we believe our inner world to be, how we regard its strengths and resources—and, most of all, by our familiarity with it.

All but the youngest or most highly extroverted of us needs regular times to be at least a little more inwardly focused than the usual demands of life allow. We need time for reverie and daydreaming, a necessary precursor to any kind of original thinking or creativity, and so often ignored as we sit in front of electronic screens both for work and rest.

We need time and inner "space" to be sensually observant, relishing the smell of freshly mown grass, or the sound of birds singing or a favorite aria emerging from the apartment next door, or the touch of the sun on our bodies after days of rain—and the sound and feel of rain as we turn our faces up to receive it rather than down to avoid it. We need time to taste our food as we eat it. And to think about how it is grown. We need time to care for and appreciate our bodies, to keep them fit and strong, lithe and flexible for as long as we can. We also need time for more explicitly inwardly directed activities such as when we commit periods of time for a spiritual retreat or prayer, for reading and reflection, or when we "make" time to sit with a friend without rushing or thinking about what we're doing next.

Douglas Purnell is a gifted, committed visual artist, a writer and also a Uniting Church minister. In his book *Being in Ministry*, where he reflects with honesty and exceptional insight on all those roles as well as his essential questions of "being," he describes a situation of getting physically "lost" on his way to an appointment and the frustration this caused him. He goes on: "Being lonely, setting limits, being bored and . . . getting lost are all ultimately about what is going on inside me. It is easy to blame the other person, to keep it 'out there.' All the things that happen to me in my living become the stuff of my daily reflection. If . . . I pretend that being lost has nothing to do with me, if I see it as a matter of bad maps or being in a rush, I learn little. Each incident like this . . . is about accepting responsibility for the life I live."

⁓ↄↄↄↄ⁓

Basic to our existential well-being is the capacity to reflect without falling into the pits of self-criticism or inflation. *Reflecting*, we discover that we can observe our thinking and not be lost in it. This feeds our vital capacities to "be" and not just "do." *Doing* may be involved in it. But we lose self-consciousness as well as anxiety when we allow ourselves to be absorbed in the moment and what the moment is offering us.

This process is a means of "fertilizing" our thinking, and therefore our lives. It is also a means of "harvesting" our thinking. In this, my own children have been my most convincing teachers. They are adults now, in their middle twenties and each with a partner and busy, fulfilling lives. I am so grateful for the mutual adult friendships as well as parent–child love we now have, but it was when they were little that I learned from them how essential it is to be able to surrender gracefully—with no trace of resentment or impatience—to the simplicity and engagement of the present moment.

Taking long, slow walks around the streets and parks of our neighborhood, making cakes that took hours for the children to measure, mix and beat, building sand castles and making mighty dams down to the ocean on our frequent visits to the beach, building towers out of wooden blocks on a daily basis on our sitting-room floor, singing the same songs or reading the same stories a hundred times, I learned to slow my hectic, future-driven self down, at least somewhat. I also learned what treasures of perception and under-standing emerge when we make way for a more considered pace.

In his highly poetic book *A Hidden Wholeness*, American writer Parker J. Palmer points out that "The soul is like a wild animal— tough, resilient, resourceful, savvy, self-sufficient . . . But it is also shy. Just like a wild animal, it seeks safety in the dense underbrush. If we want to see a wild animal, we know that the last thing we should do is go crashing through the woods yelling for it to come out. But if we will walk quietly into the woods, sit patiently by the base of the tree, and fade into our surroundings, the wild animal we seek might put in an appearance."

Little that is subtle or considered is achieved in haste. Nor much that is meaningful or sacred. Beauty is not "caught" in haste. Nor is love. A Sabbath is essentially a time to honor and relish our lives rather than hurtling through them. It's a time for simple gestures: lighting candles, putting a fresh flower into a shining vase, making a meal to share.

I suspect we need a mini-Sabbath each day. And often we need to make a commitment that we will mark out such time as a priority. My most dedicated meditation friends rise before dawn each day to spend the last hour of darkness in the conscious presence of God. There is no doubt that's sometimes hard. Bed can feel tremendously attractive on a cold morning or after a late night. But the rhythm of that commitment has its own beauty.

It's just as likely that we also need extended Sabbaths—sabbaticals—more often than we assume. Establishing the rhythm of our lives to honor the inner rather than the outer life may seem onerous or impossible. But even the smallest shift can reveal immense peace of mind and happiness, especially when we recognize what a privilege it is to have that choice.

Shirley Williams captures this. An elegant, active woman in her early seventies, I love to remember that seven years ago, when she was leaving her first retreat with me at Mana Retreat Centre in New Zealand, she stood at the door of the Octagon, the spacious, light-filled room where we had gathered each day, and gaily said, "Well, if I am not back next year you will know I have died!" And each year since, thank heaven, she has returned.

More recently, we talked about her long spiritual journey and particularly about the times of difficult loss and grief, and of painful spiritual self-inquiry. A retired social worker, mother and grand-mother, Shirley is honest enough to recognize moments in her life when her choices have been harsh and even harmful, despite her natural courtesy and kindness.

Those hard times, and the regrets that have pursued her, make it so much sweeter that Shirley can now say, "I have appreciated learning about the interconnectedness of everything. I believe I was aware of this as a child. I couldn't bear the agony of the fish caught on my first experience of fishing and never tried it again. I talked to the trees in my back garden, and stroked and murmured to my favorite rock in the sun. I refused to attend the circus because I thought the animals looked sad and I wanted no part of that.

"I was told I was 'silly' and so I believed I must be. [Yet] I have learned to value this interconnection with everyone and everything and increasingly find nature to be healing and soothing.

"In turn, of course, we need to care for our environment and for each other. It is for me no longer just God who is responsible for our world and what happens in it. It is up to us to be part of the whole and to take responsibility for that. We can ask for help, but as Gandhi said, 'You must be the change you want to see in the world.'

"My current aim is to be present to the possibility of inspiration in the small and seemingly ordinary moments in life. In fact, to wake up! Much of this depends on intuition and a lightness of heart. That doesn't come from any absurd place of perfection. It comes from where we are right now."

WHEN I CAME TO LIVE IN Australia in 1983, my personal story of transformation accelerated. I had achieved more than I could have anticipated in Britain, but I sensed that I had as far to travel inwardly as I was once again traveling outwardly.

It's Uniting Church minister Barbara Oldmeadow who makes sense of these parallel journeys, essentially a single journey, when she reflects on the idea of pilgrimage: "The thought of journey, of which pilgrimage is a special sort, reminds us that in life we travel through two landscapes. The physical journey we make through the time and spaces of our lives is always in dialogue with the inner or soul journey."

During those post-Berlin, London years, I had held two significant mainstream publishing positions and, when still in my twenties, had founded and then run a successful independent publishing house, The Women's Press. That allowed me to bring together what were then my two passions: publishing and social change. It was a dream job with a long shadow. I was able to work with stimulating, passionate writers. I was fully engaged in the front lines of change. I had generous support and backing. But tensions within the company were difficult to resolve and the personal costs were high.

Nevertheless, those years in book publishing, both before and during The Women's Press era, taught me how to be effective in the world. That's no small thing. At one level, my barely articulated ambitions had been realized—and more. But no one knew better than I did that my "brilliant career" was brilliant in patches only.

I still had much to learn about how to feel sustained by what I was doing and more "real" internally. As I have already mentioned, it was a series of compelling dreams that pushed me to realize that this move was more likely to be achieved through writing than through publishing.

Moving physically, I left a country (England) and especially a profession and circle of friends and political colleagues that had become "mine" through the most satisfying years of my life. With my English partner, I came to a country (Australia) where I had only ever been a visitor and he had visited only once. And I was taking up a profession (writing) that is about as merciless as any could be.

We planned to be away from England for a couple of years, perhaps three at most. To complicate life further, I gave birth to our son a few months after we arrived. Less than fourteen months later, I gave birth to our daughter.

I adore my children. The love I feel for them is the least complicated that I have ever experienced. It has been effortless to love them, though not effortless to be a mother who has continued to write constantly. Becoming a mother in my mid-thirties wasn't easy. Living as a mother in a new country without networks wasn't easy. I had wanted it desperately and at the same time was agonizingly lonely for my old far more certain and externally focused life.

The world of London publishing that I had left was insular, competitive, gossipy, challenging, engaging and highly social. I missed it dreadfully. I missed the friends who could remember that I was once lively and funny, not sleepless and anxious.

As I learned to be a mother, I was also deeply lonely for my own mother. After the children's births, my grief for my mother came back in the most distressing ways. It seemed newly outrageous to me that she would be missing out on knowing my beautiful children and that they and I (like my sister and her family) had missed so many years of intimacy and joy. When I was becoming a mother, I was a year or two younger than the age when she died. The injustice and grief of that provoked an inner crisis for me that was spiritual even more than it was psychological. In those early years of eventful motherhood I was lonely for my mother. I had to recognize that I was also lonely for God.

❦

*Lonely for God* was specific and complex for me in ways that this book will already have made clear. In what were to be the last years of my London publishing life, I had been increasingly fascinated by the wisdom traditions of the East. A number of people I knew were becoming more (and sometimes less) Buddhist. That seemed to make sense. The contemporary Buddhist schools or philosophies are extremely attractive to people like me: people who are spiritually inclined, veterans of social activism and also psychologically minded. But as attractive and convincing as I found many Buddhist teachings, practices and rituals to be, I needed an inner relationship that was more personal.

A relationship with whom? Or what? I didn't want to find my way back to the God or Christianity of my childhood. I knew little then about the theistic mystical traditions. Yet I could not escape the urgings of my soul.

Into my life came an opening, so obvious and simple that it felt like an invitation with my own name on it.

As the children grew old enough, I left them for an hour or so most Sunday mornings to slip into the back row at the Quaker Meeting House in Devonshire Street in Sydney where, in the undemanding gathered silence, I could tentatively meet the Holiest of spirits. Just as tentatively, I could begin to know my own deepest yearning self.

To my far greater surprise, I would also begin to recover a new relationship with Jesus Christ, based not on sin, fear and atonement but initially on the dream I recalled earlier where Christ was inviting me into the dance of life with delight and unreserved love.

I had first learned about the Quakers in my childhood. My father's devotedly Anglican mother carefully explained to me why Quakers were exempt from military service and did not take part in war other than as medical support. That brief conversation—we were standing close to the window in her small, cluttered dining room when it took place—lodged itself in my memory and heart. The unconditionality of what I came eventually to know as the Quaker "Peace Testimony" made sense to me.

The simplicity of this spoke to me of truth. Quaker life and worship more generally spoke to me of truth. Inclusive and nonhierarchical, neither Catholic nor Protestant, mystical yet abundantly practical in their modest but unswerving commitment to justice for all and the value of all lives, I learned from the Quakers that there is "that of God" in everyone, without exception. I also learned that each of us is capable of ministering to others and that our relationship to our inner world or soul, like our relationship to the sacred or divine, can be direct and unmediated.

With this I came to trust one of my most transforming insights: that there may be just a single Eternal mystery but that no single person, authority, or body of teachings or most refined beliefs has all the answers or the answers for all.

That was and remains a deeply held view and, for those essential two decades, as my spiritual vision and assurance grew, the Quakers, and especially the silence of each Sunday's Meeting for Worship, gave me the context to affirm it.

⟿⟾⟾

Years went by. I wrote my books. *Intimacy and Solitude* alone took six years and required far greater constancy and discipline than I knew I had. Patching together a freelance life, I also wrote innumerable articles and reviews, and taught writing. I returned to publishing on a part-time and very happy basis for a couple of years. For many years after the children's infancy I also saw clients in a small psychotherapy private practice, while continuing always to write. My children's father and I parted ways; the children grew. They were years of intense joys, constant work and some nearly unbearable sorrows. I stayed with the Quakers faithfully for almost all of that time and am filled with gratitude for everything I learned and was given. But my spiritual transformation and journeying did not end there.

~ひこ~

A few years ago I was asked to write an article for an online Catholic publication that required the point of view of someone who was "not a Catholic." I suspect I surprised the person who was making the request when I laughed out loud and said, "But I am *not* 'not a Catholic!'"

Speaking to that journalist, I realized I had turned my back on little of my spiritual history. Catholicism had been crucial for me in generating an intensity of spiritual commitment and practice that suits my nature. What's more, for at least a decade before that formative conversation I had been working on an intermittent basis with all kinds of Catholic groups. This included some years when I was giving occasional retreats or retreat days to women religious (nuns), relishing thinking deeply in the company of women who have given their entire lives to God. It also included working with some school staff groups, as well as offering teachings to the wider Catholic public.

Dipping back into the Catholic world, I had been astonished to find the extent to which I could claim a sense of belonging, even while I disagreed (and disagree) profoundly with some of the teachings. Unsurprisingly, I was newly struck by the persistent sexism of the institutional church and its arrogant disregard for the facts of Catholic life. Women religious and laywomen provide so much at all levels of care and scholarship. Nevertheless, in the eyes of the conservative upper hierarchy, they remain irretrievably second-class.

This concerned me as it concerns so many committed Catholics. At the same time I could not help but feel personally healed as well as touched by the warmth of my welcome, which was no less warm when it was known that I would be teaching or speaking from an interreligious perspective.

Perhaps it is the depth of symbol and spirituality most profoundly expressed in the daily mystery of the Mass that makes it a little easier for seeking Catholics to open to the most authentic and profound wisdom and mystical teachings, whatever their source. Perhaps it is less reliance on the "word" and more on where "words" and silence take us. If so, then this may be why there is such a remarkable phenomenon of Catholic priest/writers who have immersed themselves also in the mysticism of other faith paths, without losing their own. Thomas Merton, Dom Bede Griffiths, William Johnston, Anthony de Mello, Henri Nouwen and Raimon Panikkar are just some of the most obvious names.

In 2006, a year after my ordination in New York as an interfaith minister, I formalized the association I now have with a wonderful city church, part of the Uniting Church of Australia. With the generous support of a lively congregation and their minister, Ian Pearson, I am able to lead spiritually inclusive services on a regular basis, opening the doors wide to seekers of all faiths and none.

～⚬⚬～

The emphasis in my writing and teaching moved in a natural, even organic way over those years from the psychological to ethical and spiritual. The shift was more gradual than the move in professional focus from publishing to writing had been, but it was no less momentous. As it evolved, I increasingly found the need within myself for more ritual and more concentrated teaching than is available at Quaker Meeting. This was not a comment on Quakers, who together create something so uniquely uncluttered and direct. It simply describes the direction of my own seeking.

For many years I had learned a great deal from peace activist and monk Thich Nhat Hanh—perhaps as much as from any other living teacher. I had also learned from Tibetan, Zen and Theravadin Buddhists about the depth of ethical scrutiny that a spiritual life demands and where followers of all paths, including Buddhism and unaligned "spirituality," may sometimes dramatically fail. For the last fifteen years or so I have been inspired by the Sufi teachings of Hazrat Inayat Khan. And I have learned to embody as well as love the Hindu Upanishads and Bhagavad Gita for their rare mix of poetry and practice.

By observing skillful teachers from the Eastern traditions over many years I discovered my own learning as well as teaching needs and "style." I understood how essential it is to pay attention to the many "small" moments that create a life. I saw how much more communal and respectful it is to circle a profound moment rather than pounce on it or analyze it into dust. I learned how much more spacious it can be to open up questions rather than worrying too much about whether I (or the teachings) could supply immediately satisfying answers. I learned to trust the inspiration of the teachings themselves, and to see my role as being at their service, discovering from the inside out what it is to live with them on a daily basis and to be *formed* as much as transformed by them. The "teachings" are, in my case, the most profound mystical teachings on love, behavior, appreciation, adoration and awe. And I know, as I live them, that they come to life repeatedly, timelessly as they move from the page to the mind to the heart to the body to the attitudes to the actions to the influences to the very being each of us is constantly becoming.

∼ઝ૯૭ઌ∼

My life centers on study and writing and, of course, the precious, private world of home. It also includes friends, teaching, *engaging*, as well as the journalism I continue to do and the talks, retreats and services I continue to give. Yet as I have been thinking about my life's incremental changes and the inner transformations they have brought, I feel sure that what has changed me most is "everyday life" and, most of all, the selflessness that children need. I'm tempted to go further: that it is only the absolute unconditional constancy of parenting that has taught me what selflessness is and how much it contrasts with my pre-parenting life.

Saying this, I risk offending some of you who are not parents. So let me qualify it and add that it was vital for me, personally, to discover that my children could attach me to the robust complexity of life and this earth as nothing else has.

This has transformed my relationships with my dearest ones more generally. It has allowed me to be more spontaneous, tolerant and accepting, qualities I am also more easily able to offer to myself now as well as others. It has certainly taught me humility. And a great deal about the *interdependency* that is integral to intimacy: the exquisite flow of receiving as well as giving.

The invitation to join the new organization "Global Spirituality" includes the lines: "When we are rooted in our heart, we realize the interdependency of everything . . . Our heart has the capacity to respect differences and celebrate unity simultaneously." That's real for me. And it teaches me that there is little or no difference in my life between "life" and "spiritual life." *Life* is spiritual. *Everything* is a source of learning. Everything, at least potentially, is grist for transformation—and self-realization.

Parenting began and continues that "knowing" for me. It exposed and exposes to me my own vulnerability and the vulnerability and fragility of all beings, exactly as is evoked in this profound teaching from the Buddhist tradition:

> *Just as a mother would protect her only child,*
> *even at the risk of her own life,*
> *even so, cultivate a boundless heart toward all beings.*
> *Let your thoughts of boundless love*
> *pervade the whole world.* (Sutta Nipata, 149–150)

"I got a new idea of myself," said the peerless Australian poet Les Murray, recalling in a recent television interview the moment in which his grim childhood was relieved utterly by the discovery of poetry.

If I look back just as far as the time when I came to Australia twenty-six years ago, I see the extent to which I have also "got a new idea of myself," though not in a single flash. My transformation has been slow and patchy. It has also been unceasing.

CHANGE, THOUGH, IS NOT ALWAYS welcome. Transformation is not always desired.

A remarkable account of grief comes in Virginia Lloyd's memoir, *The Young Widow's Book of Home Improvement*. I finished the book one pre-dawn morning when I had woken in the darkness, prayed, and then had failed to go back to sleep. I rarely weep but as wintry light came into my room tears were pouring down my cheeks even while I felt gratitude to Virginia for articulating with such tenderness the profundities of loss.

Thirty-two when she met her adored husband, John, thirty-three when she married him and thirty-four when she became a widow, Virginia writes, "At unexpected moments I found myself overpowered by a wave of grief that swamped without warning. When I reached for a saucepan in its cluttered drawer; when I folded the sheets, washed and dried, to put them away; when I sat on the couch flicking through a magazine; sometimes while I stood in the hallway, keys still in my hand from letting myself in the front door. On occasion these waves of grief felled me: I dropped to the ground, slumped as if the puppet strings I had been relying on to hold me up had failed."

In that first year of grief Virginia also describes landing at Melbourne airport on a business trip and calling John to let him know she had arrived safely from their Sydney home, forgetting that he was dead. "For a long moment I had forgotten he was dead," she writes, "and suddenly was forced to know it again as for the first time. The bliss of forgetting. The agony of remembering. None of this was normal. I propped my elbow on the inside window ledge so as to support my hand as it shielded my face from the taxi driver, and quietly sobbed all the way to the office."

Death is the most inevitable and dramatic transformation of all. It is also the one we approach least willingly. How we understand or accept the inevitability of death will starkly affect how we regard life, and move through it.

The transition from life to death is frequently profoundly transformative for those witnessing it. When I was writing my book about the visionary poet Rainer Maria Rilke I was moved as much by the brief, intense firsthand account of his death as any other factor of his complex life and work. Aged only fifty-one, he was dying reluctantly and in great pain. Nonetheless, when dying came, he "took three deep breaths, opened his eyes wide and looked out into space with a shining gaze."

It's another poet, the American Walt Whitman, who asks (in "Song of Myself"):

*What do you think has become of the young and old men?*
*And what do you think has become of the women and children?*

Whitman's poem continues:

*They are alive and well somewhere,*
*The smallest sprout shows there is really no death.*
*And if ever there was it led forward life, and does not wait at the end*
*   to arrest it,*
*And ceas'd the moment life appear'd.*
*All goes onward and outward, nothing collapses,*
*And to die is different from what anyone supposed, and luckier.*

From Stephen Levine's book *A Year to Live* we receive some extraordinary "news" about death. "[T]he heart never stops, for when it is no longer contained between opposing ventricles it expands slowly into its inherent vastness without missing a beat, expressing the truth it has embraced for a lifetime ...

"Death, like birth, is not an emergency but an emergence ...

"Just before we feel the lightness lifting us from our body, while we are still trying to capture each molecule of oxygen just to stay alive another instant, we suddenly remember we are not the body, never have been, never will be! Resistance vanishes into a glimpse of our long-migrating spirit. We cut the moorings and dive into the ocean of being, expanding from our body, the mind floating free."

Are you asking, "How do they know?"

How do any of us know? Or how can we be truly confident about our own ignorance?

Here is an account shared with me by Diane Winder that opens our eyes and minds at least a little. Diane is a generous, gentle woman of great integrity who works in a range of spiritual and healing arts and, with her husband, Jon, with adolescent boys and their families in an innovative therapeutic setting.

As Diane comments, "It is not uncommon for a death to signal a transformation." Diane's mother's death was that, and more.

"I was twenty-three. She was sixty-one, young in our modern concept of aging. As a smoker for forty years, a routine doctor's exam revealed a 'spot' on her lung. By the time it was discovered, the cancer had already spread throughout her body. I imagine she was as frightened as the rest of us.

"After the surgery and chemo, she was weak and tired for a year. The doctors quietly explained that they weren't sure they 'got it all.' For those who have undergone such an experience, those words turn your world upside down.

"I had just shifted from the Harvard teaching hospital in Boston, where I started my then medical career, to work in a private medical laboratory. The phone call came to me at my bench in the middle of the day. I don't think the wheels of my car touched the hundred-mile journey to the hospital. When I arrived, the nurses, nuns of the Sisters of Providence, related that she was admitted because she wasn't able to breathe. They couldn't pinpoint a date or a time, but my intuition guided me to stay with her during that day and night.

"After my siblings left at the dinner hour, I sat in silence beside her, arranging the bedclothes now and then to make her (or me) more comfortable. During one of her lucid moments I asked if she wished me to leave. I remember that she replied with her customary and practical wisdom, 'No, don't leave. Don't worry. Everything happens for a reason.'

"Around ten o'clock that evening, she slipped into the unconscious and the next few hours were like a dream. The room became filled with a tangible sensation of peace, as if the air expanded in all directions. By that time she seemed to be 'responding' to questions with *yes* and *no*, speaking too softly for me to hear. I recall thinking that I was witnessing a very sacred act.

"As she crossed over, the silence and peace was beyond belief. Surprisingly, I was not overcome with profound grief or the urge to weep, such was the immensity of love surrounding us."

⁓ભ⦿ન⦿

Accepting that every life involves suffering (and will end in the transition we call death) can be a way of living more intensely and appreciatively and perhaps less fearfully.

What this might mean is that we don't rail against suffering when it arises ("Why me?"). Or, if we do rail, we don't stay stuck in that place of outrage. We may find ourselves, instead, willing to inquire, "What does this situation need? What strengths and help do I already have, or do I need? How can I bring compassion to my situation? How can I offer the kindness of a true friend?"

This may not change the situation. It may not change the sorrow we feel. What it may change is the sense of helplessness and hopelessness that worsens our anguish.

This is not a question of earnest belief or even of hope. Far more basic than that, it is a way of living through the darkest of nights that keeps us connected to our spiritual resources and roots. My own life, my devastating losses, times of anguish, rage, guilt, shame and utter uncertainty, have shown me unequivocally that there is comfort in this, even in the presence of confusion.

I have never prayed more fiercely than in my own darkest times. I have never yearned more fiercely to know God and to be known. That my prayers were a wild mixture of helplessness, anguish, confusion and pleading did not prevent them from opening my awareness to what I can only describe as the absolute fidelity of the Holy Spirit, and to a place of peace within myself that is beyond sorrow.

This did not immediately heal my heart or quell my anguish. It did not mean that I ceased to worry or blame myself for what I could not change. But what it did do was profoundly soften the pain and transform my thinking. "This too will pass" is only partly true when it comes to grief or anguish. So is "Let me meet this with kindness." Or "Peace be with us all." Yet even these most familiar and simple of mantras were sometimes enough to remind me that in every life there is suffering. *And* there is also compassion and vision.

This firsthand knowledge has transformed me. Yet, in thinking of you reading this, and particularly if your own sorrows are raw or if your questions feel unbearable, I need to emphasize that what I have discovered in those times is highly textured and multilayered.

My sister, Geraldine, makes beautiful and excitingly original quilts. When I look at them, I know it is impossible to take them in other than incrementally. There is the initial "dazzle" and then there will continue to be discoveries for the eye and mind for months, perhaps years. A quilt becomes "itself" through the unifying of innumerable choices and decisions, many of them long preceding the quilter's own choices. Each square represents time spent to create something beautiful. That beauty continues to unfurl. It is shaped, sometimes shadowed, sometimes enhanced but always affected by what sits around and alongside it.

I can't think of a more apt analogy for the life each of us is creating. That too is made up of multiple "pieces." We initiate some. Some we do not. We welcome some and they please us. Others, we do not. The "whole" is evolving. And we rarely take it in at a single glance.

Reading this book, you will know that I am passionate about spirituality as a transformer of social as well as personal consciousness. As Paramahansa Yogananda does, I believe that "Only spiritual consciousness—realization of God's presence in oneself and in every other living being—can save the world."

Idealism has been a key factor in my own development. It has never deserted me and I have never outgrown it. Spiritual idealism is the highest form of this human seeking for what is healing and nourishing and transformative. My relationship with the sacred is at the center of my existence. And yet on a daily basis I live with doubts. I observe my own carelessness and patchiness of commitment. I assume that there are some things I will still have time for "whenever." I can waste an afternoon reading something instantly forgettable. I can cut short my meditation or prayers because I am restless or distracted. I claim to be interested in all religions even while knowing that some religious teachings and forms enrage me and others leave me cold. I am easily bored, occasionally lacking in kindness as well as compassion. I worry about things which are not worth that worry. I can turn my back on things which should concern me. I struggle to love unconditionally.

All those responses are very human, recognizable and true. What is also true is that beneath all those familiar resistances some version of inner knowing and conviction continues like the movement of the tide that never ceases. Nor ever loses its connection to the light that governs it.

⁓

One of the most famous accounts of transformation comes from monk and writer Thomas Merton who, on March 18, 1958, a little more than ten years before his untimely death, had this experience. It is reported in his book *Conjectures of a Guilty Bystander*.

"In Louisville, on a corner of Fourth and Walnut, in the center of the shopping district, I was suddenly overwhelmed with the realization that I loved all these people, that they were mine and I theirs, that we could not be alien to one another even though we were total strangers. It was like waking from a dream of separateness, of spurious self-isolation in a special world ... The whole illusion of a separate holy existence is a dream ...

"This sense of liberation from an illusory difference was such a relief and such a joy to me that I almost laughed out loud ... As if the sorrows and stupidities of the human condition could overwhelm me, now that I realize what we all are. And if only everybody could realize this! But it cannot be explained. There is no way of telling people that they are all walking around *shining like the sun!*"

Could there be a call to the sacred more profound or joyous?

Labels, no-labels, dogma, no-dogma, doubts, no-doubts, all would fade into forgetfulness with this single insight and all that it implies: that each of us is "walking around *shining like the sun.*"

༜

As a young man, scarcely more than a boy, Francis of Assisi, that famed lover of all creation, asked: *My God and All: What are You and what am I?*

Opening our minds and hearts to the spiritual depths of our own existence, perceiving the holy as well as the fragility in one another; receiving inspiration and grace and good humor gratefully and humbly; taking refuge in compassion, kindness, joy, appreciation and gratitude; truly understanding what forgiveness is: these are no small things. They require commitment and trust. They ask a willingness to rise up again when we have fallen. They require discipline, in the best sense of that word. They require the most generous possible openness to the depths and mystery and abundance of life.

*My God and All: What are You and what am I?*

If we were to meet no other spiritual challenge but the living of that question, kindly, gratefully and with awe for the rest of our days, we might be joyfully and humbly enlightened.

We might also have discovered the sacred.

# SELECT BIBLIOGRAPHY

Of the many different editions of primary sacred texts that are widely known and available I have included only those few where I have drawn on the commentaries or introduction.

Allison, John, *Walking Out of Another World*, Immortal Books, South Murwillumbah, NSW, Australia, 2010.

——, *A Way of Seeing: Perception, Imagination and Poetry*, Lindisfarne Books, Great Barrington, MA, 2003.

Arberry, A. J., *Sufism: An Account of the Mystics of Islam*, Mandala/Unwin, London, 1979.

——, *The Mystical Poems of Rumi*, Vols 1, 2, University of Chicago Press, Chicago, 1974; 1991.

Armstrong, Karen, *The Case for God*, Knopf, New York, 2009.

——, *The Spiral Staircase: A Memoir*, HarperCollins, London, 2004.

Batchelor, Stephen, *The Faith to Doubt: Glimpses of Buddhist Uncertainty*, Parallax Press, Berkeley, 1990.

Bodhi, Ven Bhikkhu, "Love and Compassion," in *Parabola*, Spring 2010 (Denville, NJ).

Borg, Marcus, *The God We Never Knew*, HarperSanFrancisco, San Francisco, 1997.

Bourgeault, Cynthia, *The Wisdom Jesus*, Shambhala, Boston, 2008.

Brabhavananda, Swami & Frederick Manchester (trans.), *The Upanishads: Breath of the Eternal*, Vedanta Press, Hollywood, 1983.

Brussat, Frederic and Mary Ann, *Spiritual Literacy: Reading the Sacred in Everyday Life*, Touchstone, New York, 1996.

Burr, Chandler, *You or Someone Like You*, Ecco, New York, 2010.

Campbell, Joseph, with Michael Toms, *An Open Life*, HarperPerennial, New York, 1990.

Chardin, Pierre Teilhard de, *The Divine Milieu*, Harper & Row, New York, 1960.

Dowrick, Stephanie, *Choosing Happiness: Life & Soul Essentials*, Allen & Unwin, Sydney, 2005; Tarcher, New York, 2008.

——, *Creative Journal Writing*, Allen & Unwin, Sydney, 2007; Tarcher, New York, 2009.

——, *Forgiveness and Other Acts of Love*, Viking, Melbourne, 1997; W. W. Norton, New York, 1998; Allen & Unwin, Sydney, 2010.

——, *Intimacy and Solitude*, W. W. Norton, New York, 1994; (revised edition) Random House, Sydney, 2002.

——, *In the Company of Rilke*, Allen & Unwin, Sydney, 2009; Tarcher, New York, 2011.

——, *The Universal Heart*, Viking, Melbourne, 2000.

Eck, Diana L., *Encountering God*, Beacon Press, Boston, 1993; 2003.

FitzGerald, Constance, "Impasse and Dark Night," in Edwards, Tilden (ed.), *Living with Apocalypse*, Harper & Row, New York, 1984.

Frankl, Viktor E., *Man's Search for Meaning: An Introduction to Logotherapy*, Hodder & Stoughton, London, 1964.

Griffiths, Bede, *The Cosmic Revelation: The Hindu Way to God*, Templegate, Springfield, 1983.

——, *River of Compassion: A Christian Commentary on the Bhagavad Gita*, Templegate, Springfield, 2001.

——, *Universal Wisdom: A Journey Through the Sacred Wisdom of the World*, HarperSanFrancisco, San Francisco, 1994.

Groll, Ursula, *Spiritual Unity of East and West*, Swedenborg Association of Australia, Sydney, 2008.

Hanh, Thich Nhat, *Anger: Buddhist Wisdom for Cooling the Flames*, Rider, London, 2001.

——, *The Heart of the Buddha's Teaching*, Rider, London, 1998.

——, *Living Buddha, Living Christ*, Riverhead, New York, 1995.

Harris, Sam, *The End of Faith: Religion, Terror and the Future of Reason*, W. W. Norton, New York, 2004.

Harvey, Andrew, *The Direct Path*, Broadway Books, New York, 2000.

——(ed.), *The Essential Mystics: The Soul's Journey into Truth*, Castle Books, Edison, NJ, 1998.

Hedges, Chris, *American Fascists: The Christian Right and the War on America*, Free Press, New York, 2006.

Heschel, Abraham Joshua, *God in Search of Man: A Philosophy of Judaism*, Farrar, Straus & Giroux, New York, 1997.

——, *Who Is Man?*, Stanford University Press, Stanford, 1965.

Hick, John, *An Interpretation of Religion: Human Responses to the Transcendent*, Palgrave Macmillan, Houndmills, Basingstoke, UK, 2004.

——, *The Fifth Dimension: An Exploration of the Spiritual Realm*, OneWorld, Oxford, 1999.

Hillman, James, *A Terrible Love of War*, Penguin, London, 2005.

Johnston, William, *The Inner Eye of Love: Mysticism and Religion*, Fount/Collins, London, 1981.

——, *Mystical Theology: The Science of Love*, Fount/Collins, London, 1995.

Junger, Sebastian, *War*, Twelve, New York, 2010.

Kelly, Thomas R., *A Testament of Devotion*, HarperCollins, New York, 1992.

Khan, Hazrat Inayat, *The Divinity of the Human Soul*, Motilal, Delhi, 1990.

——, *Mastery Through Accomplishment: Developing Inner Strength for Life's Challenges*, Omega, New Lebanon, NY, 1985.

——, *The Wedding of Body and Soul*, www.wahiduddin.net/purpose

Khan, Pir Vilayat Inayat, *Awakening: A Sufi Experience*, Tarcher/Putnam, New York, 2000.

King, Martin Luther Jr., *Strength to Love*, HarperCollins, New York, 1977.

Kornfield, Jack (ed.), *Teachings of the Buddha*, Shambhala, Boston, 1997.

Levine, Stephen, *A Year to Live*, Bell/Crown, New York, 1997.

Lewis, C. S., *Mere Christianity*, Collins, London, 1952.

Lloyd, Virginia, *The Young Widow's Book of Home Improvement*, UQP, Brisbane, 2008.

Malone, Nancy M., *Walking a Literary Labyrinth: A Spirituality of Reading*, Riverhead Books, New York, 2003.

McLaughlin, Corinne and Gordon Davidson, *Spiritual Politics: Changing the World from the Inside Out*, Ballantine, New York, 1994.

Meher, Baba, *The Path of Love*, Awakener Press, Hermosa Beach, CA, 1986.

Merton, Thomas, *Conjectures of a Guilty Bystander*, Image/Doubleday, New York, 1989.

——, *New Seeds of Contemplation*, New Dimensions Press, New York, 1961.

Miller, Robert J. (ed.), *The Complete Gospels*, HarperCollins, New York, 1994.

Moore, Thomas, *The Soul's Religion: Cultivating a Profoundly Spiritual Way of Life*, HarperCollins, New York, 2002.

Mowaljarlai, David, in Bradley, Rosalind (ed.), *Mosaic: Favorite Prayers and Reflections from Inspiring Australians*, ABC Books, Sydney, 2008.

Nouwen, Henri J.M., *The Inner Voice of Love*, Darton, Longman & Todd, London, 1997.

Novak, Philip, *The World's Wisdom: Sacred Texts of the World's Religions*, Castle Books, Edison, NJ, 1994.

Osbon, Diane K. (ed.), *A Joseph Campbell Companion: Reflections on the Art of Living*, HarperPerennial, New York, 1991.

Otto, Rudolf, *The Idea of the Holy*, Oxford University Press, Oxford, 1958.

Palmer, Parker, *A Hidden Wholeness*, John Wiley & Sons, San Francisco, 2004.

Panikkar, Raimon, *The Intrareligious Dialogue*, Paulist Press, New York, 1978.

——, "The New Innocence," interview with Raimon Panikkar by Carmen Font, in *Share International*, North Hollywood, October, 1996.

Patel, Eboo, *Acts of Faith: The Story of an American Muslim, the Struggle for the Soul of a Generation*, Beacon Press, Boston, 2007.

Peck, M. Scott, *The Road Less Traveled*, Touchstone, New York, 1988.

Pemell, Judith Shepherd, *The Soul Illuminated*, 2nd ed., O Books, Ropley, Hampshire, UK, 2010.

Purnell, Douglas, *Being in Ministry*, WIPF & Stock, Eugene, Oregon, 2010.

Renfer, Linda Hill, *Daily Readings from Quaker Writings Ancient and Modern*, Serenity Press, Grants Pass, Oregon, 1988.

Rilke, Rainer Maria, (trans. M.D. Herter Norton), *Letters to a Young Poet*, W.W. Norton, New York, 1934.

Sanghera, Sathnam, *If You Don't Know Me by Now*, Viking/Penguin, London, 2008. (Published in paperback as *The Boy with the Topknot*.)

Smith, Huston, *Beyond the Post-Modern Mind*, Quest Books, Wheaton, IL, 1984.

——, *Forgotten Truth: The Common Vision of the World's Religions*, HarperSanFrancisco, San Francisco, 1992.

——, *The Soul of Christianity: Restoring the Great Tradition*, HarperSanFrancisco, San Francisco, 2005.

——, *Why Religion Matters: The Fate of the Human Spirit in an Age of Disbelief*, HarperSanFrancisco, San Francisco, 2001.

Steiner, George, *My Unwritten Books*, Weidenfeld & Nicolson, London, 2008.

Tarrant, John, *The Light Inside the Dark: Zen, Soul, and the Spiritual Life*, HarperCollins, New York, 1998.

Tillich, Paul, *Dynamics of Faith*, Harper & Row, New York, 1957.

Underhill, Evelyn, *The Spiritual Life*, Hodder & Stoughton, London, 1955.

Vaillant, George E., *Spiritual Evolution: A Scientific Defense of Faith*, Broadway Books, New York, 2008.

Vivekananda, Swami, *What Religion Is*, Advaita Ashrama, Calcutta, 1998.

Wilde, Oscar, *De Profundis and Other Writings*, Penguin Classics, London, 1976 (1905).

Wilson, Andrew (ed.), *World Scripture: A Comparative Anthology of Sacred Texts*, Paragon House, St. Paul, 1995.

# ACKNOWLEDGMENTS

THE MOST DELIGHTFUL PAGES FOR ME to write in any book are those that give me the opportunity to express my thanks to all who have helped to make the book possible. But first a story. Someone who regularly attends the services that I give at Pitt Street Uniting Church in Sydney quite recently asked me who writes the liturgies for those gatherings. "I do," I replied, slightly confused by her question. "No, who else?" she insisted. "Who puts them together and gets them into our hands?"

Wendy's confusing question became a clarifying one. No matter who finally gets to be "author" of any book (and can endure the years-long marathon that a book demands), the company of many others is indeed always needed to "get it into your hands."

This book offers personal recollections and insights from many others, and from countries as diverse as Latvia and Indonesia, the

United States and New Zealand, Germany, Britain and Australia. Gathering them was a joy and a privilege. Not all the accounts that I listened to for this book have made it directly onto these pages. Some brew between the lines. But all have shaped and encouraged it. What people spoke about in their discussions with me was deeply heartfelt. Those who read the manuscript during its production stages were passionate about the honesty of those personal reflections. So am I, particularly knowing what fidelity to the complex sacred journey of life they represent. Some people have asked not to have their names mentioned for a variety of reasons. The finished book is nonetheless an expression of gratitude to them also.

Those I am able to thank by name include Judith Ackroyd, John Allison, Maggie Attard, Subhana Barzaghi, Reverend Keri Bas, Juliet Batten, Jolyon Bromley, Sande Bruch, Monica Cable, Georgia Carr, Reverend Siobhan Christian, Susan Christian, Clare Coburn, Rodney Cole, Ali Coomber, Kim Cunio, Kim Gotlieb, Catherine Greer, Ursula Groll, Rebekah Hunter, Bill Idol, Donna Idol, Jack, Neville Jarvis, Kerstin Kamm, Dr. Varuni Kanagasundaram, Zuleyha Keskin, Igor Kukushkin, Murray Lloyd, Susan MacFarlane, Mariella, Mary Ann, Nigel Marsh, Walter Mason, Harumi Minagawa, Jane Moore, Freda Morgan, Mark Muirhead, Julie O'Brien, Reverend Barbara Oldmeadow, Reverend Helen Palmer, Judith Pemell, Jessica Perini, Reverend Dr. Douglas Purnell, Reverend Heather Roan Robbins, Kalvinder Shields, Jane Sloane, Reverend Hilary Star, Reverend Dennis Swartz RScP, Thang, Sue de Vries, Caroline Ward, Father Michael Whelan, Lorraine Whitley, John Williams, Shirley Williams, Diane Winder and Yulianto Yukito.

I would also like to thank the following people for more general support during the time of writing: my son Gabriel and his wife,

Aokie; my daughter Kezia and her husband, Sean; Kezia again for her wonderful home cooking and skills in interpreting contemporary issues; my sisters, Geraldine and Mary; Barbara and John Oldmeadow; Jane Goodall for wonderful writerly exchanges. As always, very particular thanks must go to Jane Moore for her love, unfailing kindness and care and the most stimulating of discussions. Thanks too to my dear friend Hanan al-Shaykh who translated a poem from Arabic for me especially for this book, and to Kim Cunio, Peter Damo, Charlie Hogg and Paul Wilson for invaluable "godly" conversations and always much laughter (thank heaven the two can go together).

Both Hilary Star and Jane Moore read this work in late drafts. The fault for any errors or unrealized intentions is entirely mine, but in those last months I depended on their keen minds as much as on their unlimited enthusiasm for the discoveries of a spiritual life. My gratitude for the time and interest they offered me is boundless.

The communities at Mana Retreat Center, Coromandel, New Zealand, and the congregations at Pitt Street Uniting Church, Sydney, Australia, encourage my continuing spiritual development. I want especially to mention Hilary Star again, also Donna Idol and the Mana Trustees for the true gifts of Mana and, with loving gratitude and respect, Jolyon Bromley and particularly Reverend Ian Pearson at Pitt Street Uniting, as well as all those who attend and help create our beautiful services.

My thanks for years of fruitful contact also go to Breast Cancer Network Australia and its inspiring founder and CEO, my friend Lyn Swinburne. And I cannot overlook Australian Quakers (Religious Society of Friends) and especially Devonshire Street Meeting, Sydney, for two essential decades of spiritual sustenance.

My Australian publishers are again vital in this process. I am proud to have been associated with Allen & Unwin for many years and I am particularly grateful to my good friend and fine publisher, Sue Hines, for her constancy, her real care about the themes of my work, and her personal encouragement. I am also grateful to Kelly Fagan, my delightful publicist; to Lisa White for her gifts of designing beauty; to Christa Munns for her vital and careful production editing and, once again, to Ali Lavau for her thoughtful editorial reading and interest. I also want to mention with gratitude the marketing and sales teams, under the direction of Karen Williams, and of Managing Director, Robert Gorman.

I would like to acknowledge Reverend Graham Long of Sydney's Wayside Chapel for permission to use a story from his ministry and David Mowaljarlai and Magabala Books, Broome, Western Australia, for their gracious permission to use Mr. Mowaljarlai's words. Other sources are acknowledged in the text and Select Bibliography. Special thanks to John Allison, Douglas Purnell, Virginia Lloyd and Ursula Groll for kind permission to use brief extracts from their published works.

Monty Coles

Stephanie Dowrick has the rare distinction of having written five number one best-selling books. These include *Intimacy and Solitude, Forgiveness and Other Acts of Love*, and *Choosing Happiness*. Her most recent book is *In the Company of Rilke*. Formerly a publisher, and founder of The Women's Press, London, Stephanie Dowrick was born in New Zealand and also lived in Europe for many years. The mother of two children, she has lived with her family in Sydney since 1983. Stephanie Dowrick has been "Inner Life" columnist for *Good Weekend* since 2001. A trained psychotherapist, she is also an ordained interfaith minister and has been giving spiritually inclusive retreats and talks for many years. Stephanie Dowrick completed her research doctorate with the Writing and Society Research Group at the University of Western Sydney and is currently an Adjunct Fellow. For more information: www.stephaniedowrick.com